W9-BQK-254

Growing Up Forgotten

Growing Up Forgotten

A Review of Research and Programs Concerning Early Adolescence

Joan Lipsitz

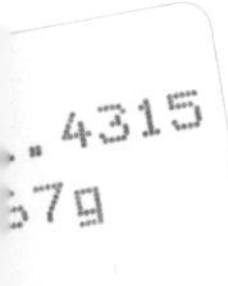

Transaction Books
New Brunswick (U.S.A.) and London (U.K.)

Library of Congress Catalog Number: 79-67002
ISBN: 0-87855-792-X (paper)
Printed in the United States of America

Library of Congress Cataloging in Publication Data
Lipsitz, Joan.
Growing up forgotten.

Reprint of the ed. published by Lexington Books, Lexington, Mass.
Bibliography: p.
Includes index.
1. Adolescence. 2. Adolescent psychology.
3. Social work with youth—United States. 4. Adolescence—Research—United States. I. Title.
[HQ796.L54 1980] 301.43'15 79-67002
ISBN 0-87855-792-X

Jonathan approaches early adolescence. Annie is there now. Joan Scheff is the young adolescent who lives on inside me. All three have had their say in this effort. This report is dedicated to them.

Contents

	List of Figures	ix
	List of Tables	xi
	Acknowledgments	xiii
	Introduction	xv
Part I	*Research on Early Adolescence*	
Chapter 1	**Research Review**	3
	Concepts of Adolescence	3
	Overview of Research on Early Adolescence	8
	Biological Research	15
	Socio-Emotional Research	26
	Cognitive Research	36
	Federal Funding for Research	56
	Research Recommendations	74
Part II	*The Young Adolescent and Social Institutions*	
	Introduction to Part II	81
Chapter 2	**Schools and the Young Adolescent**	83
	Introduction	83
	The Purpose of Schooling	85
	Historical Development of the Junior High School	88
	Junior High Schools Today—The Reformers	92
	Schooling for Minority Youth	108
	Emerging Trends	115
	The Abyss	121
Chapter 3	**Service Institutions and the Handicapped Young Adolescent**	125
	Introduction	125
	Physically Handicapped	127
	Emotionally Handicapped	133
	Mentally Handicapped	143

Special Education 147
Afterword 157

Chapter 4 **The Family and the Young Adolescent** 159

Introduction 159
Research on the Family and the Early Adolescent 161
Afterword 171

Chapter 5 **Voluntary Youth-Serving Agencies** 173

Introduction 173
Youth-Serving Agencies 173
Changes to Serve Today's Youth 177
Conclusion 180

Chapter 6 **The Young Adolescent in the Juvenile Justice System** 183

Introduction 183
Who Are the Juvenile Delinquents? 183
Prediction and Prevention 189
Control and Treatment: The Juvenile Justice System 192
Emerging Trends in Juvenile Justice 194
Conclusion 204

Chapter 7 **Conclusion** 207

Appendix 211

Notes 215

Bibliography 241

Index 255

About the Author 269

List of Figures

1-1	Percent of Total Number of Research Projects by Kinds of Research, FY '73	62
1-2	Percent of Total Number of Research Projects by Adolescent Research, FY '74	63
1-3	Percent of Total Funding by Kinds of Research, FY '73	63
1-4	Percent of Total Funding by Adolescent Research, FY '74	64

List of Tables

1-1	All Agency Distribution and Rank Order of Areas of Research, FY '73	64
1-2	Numbers and Percent of Areas of Adolescent Research, FY '74	65
1-3	Projects Focusing Primarily Upon General Adolescent Development Problems by Type of Research Activity	65
1-4	Projects Focusing Primarily Upon Organizations That Serve Adolescents, by Type of Research Activity	66
1-5	Adolescent Target Population: Percentage Involving the Physically Handicapped by Type of Research	67
1-6	Adolescent Target Population: Percentage Involving the Intellectually and Emotionally Handicapped and Others, by Type of Research	68
1-7	Specific Adolescent Development Problems, by Type of Research Activity	69
1-8	Projects Relating to an Adolescent's Social Environment, by Type of Research Activity	70
1-9	Research Projects Involving Personnel Affecting Adolescents	71
1-10	Projects Investigating New Techniques for Influencing Adolescents	71
1-11	Current NIMH Research Projects Focusing on Adolescence	72

1-12	Number of NIMH Adolescent Research Projects by Termination Year and Subject Area	73
1-13	Funding for Adolescent Research Projects by Termination Year	74
3-1	Estimated Number of Total Terminations from Outpatient Psychiatric Clinics by Mental Disorder and Age, 1969	135
3-2	Number and Percent of Patients Served in Mental Retardation Clinics by Their Status and Age	145
3-3	Number of Professional Personnel and Type of Instructional System by Handicapping Condition and by Level of School	152
3-4	Number of Handicapped Pupils in Local Public Schools, and Number and Percent that Received Any Type of Special Instruction or Assistance	154
6-1	Arrests, by Offense	186

Acknowledgments

In June of 1974 The Learning Institute of North Carolina (LINC) received a grant from The Ford Foundation for a review of programs and research on early adolescence in the United States. No review would have been possible without the help of many professionals who gave freely of their time and energies in response to requests for information. Many are cited in this report; many are not. They contributed, hoping for nothing in return except a growing social commitment to young adolescents.

We drew upon Sara Haig's skills, sensitivity, and companionship as research and editorial assistant. She gave unstintingly. She is a good researcher, a good editor, and a good friend.

Sharon Ferguson joined LINC as research assistant for this study. Her generosity of spirit, humor and intelligence under trying circumstances cannot be measured.

LaRue Hines began as secretary for the project. When she left LINC, Margie Mitchell took her place. Both have been the secretary everyone dreams of having and very few find. Without the sense of order, the commitment, and the critical asides provided by Margie Mitchell, it is doubtful that this study would have seen the light of day before the next generation of young adolescents presented themselves to us.

John Niblock of LINC and Don Wells of the Carolina Friends School always had time to listen, to guide, and to contribute.

Joan Lipsitz is the author of Chapters 1 and 2 of this report, with assistance on school-related legal issues from Burton Goldstein and from Sara Haig on schooling for minority youth. The remaining chapters represent the work of several coauthors under the editorship of Joan Lipsitz. Sara Haig, Joan Lipsitz, and Sharon Ferguson coauthored the section on the handicapped young adolescent. Burton Goldstein also contributed material on legal issues and drug programs, and Bernice Willis contributed material on retarded and learning disabled youth. John S. Niblock and Julia Slebos coauthored the chapter on the family and the young adolescent. Judith Tulchin wrote the chapter on voluntary youth-serving agencies, with assistance from Sharon Ferguson. Sharon Ferguson and Sara Haig coauthored the chapter on the juvenile justice system.

Several people have commented on rough drafts of this report. We would like in particular to thank Dr. Judith Gallatin of Eastern Michigan University for her insightful criticism coupled with her continuing encouragement.

Personal thanks are due John R.B. Hawes, Jr., Executive Director of LINC, and to the LINC Board of Directors who relieved me of my regular work responsibilities for much longer than they were given to expect in order that I could pursue this research.

Special warm thanks go to Terry Saario of The Ford Foundation. She remained confident of our ability to bring reason and order to the impossible task we had set out upon. She has never failed to be supportive and challenging. We hope we have not abused her trust.

Joan Lipsitz
Project Director

Introduction

There are more than sixteen million people in this country who are twelve, thirteen, fourteen, and fifteen, the years referred to as "early adolescence" and sometimes, inelegantly, as "transescence." Who is doing what, where, for this age group? It is this question that we address in this review of research and programs concerned with young adolescents.

Early adolescence has been overlooked in research and services. Most professionals and policy makers appear to be unaware of this void.

Terry Saario of The Ford Foundation requested a documentation, in an overview or "topographical map," of the highlights, gaps, and emerging trends in research and programs for young adolescents ages twelve through fifteen. This report is the result of her request, made possible by funding from the Foundation.

We started out with the assumption that young adolescence is the most overlooked age group among minors in America. We would have been happy to have been proven wrong. Instead, our view was reinforced by nearly every person we consulted, in every area. We have been startled by the extent to which this age group is underserved.

In Chapter 1 we review research on early adolescence in three areas: biological, socio-emotional, and cognitive. What is discussed over and over again is how much is not known about this time of life, and yet how critical most researchers feel early adolescence is to the healthy and productive functioning of the individual throughout the rest of the life span. Also documented is how few researchers are devoting themselves to answering the many unanswered questions about early adolescence. Even more serious is how few are asking in reference to early adolescence the questions that are prerequisite to developmental research. Despite the critical importance of this age group, the intellectual and economic resources of the research community are not being allocated to its study. In fact, where this age group is concerned, there appears to be no research community at present.

In Chapters 2 through 6 we look at some of the various social institutions that interact with young adolescents: schools, agencies serving the handicapped, families, voluntary youth organizations, and the juvenile justice system. Just as there is no research community dedicated to this age group, there is no "service community" for young adolescents. The researchers lack a theoretical framework to undergird their research on adolescence; the society at large lacks a coherent concept of adolescence to inform its service agencies, which therefore all too often lack rational sets of purposes to guide policy making and service delivery.

Instead, American society functions on the basis of several widespread myths about adolescents, who they are and how they are best served.

One such myth is that adolescence is a time of tumultuous upheaval during which the best we can do is to hold our breaths, wait for it to pass over, and meanwhile segregate as best we can the turbulent from the rest of society. Research showing adolescence for the majority of the population as being marked by stability rather than change, and relative serenity rather than turmoil, cannot compete with the stereotypical teenager who informs not only our mass media but, unfortunately, many of our social institutions as well.

A second myth is that junior-high-aged adolescents are children, or at most in a transitional stage between childhood and adolescence. Research showing that every decade the onset of puberty occurs four months earlier has had no effect on policymakers, and little on parents and professionals. We have not been willing to change our concept of who young adolescents are and what their needs are, despite our positive experiences of them as mature, personable young people and our negative experiences with this age group during which such antisocial behavior as drug abuse is now peaking.

A third myth that we see causing the malfunctioning of social institutions daily is the belief we insist upon holding onto that "teenagers" form a homogeneous age group. The variability of the various ages that adolescents must juggle—chronological, social, academic, biological, emotional, intellectual—is probably the most striking characteristic of this time in the life span, and the least acknowledged by societal structures.

There are other myths; in fact, they are so pervasive that this report might have been organized around popular misconceptions about young adolescents. These misconceptions are important because they are destructive. At their heart, they reflect a deep mistrust or even dislike of young people in formative years of their lives.

It is at the very least cost ineffective to expend considerable sums of money on the very young without the followthrough necessary to make good on our investment. We would hope, however, that our society could dedicate itself to the welfare of young adolescents for reasons a bit more admirable than cost effectiveness. Early adolescence is a time of growth and change second only to infancy in velocity. Social institutions for children and youth are society's mechanism for acting out its concerns. The paucity of programs serving early adolescents, the small number of professionals knowledgeable about and dedicated to their welfare, the lack of training programs for future professionals, the absence of dialogue about this age group, all these point to an acting out not of concern, but of fear; if not fear, then indifference.

It is the immodest aim of this report that the myths, mistrust, fear, and indifference be questioned and rejected in favor of a new social concern for early adolescence, an exciting and critical time in the life of every human being.

Part I:
Research on Early Adolescence

1 Research Review

Concepts of Adolescence

> It is my conviction that each life period has its sorrows and exhilarations for the individual who experiences them as well as for those surrounding him and that each period has its significance for the continuous development of the human race. Youth is neither golden nor rotten. It has the potential of all human experience.[1]

This report reviews current research and programs concerned specifically with young adolescents, approximately twelve through fifteen years old. Anyone who has worked with this age group knows the arbitrariness of isolating such years within a self-contained category. At the same time, it is precisely this arbitrariness that must become one of the subjects of this report. The ages were chosen because society, through institutions like junior high schools, sees the years from twelve through fifteen as forming a coherent stage in life. Young adolescence is a socially defined category, labeled as a "stage" and then neglected. It is the central irony of this study that we are concentrating on an age group, limiting our attention to it as much as possible, in order to help eliminate it as an arbitrarily segregated age category within broader concepts of adolescence.

Friedenberg says that if a people have no word for something, either it does not matter to them or it matters too much to talk about.[2] We have no name for these adolescents who are neither "preadolescents" nor the "youth" writers refer to when speaking about high school and college age people. They are "young" or "early" adolescents. As such, they belong to that large amorphous group we have so much trouble accounting for in our society: adolescents.

Our purpose in this section is not to provide new definitions of adolescence, but rather to review concepts of adolescence that are currently informing research. As a society we have no coherent concept of adolescence. The various theories of adolescence with which scholars and practitioners deal all emphasize similar features, like physical growth, sexual maturation, increasing autonomy, increasing cognitive sophistication. Even so, biological, psychological, and sociological concepts stand apart from one another because there is little dialogue among the disciplines.

Biologically, adolescence spans the years between the onset of puberty and the completion of bone growth. Puberty is defined biologically as that phase of bodily development during which the gonads secrete sex hormones in amounts sufficient to cause accelerated growth and during which secondary sex characteristics appear.[3]

Psychologically, Erikson's concept of adolescence as a time of both identity crisis and psychosocial moratorium dominates the literature. The adolescent's task is to integrate what he appears to be to others with what he feels he is.

According to Erikson, the adolescent identity crisis demands the simultaneous resolution of seven conflicts: temporal perspective versus time confusion, self-certainty versus self-consciousness, role experimentation versus role fixation, apprenticeship versus work paralysis, sexual polarization versus bisexual confusion, leader-and-followership versus authority confusion, and ideological commitment versus confusion of values. Other stages in life demand resolution of conflicts, but "not until adolescence does the individual develop the prerequisites in physiological growth, mental maturation and social responsibility to experience and pass through the crisis of identity."[4]

Not until adolescence does the individual see himself as having a past and a future that are exclusively his. Adolescence is thus a pivotal time of recapitulation and anticipation. It is a time when the individual seeks his distinctive identity, consisting of a conscious sense of personal uniqueness, an unconscious striving for continuity of experience, and a solidarity with group ideals.[5]

The moratorium Erikson describes is a time of delay granted by society to people at the end of childhood who are not ready to accept the obligations of adulthood. It allows for a delay of adult commitments. It permits experimentation, sometimes provocative and sometimes intense, with various commitments. It is a time of socially approved exploration and experimentation which, if truncated, can lead to the premature foreclosure of identity development.

In sociological definitions of adolescence there is a lack of consensus as to the boundaries of contemporary adolescence. The editors of *Adolescence in the Life Cycle* use what they see as the clearest social markers: the years between seventh grade and (relatively) complete independence from the family of origin. The young come to maturity within social contexts that are subject to societal, historical, and ecological variation. These variations, sociologists urge, must inform our view of adolescence.[6]

Bakan contends that adolescence was invented or discovered in America in response to social changes in the late nineteenth and early twentieth centuries, its principal purpose being to prolong childhood. Three movements combined to create adolescence as a socially determined stage of life: compulsory education, child labor legislation, and special legal procedures for juveniles. Thus, adolescence became defined by legislation associated with these three movements as the period between pubescence and the legal ages for termination of compulsory education, employment, and criminal procedure.[7]

Precisely because adolescence was added to childhood to prepare youngsters for a labor market that no longer exists, Bakan finds Erikson's approach an "idyllic vision." This vision, that adolescence can be viewed as a period of psychosocial moratorium during which the individual experiments and finds a niche for himself in his society, a niche which, according to Erikson, is firmly defined and yet seems to be uniquely made for him must, says Bakan, be viewed cynically given the exclusion of adolescents from the larger society.[8] (We suspect that Erikson would agree, since he sees variations in moratoria as linked to cultural and subcultural variations.) John P. Hill would agree with Bakan that there is no firmly defined niche. We have no important rituals, the *rites-de-passage*, which mark transitions into and out of adolescence.[9] American socialization processes may place extra burdens on adolescents, expecting each child to forge himself into a distinctive, separate individual. Unlike cultures in which an adolescent comes to define selfhood by being most like adults, American adolescents have difficulty finding a preordained place in the social unit. Our society confers on young people a long period of emphasis on self-definition, with expectations of social mobility and open choice—a social "frontier." (An additional burden is imposed on those adolescents who, while going through this process, experience the discordance of knowing that the "frontier" is closed.)

In contrast to negative assessments of the origins and roles of adolescence in American society, the Joint Commission on Mental Health of Children takes a positive view of the role of industrial societies in fostering adolescence. In fact, they recommend that "American society must take vigorous steps to grant to all its youth the right to developmental experience appropriate to the adolescent years."[10]

It may well be that one of the most defining characteristics of adolescence is its vulnerability to external events. Even biologically, one must take care to speak of adolescence within given historical contexts, as we shall see. Socially, one takes one's professional life in one's hands by making pronouncements that are to serve as definitions for even a decade. Witness the following statement in *The Vanishing Adolescent*, written in 1959:

> Adolescence is not simply a physical process; there is more to it than sexual maturation. It is also—and primarily—a social process, whose fundamental task is clear and stable self-identification.
>
> This process may be frustrated and emptied of meaning in a society which, like our own, is hostile to clarity and vividness. Our culture impedes the clear definition of any faithful self-image—indeed, of any clear image whatsoever. We do not break images; there are few iconoclasts among us. Instead, we blur and soften them. The resulting pliability gives life in our society its familiar, plastic texture. It also makes adolescence more difficult, more dangerous, and more troublesome to the adolescent and to society itself. And it makes adolescence rarer.[11]

As evidence for this argument, Friedenberg cites the beat and silent generations. "It is the fully human adolescent—the adolescent who faces life with love and defiance—who has become aberrant."[12] If this argument holds for the 1950s, it certainly does not for the 1960s, a decade which saw "love and defiance" among the young to the great distress of many. Perhaps the argument now holds for the 1970s, when we are seeing a new, eerily quiet generation. Any global statement about adolescence may hold for a decade, if one is lucky.

Glen Elder asks questions that highlight the fallacies of discussing adolescence outside of a socio-historical perspective. Elder points out that "cyclical change in the economy differentiates birth cohorts [people born in the same time period], and thus the experience of adolescence and youth." If prolonged dependency is a function of affluent societies, what, for instance, was the nature of adolescence during the Great Depression?[13] This observation has implications for the present. For instance, in the development of adolescents, what is the role of the energy crisis, inflation, of our present awareness of growth limitations within our economy? Department of Labor figures indicate that almost half of unemployed Americans are aged sixteen to twenty-four. More than forty percent of all black teenagers in the country were unemployed during 1975 and 1976. We can only speculate about the influences that anticipated unemployment may have on development during early adolescence. At the very least, we can say that adolescents are vulnerable to economic fluctuations.

They are also vulnerable to social fluctuations. For instance, we do not know what it means to be an adolescent during a time when adults provide less guidance about adulthood, going through their own "second adolescence" of sexual experimentation and exploration in second careers—their own psychosocial moratorium, as it were.

Konopka states that "there is often discussion in the literature whether 'adolescence' is a natural developmental stage or is purely sociologically determined, and especially a product of Western industrialized society. My view is that it is a developmental stage, universal because of biological endocrine changes. Its particular forms and stresses are culturally determined."[14] We concur with this view as a summary definition of adolescence *per se*. We are nevertheless left with the same question we will begin and end with: What does it mean to be an adolescent? What are the current assumptions about adolescents? Most important for this report, what does it mean to be a young adolescent in the United States during the 1970s?

Erikson calls adolescence an age of identity seeking. Konopka, while relying heavily on Eriksonian concepts, prefers to think of adolescence as the age of commitment, a move toward "the true interdependence of men." She sees the adolescent struggle between dependence and independence as an expression of this move toward interdependence.[15]

Adolescence is an important stage in and of itself. We often lose sight of such importance when we speak of it as a transitional stage, and when we see youth-serving institutions as "preparing" youngsters for "life." It is therefore necessary to underscore the importance of adolescence *per se* while we explore the concept of adolescence in the life cycle. This perspective, which will dominate areas of this report, insists upon the continuity of adolescence research. It is one which is being given at least verbal recognition at the outposts of program development.

The barriers to adopting such a perspective are considerable. Hill provides a lucid summary of these barriers: the "tendency to perceive the period as discontinuous from the remainder of the life cycle"; "the tendency to view adolescents as a homogeneous or, at best, little differentiated lot"; and "the tendency to view the nature of adolescence as endogenously programmed and the typical behavior of individual adolescents as determined by intrapsychic forces."[16]

If we insist upon asserting the discontinuity of adolescent experience, we are implying the inevitability of intergenerational conflict and of the aberrance of this stage in the life cycle. If we insist upon asserting the homogeneity of adolescence, we deny to adolescents the recognition of a wide range of ideologies, attitudes, customs, motives, and habits that we allow adults. And if we insist upon seeing physical and cognitive changes that begin in adolescence exclusively as self-generated, genetically programmed events, then interactional views (the ecological aspects of development) will continue to remain unexplored.

These three perspectives lead to a continuing stereotyping of adolescents by lay people, practitioners, and scientists. As Hill says, "Where adolescents are concerned, we are sufficiently prone to stereotypy to make the phenomenon an important one for study in its own right."[17]

It is not only a change in perspective that is required. It has been our experience in rethinking approaches to studying and serving young adolescents that there are serious deficiencies in our abilities to conceptualize alternative modes of thought. We are not here referring to alternative programs; we are referring to mental operations. Society serves up to us definitions through its mechanisms of service institutions. Adolescents do not fit neatly into these institutions, as we learn more painfully each day. We want to be able to talk about adolescents. Instead we talk about categories—research categories that are sloppy at best (e.g., biological, cognitive, socio-emotional), and program categories that we know are malfunctioning (e.g., schools, juvenile justice).

We have sought to break out of such categories, since we know that a youngster experiences life as a whole, not in sections. To put it another way, a youngster who has been incarcerated has probably had many interrelated experiences (reading problems, troubled family relationships, lack of scholastic achievement, emotional problems, etc.) which various institutions are called upon to respond to separately. It certainly was our intention, at the very least, not to compound this problem by preparing a report broken down into exactly those same fragmented categories.

We have tried to ask questions that get at the "ecology" of the youngster's day-to-day life: for instance, "What happens to a young adolescent with problems?" It is a clarifying question. The interrelationships among the problems and the fragmentation of research and services could not come clearer. Such questions cut across areas like reading problems, learning disabilities, criminal justice, endocrinology, nutrition, mental health facilities, etc. Everyone says we need to cut across these categories. We see few efforts to create the mechanisms for doing this, especially in research. We suspect this is because it is, first of all, a conceptual problem before it is an organizational one.

It will be a continuing theme of this book that what is lacking in adolescent psychology is a conceptual framework of adolescence, and particularly of early adolescence. Adults do not know what distinguishes the adolescent from the child and the adult. There is little theory besides Erikson's to spur much meaningful research on early adolescence or to help give definition to adequate social agencies.

How is one to reconceptualize the entire mode of thinking about and serving youth? We find this to be the central question being asked by a handful of researchers now.

Elder says that the state of theory and research on adolescence as a multidisciplinary field of inquiry appears to resemble the "Tower of Babel."[18] Gallatin says that Eriksonian theory already provides a conceptual umbrella for adolescence research.[19] Hill says that there exists no theory of human development equal to the task of describing, organizing, and rendering comprehensible the phenomena of adolescence. We require a theory that is life-span, contextual, and interactionist.[20] Elder agrees that it is within a life-span framework that we can begin to break through the isolation of that tower of Babel.

Isolation is a pervasive theme in our investigation of programs and research for young adolescents—the isolation that young people feel within themselves, the isolation of the age group from other groups, of one institution in relation to another, of each research discipline from others, and of researchers within disciplines from their colleagues who speak different methodological languages. Finally, there is the personal isolation of those few professionals who are concerned with the growth, development, and well-being of young adolescents.

Overview of Research on Early Adolescence

In this section, we will be discussing highlights, emerging trends, and voids in research as identified by researchers themselves—by those people whose major professional concern is asking and researching questions, and who are not concerned primarily with making programs function on a day-to-day basis. Research issues that are specific to social institutions, for instance to schools or juvenile justice institutions, will be included in the chapters dealing with the particular institutions in question.

The review of ongoing research will be presented in six sections: an overview of principal sources of research on early adolescence and general research trends;

sections reviewing biological, socio-emotional, and cognitive research; federal funding; and research recommendations.

Sources of Research on Early Adolescence

. . . there are few areas in which investigations relating to the key issues of adolescence have moved beyond exploratory efforts and clinically-based theoretical formulations.[21]

Not one single researcher contacted during the preparation of this report has expressed satisfaction with the state of research on young adolescence. The following excerpts from a sampling of letters and conversations give the flavor of responses to questions about the state of the art in various disciplines:

"Not much is going on,"

"People are doing little things, here and there,"

"There is no more neglected field,"

"It is an overlooked age,"

"Only the surface is scratched,"

"Our knowledge of adolescence is so astoundingly limited,"

"The twelve-to-fifteen age group is woefully understudied."

The paucity of outstanding developmental research is documented by Hill:

A list of the twenty-five leading developmental psychologists today selected on the basis of almost any criterion would not include one whose reputation was established primarily on the basis of scholarship in the adolescence area. There is no set of national centers of excellence in the adolescence area; there is not even one. It is doubtful whether more than five percent of the pages in *Developmental Psychology* and *Child Development* over the past five years have been devoted to adolescence. These pieces of information must also be seen in the light of the massive increase in developmental research, in general, during the past decade.[22]

Several people have offered explanations for this paucity of research talent and activity. For instance, Deborah Waber, whose work reflects a biological perspective on psychological problems, attributes the lack of attention paid by developmental psychologists to adolescents to two causes, first attitudinal and second intellectual.

The attitudinal dimensions are twofold. Adolescents, as she says, are difficult and frequently not the pleasantest people to work with. They do not offer the rewards that preschoolers offer to researchers. In addition, adolescence is a period of loss of childlikeness. Developmental psychology has traditionally been concerned with childhood and therefore adolescence tends to be viewed as a period of transition rather than as a period to be studied in itself.

The intellectual dimension stems from the heritage of both the Freudian and Skinnerian traditions. From these traditions we conclude incorrectly that behavioral plasticity declines with age in a linear fashion. Young children are seen as being the most malleable and open to experience. Investigators assume that by the time children reach adolescence, behavior patterns are already well established.

Waber considers this to be an unfortunate position. Human beings, unlike most other animals, experience two periods of intense growth, early childhood and adolescence. The stress on early childhood to the exclusion of adolescence leads researchers to neglect what may be a second major period of behavioral plasticity. It is likely, Waber argues, that plasticity increases at adolescence rather than decreases. "Adolescence may then be a golden opportunity for intervention."[23]

John P. Hill points out that psychologists have not been immune to the kinds of ideological constructions about adolescence discussed above. They are also apt to see adolescence as an aberrant period in the life cycle which might not provide fertile ground for testing beginning formulations of processes presumed to be universal.[24]

For whatever reasons, adolescence is inadequately represented in our present research efforts, and early adolescence even more so. The stagnation in adolescence research over the past several decades has occurred simultaneously with the surge of scientific interest in early childhood development. This interest has contributed importantly to the establishment of such programs as Head Start, Follow Through, Parent and Child Centers, and more recent concerns about day-care facilities.[25] The programs, in turn, have further stimulated investigators in the behavioral sciences to conduct research on early development and to pursue further the prerequisites for successful program development. It would be hoped that a corresponding surge of scientific interest in adolescence would stimulate program development which in turn would lead us to refine research methodology in biological and behavioral investigations having to do with early adolescence.

There are several sources of research on early adolescence that have been or may become rich resources. The National Institute of Child Health and Human Development (NICHD) was established in 1963. It has supported basic biological and behavioral research on human developmental processes, mostly concerned with early child development. In fiscal year 1971 NICHD spent less than one percent of its grants and contracts budget for research with a primary emphasis on adolescence. In the past few years, NICHD has begun to stimulate more research on human development during adolescence. The Growth and Development Branch of the Institute held three conferences that have become seminal in their respective fields: "Control of the Onset of Puberty," October 1972; "Nutrient Requirements in Adolescence," June 1973; "Adolescence in the Life Cycle," October 1973. NICHD identified five areas of major emphasis for research support: biological processes, nutrition, intellectual development, adolescent socialization, and endocrine and psychological development.

It is a small world of people in Washington concerned with adolescent development. According to members of the Growth and Development Branch at NICHD, the Interagency Panel for Research and Development on Adolescence's FY 1973 report, *Toward Interagency Coordination*, is the best summary of the federal government's involvement in research on adolescence. According to the Interagency Panel's report, most of their research recommendations on the process of adolescent development have been adopted from the NICHD conference, "Adolescence in the Life Cycle." The Growth and Development Branch of NICHD has become *the* central source for reviewing and stimulating research on adolescence.

The validity of this statement will bear scrutiny. NICHD has undergone reorganization that will affect adolescence research. A new organization within NICHD, the Center for Research for Mothers and Children (CRMC), has responsibility for three already existing extramural programs—Perinatal Biology and Infant Mortality, Growth and Development, and Mental Retardation. With CRMC's apparent stress on pregnancy, infancy, and early childhood, it is predicted by some observers that the adolescent program will not fare as well as it has in the past few years. In that case, one of the precious few sources stimulating and integrating new research knowledge on adolescence will be lost.

The Interagency Panel on Early Childhood Research and Development convened early in 1970 to coordinate work of agencies sponsoring federal programs affecting children. Organizational meetings for a similar panel on adolescence were held in October of 1972. This Interagency Panel provides a computerized data base for federally funded research having to do with adolescence, defined as the age group from ten through twenty-four.

To be stranded on a desert island with the Interagency Panel's 1973 and 1975 reports and with documents from NICHD (such as their program announcement of expanded research, their in-house document on expanded programs in adolescence, and the proceedings from their three conferences), is to be left with just about all there is to know about the federal government's commitment to research on adolescence. Add to that John Hill's document, "Some Perspectives on Adolescence in American Society," and Gisela Konopka's "Requirements for Healthy Development of Adolescent Youth," (two position papers prepared in 1973 for the Office of Child Development), and one has the basic materials summarizing ongoing research and recommendations for further investigations.

The Center for Youth Development and Research at the University of Minnesota is one of the few sources of research and programs at the university level addressing adolescents. "Requirements for Healthy Development of Adolescent Youth" was written to fill a request in 1973 by the Office of Child Development for a statement of the Center's concept of normal adolescence and impediments to healthy development. The statement was viewed as a possible basis for national policy. Whether any of the recommendations in this report will be implemented remains to be seen.

A possible future source of important research on adolescence is the new Boys Town complex. In November 1972, the Board of Directors of Boys Town approved the establishment of a national research and training complex. It is intended that this complex will meet the most fundamental institutional needs of the Boys Town Home: research of the processes by which young persons develop from childhood to maturity; training of personnel skilled in the care of youth; and program development at Boys Town itself. Two university-based regional centers have been established to conduct basic research concerning the problems of today's youth and at the same time to train researchers and practitioners who will have special concern for the problems of adolescents.

The Boys Town Centers are multidisciplinary. They are organized to put the research scientist into mutually helpful contact with the practitioner. This arrangement, it is hoped, should permit engagement with basic issues. They are of adequate size to deal with major problems of youth development. They are funded for twenty-five years in order to make possible sustained long-term research efforts. The complex of centers thus seeks to avoid pressures often associated with governmental and foundation grants to follow "changing fashions" in politics and social concern.[26]

This section has identified several of the most visible sources of research on early adolescence. Except for the Boys Town complex, whose successes and failures are yet to be gauged, there appears to be little inter- and intradisciplinary contact among researchers, little dialogue between research scientists and practitioners, and no safeguards for sustained research efforts.

General Research Trends

Physical, cognitive and social-emotional changes have a reciprocal influence on one another, with events at any one level able to impede or to accelerate developments at each of the others.[27]

There is one central thrust among researchers who are struggling with the present limitations in adolescence research: the insistence, conceptually and methodologically, on the interaction of biological, psychological, and sociocultural factors. Hill says that "individualism and autonomous action are so much a part of the core culture in our society that environmental or interactional views of behavioral determination and change are widely resisted."[28] We see the struggle to overcome this resistance as a strongly emerging trend in adolescence research.

Traditionally, areas of research in adolescent psychosocial development have been divided between studies of socialization and cognition. Socialization studies have included such areas as sex-role identification, family power structure, achievement motivation, child-rearing consistency, parent-peer cross pressures, and religious and/or moral development. Dimensions of cognitive growth have been studied in the areas of concept formation, orientation to the future, and political ideas. In the 1960s research began emerging independently in disciplines such as anthropology, education, medicine, psychology, social work, and sociology.

Now many researchers report that an interdisciplinary approach is required to draw the insights of the various disciplines together. Questions of human development do not fall into a single academic field. The resources of many disciplines are required to disentangle the interacting biological, psychological, and sociological forces. "Research findings, the new concepts they generate, and the fruit which these concepts bear in innovative programs are much more likely to result when there is close collaboration among sociologists, psychologists, biologists, philosophers and those in related fields than when any of these specialists operates solely within the confines of a single discipline."[29]

Some researchers are seeking to go beyond the "interdisciplinary" approach to "ecological" or "global" studies, in which findings are placed in a context of interaction with a complex of other variables. Examples would be the reciprocal aspects of components of development, or the interactive effects of institutional change.[30] (This approach is not synonymous with assessments of adolescents in society as a whole. Contextual variations must be taken into account. As Morris Rosenberg points out in *Adolescence in the Life Cycle*, young people do not live in society *as a whole*. They live in specific contexts–neighborhoods, schools, communities.[31]) It is Hill's contention that even when we are presented with interactionist theories, we will not deal with them as such.[32]

It is not possible to study a period of such rapid biological, social cognitive and emotional changes solely through unidisciplinary approaches. Even so, as Cohen and Frank point out, the vantage points of the emotional, cognitive, social, and biological researchers are not arbitrary. "Each has contributed to our understanding because each corresponds to an ongoing developmental system in the child. The course of development depends on the continuing complex interactions between these systems as well as the smooth functioning of each one alone."[33]

Besides the value of unidisciplinary studies, there are problems associated with other approaches. Interdisciplinary, life-span, and ecological studies are difficult to implement. Researchers usually lack theoretical models and research designs adequate for conceptualizing significant dimensions of human environments and for data collection and analysis.[34] And of course, personalities and "territorial rights" can come into play in counterproductive ways.

Life-span research was not new to researchers in the 1930s and 1940s. It is hard to assess whether the present emphasis on demanding such research again is a sign of revitalization of this area of research or of stagnation. Nevertheless, Elder may be correct that it is only through an analytic framework like life-span research that coherence can be brought to the developmental literature in the various domains.

The second thrust among researchers, less predominant than the one we have just discussed, is the attempt to integrate basic research with clinical observation. This attempt is one of the driving forces behind the work of Konopka and her colleagues at the Center for Youth Development and Research at the University of Minnesota, just as it is at the Child Study Center at Yale University. Donald Cohen from the Child Study Center says that in his review of the literature, there is a lack of integration between the kinds of information that come from clinical studies (including the kinds of things one may learn from working in such sites as court clinics, correctional facilities, and schools) and from the child development literature, and both are relatively isolated from the physiological literature. He recommends that teams with multidisciplinary skills might well focus on groups of particular clinical interest.[35]

These general research trends represent only a few voices. We hear them saying that there is little research in the area of early adolescence in both absolute and comparative terms. We hear a consistent calling out for an interactionist approach, for looking at the whole child, or at least for interrelationships among various aspects of development. We hear calls for research that sees adolescence as part of an entire life span. We hear constant articulation of society's confusion about this age group and its responsibility to it. We hear expressed a certain concern that as researchers we may be creating problems for young people by not knowing who these people really are, by making inappropriate assumptions which then undergird our research and contribute to ill-conceived programs. We hear concern about the lack of communication between people in research and people in programs.

What we conclude from these "voices in the wilderness" is that our programs are not informed by research and that our research is not informed by a coherent sense of who young adolescents are. So long as we remain in this state our research and our institutions, be they courts, schools, voluntary organizations, or whatever, will remain muddled at best. It is because of this that sensitive teachers, doctors, case workers, etc., often know more than anyone else. We become tempted to bypass research and pin our hopes on the rapid propagation of these people.

People are not fruit flies. We had better do a great deal of thinking about the insular and uncoordinated nature of our research efforts. We had better think a great deal about what we want the role of research to be in various fields.

It seems clear that the fact that we have so few means for interrelating clinical and practical observations in research efforts is not primarily an organizational problem.

We must call attention to the pleas for interdisciplinary research and the pleas for research and programs that are mutually informed by one another. We need some insights into the strength of the pleas and the paucity of the endeavors.

Biological Research

Puberty, next to birth itself, is the most drastic change we experience in life, but unlike birth, we are acutely aware of the exciting transitions through which we pass. . . . What triggers these profound metamorphoses?[36]

The second most astonishing fact about adolescence research is how little we know. The first is how few people are currently furthering our knowledge, remarkably few given the excitement of studying an age of growth that is explosive along many dimensions.

Opening sections of this report reviewed biological, psychological, and sociological concepts of adolescence and offered some general comments regarding adolescence research. We turn now to a more detailed discussion of biological, socio-emotional, and cognitive research, representing areas of early adolescent development generally acknowledged to be the most significant.

Anyone who has ever taught in a junior high school knows that there is no such thing as a "ninth grader." The variability among the students in one classroom can be bizarre. The variability within one student along the various growth dimensions (physical, cognitive, emotional, social) can be disturbing both to the students and to adults. James Tanner, author of the classic work, *Growth at Adolescence* (1962), stresses continually the different ages at which children begin their growth spurts and pubertal changes, as well as the variation of pubertal patterns. "To speak, therefore, of a 'boy aged fourteen' is to be vague to the point of leaving out almost everything that is important about fourteen-year-old boys. The same is true of talking about twelve-year-old girls (or thirteen-year-old boys or girls, naturally)."[37]

The mean age of menarche (the first menstrual period) for girls is 12.9. Their adolescent growth spurt initiates at a mean age of 9.6. Its peak velocity is at a mean age of 11.8. Comparable milestones occur two years later for boys.[38] These figures cannot be seen as absolutes:

One of the most important—and most often ignored—characteristics of the biological change at puberty is the variability in the time of its onset. . . . If this sequence is considered to end at the time of first ejaculation, it may be noted that average age is 13½ to 14 but that this may occur earlier or later depending upon when the process began. What should be remarked here is that, given two boys of the same chronological age, one may complete the sequence before the other has begun it. One is, therefore, exposed to a totally different set of internal and external stimuli (in the reactions of others) than the other.[39]

Nevertheless, the figures cited above for the mean age of menarche and the adolescent growth spurt have great personal and social significance.

The social significance of the figures pertaining to the onset of puberty has to do with what is referred to as "the secular trend": children grow more, and experience the adolescent growth spurt and the onset of puberty, approximately four months earlier each decade. A secular trend is one that persists over a period of several decades. Were this trend to remain constant, it has been estimated that at the present rate of change of one inch gain per generation, man would have doubled his standing height and have reached an average of eleven to twelve feet by the year 4000. If the age of menarche were to continue to decline at the present rate of four months per decade, by the year 2240 the average four year old would experience menarche.[40] The obvious question is whether there is a boundary to man's size. Various theorists—anthropologists and geneticists—predict a leveling off effect of this secular trend. At least one study has indicated that the trend has already ended. Tanner maintains that it is presently continuing unabated.

There are various theories as to the cause of the secular trend, usually including better nutrition. Whatever the cause or causes, we have not examined the social impact of the earlier onset of puberty. A paradoxical movement in opposite directions results from a shorter biological childhood and the longer social childhood afforded (or forced upon) adolescents. During the industrial revolution and westward expansion in America, there was less time allotted for defining one's identity by "trying on" alternatives. Now, adolescents experience an earlier onset of puberty coupled with an extended time to explore and determine future possibilities and present potentialities. The complex interrelationships among biological age, chronological age, and social age remain virtually uninvestigated.

Our expectations of youth are based on preconceived notions of the characteristics of chronological age. This frame of reference, seen malfunctioning in our schools and families, is one that demands rethinking. Definition by chronological age can be viewed as one of the myths imposed by society on young adolescents.

The Onset of Adolescence–Nutrition

In *Promoting the Health of Mothers and Children*, The Maternal and Child Health Service reports that the three groups most vulnerable to poor nutrition are infants and young children, adolescents, and women of childbearing age.[41]

The Ten-State Nutrition Survey of 1972 indicated that young people between the ages of ten and sixteen had the highest rates of unsatisfactory nutritional status, males more than females. Problems included underweight, undersize, obesity, iron-deficiency anemia, and dental caries. Hemoglobin levels were inadequate (less than 12 grams per 100 milliliters) in 10.27 percent of 13-16 year old boys and in 24.89 percent of 13-16 year old girls.[42] Also, *Maternal Nutrition and the Course of Pregnancy*, a summary report from the National Academy of Science's Food and Nutrition Board, states that "such evidence as there is" on the nutritional status and food habits of pregnant and nonpregnant adolescent girls suggests a frequency of "bizarre" dietary habits, involving inadequate intakes of iron, calcium, vitamin A, and ascorbic acid.[43]

It is generally agreed that nutrition hits one of its low spots during adolescence. What is not known is exactly what constitutes adequate nutrition for this age group.

A paper prepared for internal use by staff members from NICHD points out that although adolescence represents one of the most complex stages in human development and one of the most critical, relatively little is known about the nutrient requirements of this stage. The summary proceedings of a workshop sponsored by the National Academy of Sciences, *Extent and Meanings of Iron Deficiency in the U.S.*, support this conclusion. Participants reviewed methods of assessing iron nutriture and attempted to establish the prevalence of iron deficiency. The report, based on a review of the literature for the past twelve years which uncovered no more than a dozen relevant papers, concludes that there are practically no data on iron deficiency in adolescents.[44]

The adolescent growth spurt is second in rate of change only to infants' growth. The developmental and long-range health implications of adolescent nutrition would appear to be critical. Perhaps they are not. Most experts feel that research and intervention emphases should assure adequate nutrition during pregnancy and through the first two years of life. The brain is one of the systems most vulnerable to insult during infancy. Eighty percent of the biological development of the brain (size, cell number, cell form) is completed by age two. There is strongly suggestive evidence that early malnutrition directly affects later intellectual competence. The evidence is not conclusive as to whether and under what conditions such damage is irreversible.

It is no wonder, given the weight of the evidence stressing early intervention, that the developmental nutritional needs of adolescents have been assigned low priorities in research and in services, except insofar as they involve pregnant adolescents.

Further, the relationships among poverty, undernutrition, and subsequent development in America are becoming dwarfed by the spectre of worldwide famine. Inadequate nutrition pales as an issue before the fact of famine. The data in Birch and Gussow[45] about undernutrition, malnutrition, birth risk, and illness—all the data that came down upon us like hail during the 1960s and led to impassioned calls for action—now seem almost comfortingly familiar in comparison with discussions about "triage." In this context, American adolescents snacking on empty calories in candy bars and soft drinks seem singularly blessed.

If we are not to forfeit our continuing commitment to healthy and intact human beings, functioning optimally, we must nevertheless inquire into the attention being paid to the status of research and programs on adolescent nutrition. We must be concerned with adolescents in terms of the functional significance of early and current nutritional deficits for adolescent behavior. Other major nutritionally related events take place during adolescence, including emotional stresses, changes in caloric demands, changes in attitudes towards food, experimentation with diets, and the molding of diet patterns. We have little knowledge about the factors that determine adolescent eating patterns, and the effects of these patterns on adolescents.

We must also be concerned about the effects of adolescent nutriture on subsequent adult performance. There is almost no literature on adolescent nutriture as it affects adulthood, for instance what degenerative processes may originate in adolescence as a result of nutrition. We are told that adolescents are particularly vulnerable to poor nutrition. We must investigate what, precisely, this means.

One of the purposes of NICHD's 1973 conference, "The Nutrient Requirements of Adolescence," was to stimulate broader interest in adolescent nutrition. "Broader" may be understood in two senses. First, staff members felt that the literature in adolescent nutrition is not great because of the overwhelming emphasis on the nutrition of younger children. One aim of the conference was to help stimulate interest in a broader age range. Second, within the field of adolescent nutrition itself, NICHD has supported more studies in obesity than in any other area. A purpose of the conference, therefore, was to stimulate interest in other aspects of nutrition. The recommendations that emerged from the conference indicate that aspects identified by researchers thirty and forty years ago as needing attention are still being highlighted as serious gaps in our knowledge.[46]

Participants, divided into four work groups, asked that the recommended dietary allowances be examined with regard to adolescents. The age groupings fail to correspond to sex differences in adolescent growth, and the heights and weights imply a single figure for a three-year period during which adolescents grow rapidly. Likewise, individual dietary requirements for adolescents should be based on maturation status, body size, and body composition, not on chronological age. Research determining the distribution of growth rates for successive ages during puberty and adolescence is needed for definition of nutritional requirements and for determining long-range health implications of variations in growth velocity.

Some researchers recommended that a study be made of the psychosocial forces that influence adolescent dietary intake and that may affect nutrient needs. There were several requests for studies on the influence of drugs, alcohol, oral contraceptives, pregnancy, and athletic programs on nutrient requirements and nutritional status within the age group. One work group stated that more precise data are required for further research, e.g., "There is only one study of adolescents at the limited ages of 10-12 years for requirements of essential amino acids." One work group at the conference summarized the state of the art bluntly: "A complete study of growth, nutrition, psychology and morbidity is needed. . . ."[47]

It is clear from the Ten-State Nutrition Survey that certain individuals in our adolescent population are not in optimum nutritional status. What remains unclear, but of concern, is whether their present and future health are thereby being compromised. At this point, there is more concern than knowledge about the relationship between the nutritional status of adolescents and their previous and subsequent development.

Unfortunately, too much research on adolescent nutrition is of the quality of a study supported by the Michigan state government, whose purpose was to develop recipes to encourage increased teenage consumption of Michigan red kidney and cranberry beans. The objective of the study was the standardization of eight to ten red kidney bean formulas to encourage increased utilization of dry beans by away-from-home institutional outlets for teenage eating. Progress was made. Recipes for six menu items (bean salad, bean pizza, chili con carne, chili burgers, harvest pie, and yum yum cookies) were checked and rechecked. These recipes are available from the Michigan Bean Commission.[48] (What is good for adolescents seems to be what the state of Michigan has to offer them.)

Some specialists argue that the most provocative nutritional work being done at present takes place in the offices of pediatric allergists. The case method has developed a clinical literature suggesting relationships between diet and learning and/or behavioral disorders. There has, for instance, been considerable clinical success reported with dietary changes in hyperactive learning disabled children. Lacking adequate explanations of the biochemical mechanisms involved, such reports are not highly regarded within the medical profession.

Sol Klotz, medical advisor at The Green Valley School in Florida, reports that a very large number of adolescents with behavior problems at the school are found to be suffering from two major conditions, allergies and hypoglycemia. Remediation of academic and behavioral disabilities through dietary changes and hypodesensitization appears to be strikingly successful. Whether or not the medical intervention is the primary cause of remediation is open to question, but the findings are highly suggestive.[49]

Roger J. Williams, in *Nutrition Against Disease: Environmental Prevention*, cites a London study in which seventeen delinquent girls (eleven to fifteen years of age) were changed from a diet made up largely of white bread, margarine, cheap jams, sweet tea, canned and processed meats, to one which was far more nutritious and diversified. Their behavior quickly became less aggressive.[50]

Ray C. Wunderlich, a pediatric allergist, has found that the maladaptive child frequently has blood sugar values at the lower end of the normal scale. These children do not work well under the high sugar load common in the American diet. Wunderlich sites the findings of Dr. Ross Cameron of the Pinellas County Health Department in St. Petersburg, Florida. Cameron performed oral glucose tolerance tests on fifty 10-15 year old inmates of a juvenile detention center. Seventy percent were found to have flat oral glucose tolerance curves, forty percent were diagnosed as hypoglycemic when further analyzed according to symptoms.[51]

Michael Lerner (director of The Full Circle Residential Research and Treatment Center in Bolinas, California), who has provided background materials for this discussion, argues that we need not restrict our observations to young people in jail. Any observer skilled in the diagnosis of nutritionally related neurological disorders underlying behavioral and learning problems sees the "continuum of casualties" in every urban and suburban classroom.

Probably best known is the work of Dr. Benjamin Feingold, Chief Emeritus of the Allergy Section of Kaiser Foundation Hospitals and Permanente Medical Group, who reports that some hyperactive children with learning or behavior problems respond dramatically to a diet that removes artificial food flavors and colors, as well as the natural salicylates, from their food. The child most likely to be helped by such a diet appears to be the aggressive/assaultive hyperactive child. Dr. Feingold states that the nature of the disturbance he sees as caused by additives is yet to be determined, but the ability to "turn on" and "turn off" the clinical pattern dietetically suggests a functional disturbance rather than organic damage. He claims that the link between hyperkinesis and learning disabilities with the ingestion of artificial food colors and flavors accounts for forty to sixty percent of the disturbances of the children involved.[52]

Lerner points out that when Feingold takes children off artificial flavors and colors, he is in effect putting them on a "natural diet." Exactly what causes the behavioral changes is at present difficult to say. Relief may be caused by the withdrawal of allergenic foods or by the accompanying dietary changes. It is possible that allergies to synthetic chemicals in the diet, particularly artificial food flavors and colors, may be as important as hypoglycemia in causing neurological disorders. In any event, Lerner does not maintain that diet alone can rehabilitate the deeply troubled child. It is of critical importance because it may in many cases make rehabilitation possible.

Feingold's theories are being tested by the Food and Drug Administration and National Institute of Education. There is a need to continue this process of testing the claims being made about the effectiveness of dietary therapy in treating preadolescents and early adolescents as well as younger children. The tangled relationships among learning disorders, academic failure, juvenile delinquency, allergies, hypoglycemia, and diet need to be studied carefully in clinical and laboratory settings. If it is true that many of the children in the worst trouble in American society have marked nutritional problems, and that alleviation of these problems produces improvement in their capacity for normal behavior, then as Lerner suggests, investigating these issues appears to be a relatively inexpensive, justifiable social priority.

Another area of controversy in adolescent nutrition involves the role of nutrition, specifically weight, in the onset of puberty. The relationships between nutrition and endocrinology are not clear. Puberty, with its hormonal changes, is a critical time for hormone-nutrient interactions. Rose Frisch has asked a central question: How do physical growth and sexual maturation get synchronized? Frisch sees weight as the critical factor. Anything that delays weight (poor nutrition, high sea level) delays menarche in girls. In other words, menarche is weight-dependent. Girls reach menarche earlier ("the secular trend") because they weigh more sooner.

In 1969 Frisch and Revelle reported their finding that the time of fastest weight gain during the adolescent growth spurt occurred at the same mean weight but at differing ages. They found that the mean weight of girls at the time of initiation of the adolescent growth spurt, at the time of peak velocity of weight gain, and at menarche did not differ for early and late maturing girls. Comparable findings held for boys, but at different ages, weights, and heights than those of the girls. It was a surprise to these investigators that these three major events of human adolescence were each related to an unchanging mean weight. "We propose that there is a direct relation between a critical body weight, representing a critical metabolic rate, and menarche."[53] Frisch and Revelle hypothesize that the secular trend should end when the weight of children remains the same because of the attainment of maximum nutrition and child care.

It is known that the critical weights of different races differ; for example, Japanese girls are about six kilograms lighter at peak velocity, which precedes menarche, than are girls of the United States. Answers to questions raised by racial and ethnic differences require further research on the biological determinates of fertility.[54]

An unanswered question in the work of Frisch and Revelle is how the attainment of the critical mean weight triggers menarche. The state of the art is shaky enough that Tanner asks whether we should reverse Dr. Frisch's concept and say that a critical weight is reached at menarche. At this point there are no decisive answers.

The Onset of Adolescence–Endocrinology

Tanner, speaking about the various events of puberty, ends his discussion thus: "To give more specific endocrinological explanations of the events, their sequence and timing, is not within the scope of the present brief summary. Perhaps that is as well, for we have none at present."[55] The last three-and-one-half pages of concluding comments of *The Control of the Onset of Puberty* consist of questions that need answering. For instance, what is the basis of the clock that determines the remarkable consistency in the time of puberty for each species? Should we reverse Dr. Frisch's concept? Do such factors as olfaction, vision, and environmental lighting influence the timing of puberty? How do we best define puberty?

The Control of the Onset of Puberty is a book based on the proceedings of the NICHD conference of the same name. It is a collection of clinical and research knowledge gathered about control mechanisms associated with transition into puberty, for instance, at the level of the central nervous system, the pituitary gland, gonads, peripheral tissues, and hormonal interactions.

The book contains discussions in six areas: (1) hormonal patterns in pubescence; (2) hypothalamic-pituitary regulation of puberty; (3) central nervous system and puberty; (4) steroid receptors and target organs during puberty; (5) somatic growth patterns and puberty; and (6) gonadal maturation.

Tanner summarizes the somatic changes of puberty as follows:

> (1) A general increase in the growth rate of skeleton, muscles, and viscera, known as the adolescence growth spurt. (2) Sex-specific increase in growth rates, for example, of shoulder and hip width above the general spurt, leading to an enhancement of sexual dimorphism. (3) Changes in body composition caused by an increase in muscle, decrease in fat, and increase in cortical but not medullary bone more pronounced in boys than girls. (4) The development of the reproductive system and secondary sex characteristics.[56]

The Control of the Onset of Puberty raises more questions than it answers about endocrine-related changes at puberty. At the same time, there is an exciting sense of being on the threshold of new discoveries made possible by methodological breakthroughs.

In the introduction, Gilman D. Grave says, "The contents of this book represent a thorough compilation of the state of the art today at both the theoretical and practical level. If few of the key questions received definitive answers at the conference, at least most of them were asked. They are now gathered in this volume in which they will, we hope, stimulate more research on the control of the onset of puberty."[57]

Recent advances in methodology are making it possible for scientists to study prepubertal and pubertal hormonal changes. Julian M. Davidson of the Stanford University Department of Physiology writes in answer to a question about biomedical research needs, "I would identify research on the physiological mechanisms for controlling the onset of puberty as an important area which is still shrouded in mystery, but for which the tools are available for basic research."[58]

Davidson's contribution to *The Control of the Onset of Puberty* is a review of the current status of conceptualization about mechanisms involved in the onset of puberty. His review reflects the general sense of excitement in this area of research. "Now that reliable measurements of gonadotropin and gonadal steroid levels in the blood of immature individuals are possible, the way is open for the quantitative evaluation of concepts. This methodological revolution is just beginning to bear fruit in the field of experimental puberty."[59] Researchers' knowledge, however (for instance, of the details of the interaction between the hypothalamus and the pituitary) is still extremely limited. Throughout his article Davidson uses such words as "sketchy," "vague," "mystery," in referring to the mechanisms of the onset of puberty.

R.A. Gorski of the University of California, Los Angeles, has contributed a review of extrahypothalamic influences on gonadotropin regulation for *The Control of the Onset of Puberty.*[60] Also, J. Van Wyk's laboratory at the University of North Carolina has isolated a potent growth factor, somatomedin, which is now under intense study, funded by NIH. The Nobel Foundation sponsored the first symposium on the somatomedins in Stockholm in September 1974. Chapel Hill, Stockholm, and Zurich house the three laboratories studying this growth factor.[61] "Although growth hormone (somatotrophin) is generally regarded as the principal hormone regulating skeletal growth, evidence has accumulated that growth hormone does not itself stimulate linear growth, but rather induces the formation of a secondary growth-promoting factor. . . . This factor has been found to play a much more profound role in cell growth than initially suspected." Somatomedin is the genetic designation for these insulin-like substances. To date the mechanism by which growth hormone stimulates somatomedin production remains unclear. "Just how many substances of this description exist, the manner in which they are formed, the clarification of their roles in health and disease, and their possible therapeutic usefulness are questions which remain to be answered. The unfolding of this story should be of particular interest to pediatricians and other scientists concerned with human growth."[62]

NICHD sponsors purely organic work governing the onset of adolescence, trying to find out factors that operate normally to control growth and sexual maturation. A concern that surfaces infrequently among endocrinologists, but of obvious clinical importance, is on what basis human decisions are made, and by whom. The following is illustrative:

During the symposium on the control of the onset of puberty, Kulin and Reiter reported on delayed sexual maturation in the male. "Puzzling and difficult to diagnose at the time of expected puberty are the clinical syndromes associated with absolute or relative hypogonadotropism" (deficient development of secondary sexual characteristics).[63] It is their opinion that under any circumstances adolescence is a trying period and that the adolescent boy is "entitled to secondary sexual characteristics at an appropriate time."[64] Kulin and Reiter, because of problems in diagnosis, recommend a short-term trial treatment with agents like testosterone in any boy who is approaching the age of fourteen and does not have significant pubertal development, but has normal prepubertal size organs and levels of gonadotropins.

Tanner, in response, took great exception to this direction of treatment. "We should not forget the cultural impact of this, especially since we are talking about doing something that I would fairly violently disagree with, i.e., inducing puberty in all boys who have not got there by fourteen." Tanner's objection is based on the possible trade-off of earlier maturation for dwarfism. "Most people feel that you often jo just that (cause some short grownups). A little bit of psychotherapy and social support is best for these kids while they are waiting to do what is really normal."[65]

John Money, in response to this debate, makes a statement the major thrust of which is that each case must be judged on its individual merits. He stresses, however, that "it is very difficult for some youngsters to be caught in that no-man's land between their chronological age and their physique age, trying to keep up their social age, their academic age, their personality age, and their psychosexual age, in conformity with their chronological age."[66]

What is most striking about Money's statement is that in it suddenly adolescents emerge as people, people growing albeit with greater pain than most of their peers, but people nonetheless, anticipating their futures and experiencing their present relationships in all the complexities that being human entails. This perspective is one to be cherished for its humaneness and rarity.

Van Wyk would like to make it possible for more people to have such a perspective. In his practice he sees young people passing through adolescence with physical deviations that cause them great concern. These deviations may not be life-threatening situations, but the concerns they generate are intense and require counseling. Van Wyk and his associates are planning a training program in psychological counseling—"Psycho-endocrinology."

Incorporating psychologists into endocrinology started in the 1950s at Johns Hopkins with Lawson Wilkins. Now John Money, whom the public knows best for work on sexual identity, is studying patients with abnormalities, sorting out what is learned from what is organic. His work epitomizes the development of techniques dealing with psycho-organic problems that Van Wyk is talking about. As Van Wyk says, very few people can cut it both ways, and therefore we must set up training programs to give psychologists training in organic problems (psycho-endocrinologists).[67] Psychologists must become experts in a particular organic clinic, for instance in the relationship between endocrine functioning and behavior. Or, as Money puts it, we need to have close working relations between "behavior" and "body" people.

A fascinating non-happening occurred at the NICHD conference, "The Control of the Onset of Puberty." Money, responding to whether or not to treat delayed puberty, mentioned the difficulty certain hypogonadotropic males have in falling in love. "That is (a) term that we haven't mentioned so far in this conference. Yet I would like to remind you that one of the essential aspects of puberty is that the visual image takes on a new importance with regard to falling in love, which we all leave alone as if it were a red hot stone when it comes to scientific dicussion."[68] In the context of this conference, as reflected in the text, along with pictures of naked boys and closeups of genitals, all starkly clinical, the mention of falling in love is startling. It is suddenly all too human. No one else in the discussion picked up on this. As Money says, the participants in the conference ran away from his comments.[69]

Grinder tells us that "the relation between changes in physical growth and personality dynamics are intimate and pervasive."[70] Aside from the recommendations for future research that are found in *The Control of the Onset of Puberty* specific to the field of endocrinology, biological research concerned with the various types of growth occurring during this age period is seriously neglected. For instance, Money finds that co-relative studies on imagery and physiological growth are totally overlooked and yet the role of imagery (imagination and perception) is a critical development during the onset of puberty. In other words, research knowledge about psychosexual development at this stage in life is very limited. In fact, Donald Cohen says that there is not one study that has related endocrinological (and other physiological) changes to personality changes from latency through adolescence.[71]

Reviewing current issues in biological research on adolescence seems to underscore the losses to society caused by the lack of dialogue among researchers. Many observers have pointed to the lack of a solid conceptual framework underlying research and programs on adolescence. There is, as George Christakis has pointed out, much in the biological, nutritional, and clinical aspects of adolescence, including its biochemistry, that could provide leads to a needed theory of human development in adolescence. Perhaps, he concludes, we have yet to look in the right places or ask the right people.[72] We have certainly failed to establish adequate mechanisms for dialogue among the "behavior" and the "body" people.

As a concluding but not summary observation, it is our feeling that in endocrinology, as in so many other areas, we place our greatest emphasis on helping people who are deviant or overtly in need. Van Wyk argues, as do many other medical researchers, that in medicine and many other fields researchers gain insight into the normal by studying the abnormal. Individuals experiencing disturbances of growth and sexual maturation are not in a class completely different from normal individuals, but represent a greatly increased intensification of the normal problems of adolescents. Studying the mechanisms of abnormal physiology or psychology helps researchers to obtain "the very best handle for formulating a more generalized concept of the problems of the normally developing child," according to Van Wyk. In helping those adolescents whose needs are very great, "we are also gaining insights which make more effective our efforts towards supporting boys and girls through the normal period of adolescence."[73]

We would question whether these efforts actually occur to the extent implied. Who is doing what, where, for the young person who is not deviant, special, atypical? What *should* be done?

Socio-Emotional Research

Like biological development, growth in the socio-emotional sphere is commonly acknowledged to be one of the most important aspects of early adolescence. In assessing our current state of knowledge with respect to socio-emotional changes during adolescence, Hill touches upon some by now familiar themes:

> Little is known about . . . social roles of adolescents let alone about the relations of primary changes to them. Presumably both biological and cognitive changes should make possible deeper and broader roles as worker, friend to adult, citizen, and member of community organization. Yet these roles are little studied and one has the impression that adolescents are, in fact, excluded from opportunities to practice them, the result being that newly developing physical and cognitive capacities cannot be exercised in these arenas. . . .[74]

Adolescence in the Life Cycle, a collection of the papers presented at NICHD's conference, will probably become the seminal work in this area just as *The Control of the Onset of Puberty* has in its own area.

The book includes articles on human development: physical development and its social meaning, cognitive aspects of development, and development of ideology through the adolescent years; analytic issues of adolescent development: socialization antecedents in childhood of adolescent styles of competence, consequences of asynchrony, and "dissonant context" and self-concept. The editors' purpose in selecting these areas is to generate fresh problem foci on adolescence within a life-span framework.[75]

Just as few chapters in *Adolescence in the Life Cycle* speak directly to the years of early adolescence, likewise the National Society for the Study of Education (NSSE) Yearbook on adolescence deals mostly with later adolescents. There is no comparable work on young adolescents.

The Yearbook analyzes the experiences youths encounter in social institutions as they make their way into adulthood. Areas included are the impact of current role expectations in education, courtship, marriage, and work; changing patterns in three principal institutions affecting youth—the labor force, the family, and schools; work as a socializing agent. There are also several chapters dealing specifically with rural, black, Chicano, Oriental, and low-income youth.

Why is there no comparable work on young adolescents? Once again we have a collection of scholarship that looks at adolescents out of the context of all the changes involved in the preadolescent and early adolescent experiences.

This phenomenon does not occur for want of recognition of the importance of early adolescence. To quote Robert E. Grinder, contributor to the Yearbook, "Young adolescents are relatively neglected. . . .Priorities are many indeed. The sexist and racist dimensions of society are changing in complex ways, and I suggest that research on sex-role identification and moral behavior would be exceedingly important topics, but not any more important than the broad question of socialization for living in a culturally pluralistic society."[76]

For some reason, despite such priorities, there appears to be no impetus for promoting serious public dialogue.

Myths About Adolescents: An Illustrative Example

Gerald Bachman, at the Survey Research Center of the University of Michigan's Institute for Social Research, conducted the Youth in Transition study for the Office of Education (OE). This longitudinal study involved repeated data collections from a panel of approximately 2,200 young men, starting in 1966 when they were beginning tenth grade. The study is pertinent to this report for two reasons. First, its implications for young adolescents are easily drawn, since the first data collection occurred at the start of tenth grade. Second, the mandate for and results of the study highlight societal assumptions about adolescence that are based on myths. (Third, should one be interested in exemplary survey methodology and reporting, the volumes summarizing the research design are well worth studying.)

The mandate from OE was to study the causes and effects of dropping out as against graduating from high school. Bachman and his associates were able to identify a number of characteristics of the potential dropout: low socioeconomic level, limited scores on measures of academic ability, poor grades, limited aspirations, above-average levels of delinquency. Many personality and behavior dimensions were examined in the attempt to determine the effects of dropping out. Bachman found that there were greater differences between the groups that went on to college as against non-college-bound high school graduates than between dropouts and non-college-bound high school graduates. The conditions that are usually seen as effects of dropping out were actually pre-existent conditions showing up at the start of tenth grade. Dropping out is not a problem in its own right, but a symptom of other problems or limitations.[77]

This study was extremely comprehensive. It involved four data collections (fall 1966, spring 1968, spring 1969, summer 1970), which focused on such areas as dimensions of mental health, self-concept, values and attitudes, plans and aspirations, and behavior. These areas were linked to objectives such as identifying causes of dropping out, a study of family background and intelligence, studies of differences in schools and vocational programs within schools, and of post-high school environments.[78]

Bachman did not come up with what our society wants to hear, that "dropping out" is a problem in its own right—something to be reduced and eventually eliminated.[79] More harm may be done by promoting the myth that not dropping out, in and of itself, is critical to one's future. The harm is done through labeling youngsters and by diverting us from real issues. The mass media campaign against dropping out "implies that if the potential dropout merely remains in school he can be just like his classmates who continue to graduation. This simply is not so; by the time he reaches tenth or eleventh grade the potential dropout usually has basic problems and/or limitations that will not be 'cured' by another year or two of high school."[80] The problems have their origin earlier in life. "The difficulties experienced by the dropouts we studied—the low aspirations and accomplishments, and even the limitations in self-esteem and self-concept—were already present or predictable by the start of tenth grade, and there is little evidence that dropping out made matters worse."[81]

What are the myths that this study explicitly or implicitly attacks? First, the media campaign against dropping out misleads while labeling, thus reinforcing adult stereotypes. Second, pouring federal money into keeping older adolescents in school is cost-ineffective at best, since something is going on in schools before tenth grade (beyond family background and socioeconomic level) which is damaging to self-esteem. Third, what adjective can we apply to the assumption that more of the same will change failure and/or delinquency into success? Fourth, the funding process itself, starting with tenth graders, perpetuates the myth that young adolescents need little or no federal attention. To the slogan, "Get them while they're young," which seems to be the slogan for federal funding for preschool and elementary compensatory programs, we can add, "Keep them when they're older." Where is the middle?

Fifth, the underlying assumption is a myth: that our dropout rate is accelerating at startling rates. In fact, while the dropout rate in 1900 was about ninety percent, the dropout rate among young men in high school in 1969 was less than twenty percent.[82] While we may not find a twenty percent dropout rate acceptable, the consistent decline in percentages is encouraging. It has been lost in the media campaign.

Bachman's work on dropouts exposes a classic example of the ways in which erroneous perceptions of adolescence lead us to misconstrue data, to formulate policy based on our misconceptions, and then to expect research to validate such policy. The demands upon social researchers for independence of mind from their own society are considerable given the myths that pervade our theories and institutions regarding adolescents.

Emotional Tasks—Identity and Self-Esteem

Some men, perhaps most men, are the lifelong dupes (or beneficiaries) of self-ideals or self-pictures developed in adolescence.

—Iris Murdoch
The Sacred and Profane Love Machine

Many developmental demands impinge upon the young adolescent simultaneously. Central to socio-emotional development is the continuing task of identity formation, always challenged by the vagaries of self-esteem.

Cohen and Frank, in a paper concerned with the importance of preadolescence, point out that in middle childhood children invest in cognitive functions the energy that was previously used in maturation of social relationships in the family. The outstanding emotional quality of preadolescence is aimlessness, or unstable feelings. "The preadolescent of eleven or twelve invests himself considerably less in cognitive mastery than he had before. There seems to be a breakdown in the normal progressive mechanism of identity development through industry as the initial stirrings of sexual interest and drive appear." The transitional quality of maturation leaves the preadolescent suspended between childhood and older adolescence. There may be a return to such infantile patterns as fear of the dark. Physical fighting, moodiness, outbursts of anger may be characteristic even of youngsters who previously showed adaptive behavior and adequate defenses. It can be a time of considerable emotional confusion and conflict.[83]

Cohen and Frank argue that preadolescence may be a time of greater struggle than later adolescence. In other words, we cannot generalize about the emotional tasks of "adolescence." We have already seen Hill's argument that one of the significant barriers to healthy adolescent development is the social myth of the homogeneity of adolescents. Thus, we can add to Cohen and Frank's arguments that even within a given stage, such as early adolescence, great variability will be found.

It is the argument of Herbert Otto and Sandra Healy that we overemphasize adolescent problems, maladjustment, and social pathology. Otto and Healy administered a "strength questionnaire" to two groups of high school students. They determined from this questionnaire the general categories from which adolescents derive their personal strength. The questionnaire revealed that the adolescents' self-perceptions of their personality strengths were similar to adults'. It was the authors' primary intent to create a more positive image of adolescents because the development of a positive, realistic self-concept is so crucial for identity formation. What, they ask, is the adult's responsibility to adolescents? "To what extent does society and its use of the mass media interfere with normal development by continuously drawing attention to the maladjustments and negative behavior of adolescents?"[84]

We allow stereotyping of "teenage behavior" in our media and in general conversation that would be offensive to most were it in reference to race or religion. If such stereotyping is harmful to the self-concept of one group–e.g., blacks, Jews–why do we assume it is not to this subsection of our population, adolescents?

In his comprehensive review for DHEW, Hill chooses six psychosocial areas for discussion in reference to adolescence: detachment, autonomy, intimacy, sexuality, achievement, and identity. Of these six, most is known about achievement motivation and behavior in achievement situations. "This is not unrelated to the importance of the achievement-work-success value set in our core culture."[85] (Note the implication that researchers are influenced to choose those areas for investigation that are congenial to the central ideological thrusts of their society.)

Hill differentiates between "detachment" and "independence." "Detachment" refers to the issues of emotional independence from parents. "Independence" connotes, in addition, freedom from parental dominance in decision making, or "autonomy." We find this distinction extremely important for clarifying the emotional tasks of young adolescents. When we lump all adolescents together in a single classification, we reinforce the myth of rebellious teenagers battling their parents for dominance at all costs. In fact, as Hill, Cohen, and Bachman point out, it is the younger adolescent who experiences greater ambivalence of feelings toward both parents. Offer also reports that rebellion is seen mainly in the early adolescence of his subjects, chosen for their normalcy.[86] It is, then, the younger adolescent whose behavior is "rebellious" as part of the normal process of detachment, changing ties from parents to peers.

Hill's cautionary note that "rebelliousness," which has its roots in psychoanalytic theory of detachment, has been used as a catchall term devoid of real descriptive meaning, is typical of his general attempt to reconsider popularly held assumptions.[87] Given the variability of psychosocial development among young adolescents, the issue of autonomy may be of great significance to some and of little to others at this age. Difficult conceptual issues remain unresolved because of the lack of refinement of empirical research and analysis.[88]

Douvan and Adelson question the quality of autonomy that is freely given to the American adolescent. In achieving behavioral freedom with such ease, do adolescents also achieve a high degree of emotional autonomy [detachment] and value autonomy? "Indeed, the ease with which the adolescent acquires behavioral freedom may tend to interfere with the achievement of emotional and ideological freedom. . . ."[89] Or, as Hill asks bluntly, "What are we facilitating when we foster 'autonomy'?"[90]

Specialists are not in agreement about how much intergenerational conflict and *sturm und drang* are normal or necessary for young adolescents. Psychoanalytic literature presents adolescence as a time of turmoil during which lowered ego strength and heightened aggressive and sexual impulses create havoc within the individual. Peter Blos, a psychiatrist who specializes in adolescence, argues, as does Anna Freud, that the adolescent must struggle with parents and parental figures in order to establish identity clearly. The "understanding" of parents, teachers and other adults that blurs the boundary lines between generations makes this critical developmental task more difficult or impossible.[91]

Daniel Offer's work represents an important contribution to the dialogue in this area. The subjects in Offer's study were primarily middle class suburban high school students, functioning within what was called "the middle range of adjustment." These subjects experienced less psychic disruption than is customarily postulated for this age group in psychiatric theory. A six-year study bore no evidence of underdevelopment or inhibition. Offer suggests that investigators who spend most of their professional lives studying disturbed adolescents stress the importance of turmoil for maturing. Those who study the normal adolescent population minimize the extent of turmoil.[92]

Offer thus finds Erikson's concept of "normative crisis" more applicable to his subjects than is the concept of turmoil. He found emotional conflicts, but little behavioral disequilibrium. This leads him to speculate whether adolescents going through adolescence with much *sturm und drang* do so in every stage of development. Offer predicts that one's style of coping with crisis remains relatively constant throughout life. "*Stability, not change*, is the overriding characteristic in the psychological patterns of reaction of these modal adolescents."[93]

Douvan and Adelson, whose survey of normative adolescent behavior included the middle majority of adolescents, report data supported by Offer's study. Psychological turbulence is the norm only for the adolescent at the extremes.[94]

Gallatin lends clarity to the arguments about storm and stress by pointing out that critics are really discussing two issues, storm and stress as a norm and storm and stress as an ideal.

Storm and stress is normative, in Eriksonian theory, in the sense that every adolescent must resolve similar issues, which are formidable and potentially stressful, but typical. Storm and stress is also normative in the sense that each of the eight stages of man described by Erikson has a crisis to be resolved. Thus adolescence is not unique in its task of crisis resolution. Identity formation is an ongoing process, beginning in infancy and continuing throughout life.

Storm and stress is not normative in its distribution among the population, since variables like previous developmental experiences, future expectations, privilege, giftedness, training, and many others help determine the intensity of turmoil during crisis resolution.[95]

Whether or not storm and stress is an ideal, necessary for self-definition, separation, individuation, commitment—for identity, in other words—remains an area of contention in concepts of adolescence.

Research cited in this report appears to support Eriksonian theory as to what is normative. It cannot speak to what the ideal should be.

More popular than Blos's, Offer's, or Douvan and Adelson's viewpoint is one which holds that the "generation gap," *sturm und drang*, and age segregation are dysfunctional by-products of Western industrialized nations. Adherents of this viewpoint include such luminaries as Riesman, Coleman, Bronfenbrenner, Hill, and Elder, among many others. In fact, there seems to be close to unanimous adherence to the social-integrationist "movement" among social scientists, surprising given the strong hold that psychoanalytic views like those of Blos and Anna Freud have had for so many decades. Whatever the merits of either viewpoint, the tendency toward bandwagon effects in research is apparent.

At no point in the previous paragraphs have we used the third person singular pronoun, thus avoiding he/she stylistic problems. Yet we could have, since "so pronounced is the stereotype and the reality in our society of the paramount importance of autonomy for the male that it apparently has not been seriously studied in girls."[96] (Elder comments that his review of the professional literature on adolescence in 1968, *Adolescent Socialization and Personality Development*, might well have included a section, "Where Are The Girls?"[97])

It is more than possible that studies of the socialization of young women will become one of the fads of the 1970s. Women's studies are rising mushroom-like in a frequently congenial climate. One must hope that careful studies will remain independent of some of the popular myths at large about women's liberation. Matina Horner's work on women's "fear of success" is not to be taken lightly; we need to know more about the relationship of this fear to adolescent development. J.M. Barwick and Elizabeth Douvan say that it is at some time during adolescence that girls, who hitherto felt equal to boys in capacity and opportunity, begin to equate competition with lack of femininity or aggressiveness and therefore a threat to the heterosexual relationship. As Hill says, there is little data related directly to these hypotheses. Available data are fascinating, but composed of sparse and indirect pieces of information.[98]

Gisela Konopka's *Young Girls: A Portrait of Adolescence*, is a study of 1,000 girls, ages twelve through eighteen, using open-ended interviews lasting forty-eight to ninety minutes with each girl.[99] This is the first major study of girls to appear in the literature. In her "purposive sample," Konopka selected a sample of one-half white and one-half minority (black, Chicano, Inuit [Eskimo], American Indian, Puerto Rican), various socioeconomic levels, and locales including urban, suburban, small town, and rural. Most interesting, one-third are adjudicated delinquent, institutionalized girls, one-third are presently affiliated with youth organizations, and one-third are not so affiliated and not delinquent.

Konopka reports that self-concept, which the girls never talked about directly, permeates everything they say. There is a high level of self-consciousness stemming in part from being adolescent and more so from being female at a time of heightened self-awareness.

Two themes that emerge from the interviews are pertinent to this discussion. First, in reference to life goals, most girls want a career, marriage, a family, and think that women are able to combine them. (Adjudicated girls say twice as often as other girls that this is not possible.) The ideal of marriage is a partnership; some fear marriage because of possible subjugation of the woman by the man. A majority of the girls want children and feel responsible for them. They also increasingly desire participation in professions, but their choice of careers is influenced by life experiences, especially with adult models.

Second, Konopka found no evidence to support the phenomenon of the "generation gap" as inevitable. Instead, there is a constant cry for adults to listen and understand. Seventy-five percent of the girls felt close to adults (family members, friends, occasionally teachers) and felt that they were all equal human beings. However, there is greater expectation than ever before from both adults and youth that there be open communication; this may lead to conclusions that there is a modal "gap."

Erik Erikson is the best-known theorist of adolescence. Acquaintance with his work is widespread among researchers, practitioners, and the public at large. Erikson's work provides some psychologists with a framework for understanding adolescent development; for others, it provides a starting point that is seen as inadequate but the best we have. His influence is pervasive. Despite the fact that Hill finds Erikson's theory of adolescence insufficiently comprehensive, *Identity: Youth and Crisis* is particularly relevant to his review of psychosocial development.

Nevertheless, Hill questions the continuing reliance on the concept of identity as an integrating variable. It is, he says, an "appealing" concept because it integrates (or appears to) much of what we know about adolescence. There is however, very little empirical information outside clinical studies to help us evaluate the concept, nor is it clear how one would make operational components (motivational, behavioral, and cognitive) of Erikson's formulation. Whether or not the clinical study of articulate, upper- and middle-class neurotic adolescents leads to universally applicable principles is an unanswered empirical question. Hill is also skeptical about the incidence and social distribution of the "full-blown identity crisis" in our society. The question for Hill, then, is whether the concept of identity "helps us put together existing knowledge in satisfying ways or whether it contributes to new knowledge and increased understanding of the adolescent period."[100]

Judith Gallatin disagrees. She states that it would not be difficult, given time and money, to test various aspects of Erikson's theory. "In other words, Hill and others may be (needlessly) racking their brains trying to come up with a *new* theory of adolescence when there's already a pretty satisfactory one in existence."[101]

Some researchers insist that approximately 70 percent of young people experience relatively serene adolescence. Whether this figure is accurate, and whether these adolescents achieve detachment, autonomy, intimacy, and the other Eriksonian tasks of adolescence we cannot say. What we can say is that, barring further investigation, we remain predominantly in the realm of insufficient theory—and in the popular mind, in the realm of myth. Theories as well as social myths can be constricting or destructive.

The Social Meaning of Differential Physical and Sexual Maturation

The heading of this subsection is the title of John Clausen's contribution to *Adolescence in the Life Cycle.* In this volume, Clausen contributes a summary of his work and others' on interrelationships among variables of development (physical, cognitive, temperamental, social), stressing, for instance, body type, social class, sex, and age.[102] These interrelationships have barely been explored.

Clausen's work on childhood socialization speaks directly to these issues. His research includes (1) use of the longitudinal data at the Institute of Human Development (Berkeley) to examine the relationships among physique, early maturing, and personality development; and (2) a study of value transmission and personality resemblances in the families of the longitudinal subjects.[103]

The Berkeley studies of early and late maturers have found that early maturing adolescents evoke responses from adults that have effects into adulthood. Clausen's work, however, is broader in scope. (It is, and we must note this just as he does, based upon data from adolescents who matured a full generation ago.)

Differences in size, weight and performance between early and late maturers will be greatest for girls at ages twelve through fourteen (during the junior high period), for boys between fourteen through sixteen (toward the end of junior high and the beginning of high school).[104] Such data confirms the arguments that *early* adolescence is a time characterized by greater variability than adolescence seen as a whole.

Clausen, in reviewing general formulations of earlier research, cites the work of Peskin on early maturation. Peskin studied behavior ratings and test scores for early and late maturers (not according to chronological age but according to years before or after pubertal onset). He found no significant differences in the prepubertal period between the early and late maturers, testing a wide range of motoric, cognitive, social, and emotional dimensions. Significant differences were found with the onset of puberty, and were confined to the first few years thereafter. Early maturers became less active, less exploratory, less intellectually curious, more submissive, more anxious. Late maturers showed little or no such consistent changes with the onset of puberty. In some cases, changes showed up in ratings three to four years later.

These findings bear out Peskin's expectation that inhibition and rigidity characterize the early maturer's response to puberty. According to Clausen, "The early maturer may be forced into premature identity, having had little time during the latency period to come to grips with his own feelings and the ambiguities of his world." The late maturer has more time for flexibility in dealing with pubertal changes.[105]

Erikson sees the "identity crisis" and its resolution as the major task of adolescence. Our institutions—families and schools in particular—are highly rewarding of early development in childhood and adolescence. If inappropriate social rewards preclude the resolution of developmental tasks, the early maturer may form a premature and relatively constricting self-view.[106]

This issue, which is only one of many having to do with identity formation in young adolescents, is particularly important because of the emphasis placed in our culture on rapid development. We "hang loose," granting autonomy as gratuitously as Douvan and others note; we create "free" learning environments which may demand inappropriate independence.

Clausen points out, however, that most research findings in this area relate to boys. The implications of early maturing differ for girls, who seem to be *less* attractive than their later maturing peers. An early maturing boy may be as physically mature as the average girl in his class. An early maturing girl will be larger than most of the girls and boys. Early physical development for girls involves a different form of social acceptance and pressure than for boys. ". . . the physically mature girl, especially if she is well endowed with curves, is far more likely to be regarded as a sex object by older boys, and to be pressured into different kinds of peer relationships with the opposite sex. This is perhaps more likely to be true in the working class than in the middle class. . . ."[107]

Clausen points out that the longitudinal data from the three sample populations are not always consistent, nor can he find any basis for the vast differences he found in two groups only seven or eight years apart.

There is much researchers do not know about the consequences of one's physique and biological maturation in relation to personal development and adult expectations, and in relation to prior concepts of body image.

> Whatever their long-term consequences . . . there can be little doubt that during the years of childhood and early adolescence, physique and sexual maturation vie with and interact with cognitive skills and emotional expressiveness in contributing to the social identity of the adolescent.[108]

The extent to which this vying is biologically influenced or culturally determined remains an open question. The impact of the onset and rate of development in the young adolescent on all variables of socialization (among others, self-perception, family and peer relations, achievement, and role-taking in later years) is, to say the least, "of considerable interest."[109]

Research Instruments and Methodology

Most studies having to do with adolescent behavior as a consequence of previous socialization are riddled with methodological problems. They tend to be cross-sectional, use instruments inadequate for measuring social and emotional growth, and are out of date. Also, given recent trends toward multiple-variable assessments and toward ecological studies, basic assumptions that underlie experimental procedures are often violated. More research with a primary focus on methodology may be necessary in order to develop new research designs to cope with these problems.[110] These complaints could have been made a decade ago. The effects of stagnation permeate the field.

A first step may not be developing adequate affective measures nor proselytizing for more longitudinal, ecological studies, although both are sorely needed. It may be pulling together the biological and behavioral professionals, both researchers and practitioners, to continue to conceptualize a framework of agreed upon concepts, definitions, and language that can generate questions appropriate to facilitating the development of young adolescents.

Cognitive Research

In psychology there are experimental methods and conceptual confusions.
—Lichtenstein

We have been complaining about the lack of physiological and socio-emotional research on early adolescence, and about the need for the development and use of different methodologies. Even less attention has been paid to the nature of intellectual functioning in early adolescence. This is not to say that there has not been a good deal of attention paid to IQ and academic achievement; but it is to say that this attention is a sign of how narrow our view of cognition has been. Although cognitive changes are not as readily apparent or dramatic as physical growth and emotional turmoil, the young adolescent is every bit as much in a period of exciting and disturbing intellectual change.

Professor Benjamin Bloom of the University of Chicago says that about 50 percent of cognitive development, in terms of intelligence measured at age seventeen, takes place between conception and age four, 30 percent between four and eight, 20 percent between eight and seventeen.[111] In other words, as much occurs in the first four years of life as in the next thirteen. Partly on the basis of such arguments, we have chosen as a society to place the greatest emphasis on the cognitive development of the very young child. Therefore, studies of cognitive development in adolescence have comprised only a small fraction of the total number of studies of mental growth.[112] A point to be noted here is that so long as we see intelligence in terms of intellect measured at age seventeen, with all the narrowness of definition of intellect that this implies, there is no reason to be concerned about the relative dearth of studies on adolescent thinking. It is when we acknowledge the diversity and the complexity of adolescent thinking, and especially the inseparability of the intellectual aspects of human behavior from the physiological and socio-emotional, that we conclude that the study of adolescent intellect is important. It is important not only in its own right, but also for the implications such study will have for education and social health.[113]

Cognition, as defined by dictionaries, is the act or process of knowing "*in the broadest sense.*" As approached traditionally by researchers, cognition is the *intellectual* process by which knowledge is gained. The difference between the inclusiveness of the first definition and the relative narrowness of the second leads to fundamental confusions about what can legitimately be called "cognitive research."

Further, the interrelationships among the various intellectual processes by which knowledge is gained and emotional, social, and physiological processes are complex beyond our present comprehension.

Finally, investigations in cognition are conducted in molecular fashion.

These three factors–the fundamental confusions, the complexity of interrelated processes, and the lack of a bonding agent among current research concerns–leave us without any apparent organizational rationale for discussing adolescent cognition.

Research in the area of cognitive development in adolescence is centered on only a few problems. Elkind identifies five areas of research: (1) the self-concept in adolescents; (2) the generality of formal operations; (3) conceptual orientation shifts; (4) ethnic differences in cognitive ability; and (5) moral judgment and behavior.[114] We will approximate Elkind's categories to superimpose an external structure which actually does not presently exist.

We are encouraged by our inability to classify some of the studies we will be discussing. We prefer to superimpose an external structure than to adopt an internal coherence that may be suspect or limiting.

We are therefore wary of the one such structure that is available–Piagetian theory. We are wary because it is the only one.

Piaget's theoretical framework for cognitive development dominates the field–we might almost say, monopolizes it. His theories undergird Elkind's work on cognition and affective behavior, Kohlberg's work on cognition and moral development, and Adelson's work on cognition and the growth of political ideas–in other words, some of the most seminal work in socio-psychological research.

Briefly, developmental learning theory as set forth by Piaget holds that whereas the child reasons on the basis of objects (concrete operations), at some point during adolescence the young person begins to reason on the basis of symbols and principles (formal thought or "propositional operations").

The shift in thinking is from logical inference as a set of concrete operations to logical inference as a set of "operations upon operations." " 'Operations upon operations' imply that the adolescent can classify classification, that he can combine combinations, that he can relate relationships. It implies that he can think about thought, and create thought systems or 'hypothetico-deductive' theories. This involves the logical construction of all possibilities–that is, the awareness of the observed as only a subset of what may be logically possible."[115] During adolescence, a qualitative change in thought processes takes place.

It should be noted that this is a distinctly different mode of knowing from that proposed by Skinner and such Skinnerians as Gagné, who suggest that learning is not developmental but cumulative. This difference is of extreme importance when we approach such practical areas as programmed learning and behavior modification in the classroom. It is a difference which we do not grapple with openly in research or programs, but which we expect practitioners to deal with on a day-to-day basis through materials and procedures which at this point may be based on diametrically opposed approaches to learning. It may well be that cumulative learning theory undergirds practice, while developmental learning theory undergirds research.

It should also be noted that Piaget's maturation-learning theory of development is unconcerned with the subconscious aspects of human behavior and development. Unlike Freud and neo-Freudians, Piaget concentrates on the rational, conflict-free thought processes during stages of intellectual development. He is equally unconcerned with such variables as sex, socioeconomic class, and IQ.[116] Again, the contradictory crosscurrents of various espoused theories and practices may create unacknowledged burdens for various practitioners.

Issues concerning cognitive development "in the broadest sense" are far-ranging. In this section we will be looking at questions of current concern to researchers. What is the relationship between cognitive development and changes in self-concept during adolescence? Is the ability to think in formal terms a development that occurs universally during adolescence? Is there greater ease in shifting one's conceptual orientation that relates to the adolescent's level of cognitive ability? What is the relationship between the development of social cognition and social behavior during adolescence? Have controversies over ethnic and sex differences contributed to our understanding of adolescent cognitive development? Is moral development dependent on cognitive development? How does the young adolescent form political concepts? And finally, if concept development is culture-dependent, what implications must be drawn in a pluralistic society for social institutions, especially schools?

Adolescent Self-Concept and Cognition

David Elkind, in "Recent Research on Cognitive Development in Adolescence," says: "The domain of cognitive psychology is ill defined at best and particularly so where the self is concerned. . . . Many of the studies of self-concept reside in the never-never land between the cognitive and the affective domains."[117] It is Elkind's position that studies of adolescent self-concept lack theoretical direction and coherence. In particular, the role of cognitive growth in the development of the self-concept during adolescence needs to be explored systematically. For instance, the onset of formal operations makes it possible for the young adolescent to see himself as others see him. What impact does this new perspective have upon the self? The ability to think about thinking reveals to the adolescent "the privateness of his thoughts and the social isolation of his reflective self." How does the adolescent handle these new discoveries? How does he deal with them while coping with physical and social changes? These questions have not been explored in a systematic way.[118]

Elkind's work on egocentrism in adolescence explores an area in which development is directly related to affective experience and behavior. Elkind traces different forms of egocentrism through infancy, early childhood, childhood, early adolescence, and adolescence. "During adolescence the major problem is the conflict of thought, which is said to give rise to two mental constructions, 'the imaginary audience,' and 'the personal fable,' the former being related to self-consciousness and the latter to personal feelings of uniqueness."[119]

The adolescent's belief that others are preoccupied with his appearance and behavior constitutes his egocentrism, according to Elkind. In social situations the young adolescent anticipates the reaction of other people to himself, assuming constantly that others are as admiring or critical of him as he is of himself. In this sense, then, the adolescent is constructing or reacting to an imaginary audience. Thus, the adolescent fails to differentiate his own concerns from those of others.

At the same time, he over-differentiates his own feelings. "Perhaps because he believes he is of importance to so many people, the imaginary audience, he comes to regard himself, and particularly his feelings, as something special and unique.... This complex of beliefs in the uniqueness of his feelings and his immortality might be called *a personal fable*, a story which he tells himself and which is not true."[120]

Elkind contends, as do many others, that the mental structures of adolescence must serve us for the rest of our life span since after the appearance of formal operational thought, no new mental systems develop.

> Adolescent egocentrism is . . . overcome by a twofold transformation. On the cognitive plane, it is overcome by the gradual differentiation between his own preoccupations and the thoughts of others; while on the plane of affectivity, it is overcome by a gradual integration of the feelings of others with his own emotions.[121]

Hill and Palmquist are interested in self-concept and identity formation in general. As they interpret Erikson's work, the resolution of the identity crisis appears to require types of cognition possible only for those who have attained the level of formal operations. It is possible to argue in a chicken-egg manner about which precedes which, the identity crisis or the onset of formal operations. The main point, however, is that the phenomena Erikson has described have cognitive components. Hill and Palmquist feel that it is time we began recognizing this and studying these components.[122]

Generality of Formal Operations in Adolescence

Elkind sees the diminishing of the egocentrism of early adolescence as being interdependent with the onset of formal operations. Nevertheless, the generality of that onset is greatly in question, which should have implications for Elkind's argument about adolescents' ability to overcome their form of egocentrism.

According to Kohlberg and Gilligan, "there are two facts which distinguish the adolescent revolution in logical and epistemological thinking from the five-to-seven revolution in thinking. The first is that the revolution is extremely variable as to time. The second is that for many people it never occurs at all."[123]

Assuming the attainment of the level of formal operations, the generality of the application can still be called in question. For instance adolescent girls, for heterosexual social reasons, may be more likely to apply their formal operational thinking to interpersonal relationships rather than, let us say, to science.[124] Such variables as race and socioeconomic level seem to influence the application of formal operations to various aspects of reality. Hill and Palmquist cite a study by Dulit of gifted high school students in which 75 percent were capable of formal reasoning. They report that in samples from populations more normally distributed on IQ the range of subjects beyond the age of twelve who attain formal operations may vary from 35 percent to 70 percent. There appears to be a positive relation to social class. Dulit suggests that formal operations are a "characteristic potentiality" but not a characteristic of adolescents.[125]

Cognitive Shifts in Children and Adolescents

Elkind and his associates have been exploring what they call "conceptual orientation shifts." The assumption is that there are particular conceptual orientations which relate to the child's level of cognitive ability. For instance, the preschool child at the preoperational stage of development will tend to conceptualize on a perceptual basis. The school age child, at the concrete operational stage, will tend to conceptualize at a functional level. Adolescents, at the formal operational stage, tend to conceptualize at the abstract or categorical level. While at different levels of cognitive development young people may have a preferred orientation towards conceptualization, these orientations will interact with the stimuli to be conceptualized. In several of Elkind's studies it was hypothesized that "adolescents would shift more readily [between modes of conceptualization] than would children because formal operations provide for greater flexibility of thought than do concrete operations." This hypothesis was upheld.[126]

As Elkind points out, there is obviously a great deal of work to be done on the problem of conceptual orientation shifts. Of particular interest are the conditions that facilitate and hinder such shifting, especially since these shifts have many educational implications as well as theoretical significance. Many observers point out that a student's ability to interact with the formal educational system depends upon the match between individual cognitive abilities and the educational system. This issue of conceptual orientation shifts being researched by Elkind and his associates can help to illuminate the "match."

The work of William Rohwer is of an entirely different nature.[127] Rohwer is studying learning behavior and development of conceptual processes in the hopes of understanding major determinants of learning efficiency in childhood and adolescence. He studies such aspects of behavior in learning and memory tasks as conditions for elaboration, properties of referential events that control retrieval, developmental interactions, and the generality of effects.

The types of investigations that Rohwer is conducting with populations of learners eleven to fifteen years of age have been conducted only with much younger subjects. For instance, he is interested in those adolescents who do not perform optimally under conditions of minimal prompting. It is his feeling that they lack only a problem-solving orientation toward learning and memory tasks. Rather than dealing with concepts, the way such researchers as Elkind do, Rohwer is interested in whether a problem-solving orientation could not be achieved through training provided at critical times for learners, for instance the time when, as he puts it, the "minimal prompt shift" naturally occurs (11 to 15 years). One of Rohwer's studies indicates that learning skills can be taught effectively to junior high-aged students. Older, wealthier students require fewer hints, less wealthy students require hints throughout the higher grades on memory tasks.

At this point, Rohwer's research has been limited to pair-association learning. Whether his work has any utility beyond tasks that require the learning or memorization of noun pairs remains to be seen. His work is an example of the type of learning theory (as against developmental) research being conducted in relation to cognitive shifts taking place in early adolescence.

We note here, as we can in each section having to do with young adolescents, that shifts that take place in conceptual orientation occur with great variability as to time and rate. The importance of this central theme of variability cannot be overemphasized. Since this variability is one of the aspects of being a young adolescent that contributes to the potential painfulness of this time of life, we underscore it time and time again in the hopes that those working with and living with young adolescents will be extremely sensitive to the issues involved. Changes in cognitive structure may begin to appear around age eleven in some children and not until the early twenties in others—and not at all in some. "The cognitive abilities of any given group of adolescents are thus subject to extreme variability across individuals. The impact of this variability has not been studied, but is likely to be considerable, as cognitive function is the basis for both individual behavioral decisions by the individual and societal decisions about the individual."[128]

Social Cognition

Hill and Palmquist are concerned with researching social cognition and socialization in adolescents who are approximately eleven to fifteen years old. They emphasize the development of cognition of the social world from preadolescence through adolescence. Although, as we have said before, the work of Piaget dominates the field of cognition, the research about formal operations has been very limited in comparison with that devoted to the preoperational and the concrete-operational stages. In fact, as Hill and Palmquist point out, there are few studies that include subjects who are older than twelve years, and those which do include subjects older than twelve present data in terms of broad age categories which obscure changes that may be occurring around the time of puberty. (We can note here the parallel with biological research.)

Hill and Palmquist raise questions for their own research which integrate a great deal of what we discuss in this report:

> We can find neither cross-sectional nor longitudinal studies designed to examine Inhelder or Piaget's assertion that the assumption of adult social roles is indispensable to the emergence and development of formal operations. This gap in the literature is especially striking given the wide range of individual differences in the onset and ultimate appearance of formal operations reported above. We do not know whether opportunities for adult role assumption are related to the onset and further development of formal operations.[129]

Another example of the integrative conceptual approach to their research has to do with the great discrepancy between *sturm und drang* views of adolescence and what we know about the new competencies in social cognition among adolescents: "The potential of the adolescent to integrate and operate upon impressions of the social world . . . [and] to consider the *possible* in persons and social systems . . . are difficult to reconcile with the *sturm und drang* view of the adolescent as malcontent, interpersonal troublemaker, and social klutz."[130] Hill and Palmquist also point to the lack of studies on the effects of the onset of formal operations in family interactions. Parent-child interactions may well be facilitated or impeded by levels of parental tolerance in the face of adolescents' new perspectives on parental behavior. For instance, for the first time children will be comparing actual parental behavior with possible or ideal parental behavior.[131]

As Hill and Palmquist report, the task ahead for research in social-cognitive and social-relational areas are not easy ones for they have not been well mapped, have been more empirically than theoretically inspired, and rely on survey questionnaire methodologies too often and too little on field observation and experimentation.

Demographic Variables

There is no statement that can be made about cognition in relation to demographic variables, in particular race and sex, that is not open to challenge.

Hill has been unable to locate any evidence relative to sex difference and the onset of formal operations, although he sees as feasible a sex difference favoring earlier onset for girls given their earlier endocrinological maturation. (As we will see, Deborah Waber's work bears on this issue.)

Also, Hill says that there is no solid evidence as to earlier onset of formal operations in persons of higher social class, although studies relating IQ measures to formal operations would suggest that the earlier onset is at least a tenable hypothesis.[132] (We will see that the work of Judith Gallatin speaks to this issue.)

And certainly, there is no area that has received more public as well as professional attention, without adequate clarification, than that dealing with racial differences in cognitive development. This issue is clearly an extraordinarily complicated one, socially, methodologically, and conceptually, at this time in the United States. Researchers and practitioners veer away now from any comment about race and cognition—and many have changed their professional emphases in order to remove themselves from this explosive arena. There is therefore little research being conducted at present about an issue of considerable social import.

We would like to comment indirectly about race and cognition by citing the work of Elkind. We choose this work because it deals directly with adolescents, including young adolescents, and because it deals with an area that is discussed elsewhere in this report.

Elkind is discussing Jensen's work (and the subsequent uproar concerning it) relating to the intellectual ability of blacks. He asks to what extent black adolescents may be deficient in abstract thinking and to what extent, if any, this deficiency may be attributed to genetic factors. Building upon his decade of experience working with delinquent adolescents, Elkind asserts that intelligence test scores of low-income adolescents are meaningless when they are interpreted independently of the social context in which they are obtained.

In clinical settings two types of low-income adolescents score low on intelligence tests but give other indications of average intellectual development. One type Elkind calls "prematurely structured," having had to cope with harsh realities from an early age. Their cognitive skills have developed "in the service of survival." The second type of low-income adolescents who score low on IQ tests, whom Elkind labels "alternatively elaborated," have in fact developed remarkable abstract intellectual skills.

. . . They know how to stay out of trouble with the law, how to con the "John's" and other "dudes" and how to dominate women and other men. They have a rich vocabulary of words and phrases that one would never find in

Webster's dictionary and an array of interpersonal skills and talents that would be the pride of any used car salesman.[133]

Intelligence tests are reasonably good predictors of academic performance regardless of the socioeconomic background of individuals tested. As such, and when used only within the confines of this particular predictive situation, they provide useful information about possible school achievement. They do not begin to touch questions about the "prematurely structured" or the "alternatively elaborated" intelligence which Elkind has noted in low-income adolescents. And since "low-income" differences are often synonymous with ethnic and racial differences, the relationship between ethnicity and cognitive development remains a mined field for the researcher.

If there was ever an area of research troubled enough to indicate the desperate need for new conceptualization, interdisciplinary work, the cooperation of researchers and practitioners, and new methodologies, it is the area of race and cognitive development.

Deborah Waber's work is in an area that has retained more rationality in research, even if not in the society at large: gender differences in mental ability. Waber's doctoral dissertation, "Developmental Trends and Biological Bases of Gender Differences in Mental Abilities," draws upon the insights of different fields, as we repeatedly say is necessary.

Waber combined the following observations to form her hypothesis: (1) we have observed that female performance is superior at tasks of articulation and word fluency, and that male performance is superior at tasks of spatial visualization; (2) we also know that as a result of lateralization of the brain, verbal abilities usually become concentrated in the left hemisphere and spatial abilities in the right. Less complete lateralization leads to excellence in processing verbal information, since such processing can occur in both hemispheres. Individuals who are more completely lateralized may be less competent at processing verbal information, but may excel at spatial processing; (3) the end of the lateralization process is thought to be associated with the adolescent growth spurt. Studies of physical growth show that the early maturer tends to have a relatively short, intense growth spurt, and the late maturer a longer, less intense growth spurt period. In absolute terms, at the end of adolescence, the early maturer tends to have grown less than the late maturer.

From these observations, Waber hypothesized "that variation in age between individuals at the onset and cessation of the adolescent growth spurt is systematically related to variation in the ultimate extent of cerebral lateralization;" that "the early maturer lateralized more quickly but in the end is less completely lateralized in absolute terms than the late maturer. Therefore, the late maturer, being more completely lateralized, could be predicted to be relatively better at spatial skills than verbal ones." Since females can be construed as early maturers in relation to males, "the difference in timing of the growth spurt causing differences in lateralization between the sexes could then explain the reported differences between them in performance on verbal and spatial tasks."

Waber hypothesized further that early maturing females will show a pattern of abilities in which verbal skills are relatively better than spatial skills, while late maturing and therefore more completely lateralized females will show a pattern in which spatial skills are equal to or better than verbal skills. A similar hypothesis was predicted for males.

In a study involving females at ages ten and thirteen, and males at ages thirteen and fifteen, the results supported the hypotheses.[134]

Waber's work provides data concerning very important questions: (1) how the brain participates in the adolescent growth spurt, and the consequences of this in terms of cognitive development; (2) the biological determination of gender differences in adult cognitive abilities; and (3) ability differentiation at puberty as a consequence of the adolescent growth spurt.

According to Waber, our knowledge of adolescence is so limited that it is difficult to do much more than speculate about conceptual shifts in early adolescence. "My own research showed significant changes in the brain which set the adult pattern of mental abilities, and I suspect that if we dig deeper, we may find many areas of intellectual and emotional development which assume a form at adolescence which persists throughout adulthood."[135] It is Waber's opinion that one cannot emphasize enough the "last chance" aspect of adolescence and its potential for having a productive or destructive effect on the individual.

Moral Development

"The ultimate evil is man's ability to make
the concrete abstract.
—(Sartre or Camus)

Sartre or Camus never read about Piaget's
4th stage."
—Grafitti on a
university wall

Twenty years ago a discussion of moral development would have been included in a section entitled "social development" or "socialization," rather than in a section entitled "cognitive development." It is not incidental to trends in adolescent research that moral development is more appropriately placed in this section. First, researchers are interested not so much in the content of adolescents' moral thought as in their style of thought, once again reflecting the influence of Piaget. Second, cultural trends affect approaches to research. A society that is less and less sure of what is right and what is wrong, and of the values it is willing to inculcate through its institutions, and which feels that in fact the young may have more to teach the old than the old have to teach the young, will produce research that investigates objectively cognitive stages of moral development rather than investigating the acquisition of moral content.

Kohlberg's work on the structure of moral thought is the most significant in this area. It is significant because of the contribution it has made in its own right, because of the research that it has stimulated in attempts to verify and expand its concepts, and because of articles in reaction to his research that call into question the universality of his concepts and the appropriateness of his methodology. Whether in support, in extension, or in opposition to Kohlberg, the current body of research in the area of adolescent moral development is a testimony to his overriding influence in this field.

Kohlberg posits three levels of moral judgment: the pre-conventional level, the conventional level, and the post-conventional level. Within each of these levels there are two stages (or "types") making a total of six stages of moral development. The child develops from having no conception of right existing beyond the individual's point of view (level one), through the conventional level where socially shared expectations about right and wrong are seen as legitimate (level two), to level three, the post-conventional level, in which the individual starts with principles and judges the conventions on the basis of their realization of these principles.[136]

Kohlberg sees individuals as developing through the stages of moral thought stepwise in an invariable sequence. This is not to say that everybody achieves all stages of development. In fact, one of the areas of criticism of Kohlberg's work is that cross-culturally many people do not score beyond level two.

The importance of Kohlberg's work has been his departure from the leads of such figures as Freud and Durkheim. Moralization has been seen as a process of internalizing culturally given external rules, a process of "stamping in" the prohibitions of the culture upon the child. Kohlberg, following the perspective of developmental psychology proposed by Piaget, holds instead that internal moral standards are the outcome of internal transformations accompanying cognitive growth and social experience. Changes in modes of moral thought are not successive acquisitions or internalizations of one's culture. Instead they represent the ways in which the child organizes cognitively structures that emerge from his interaction with his social environment.[137]

Carol Gilligan, co-author with Kohlberg of "The Adolescent as Philosopher," has written an extremely helpful summary of Kohlberg's work for teachers. What is of relevance to this book is her description of what happens during early adolescence, a time when shifts should be taking place in moral development parallel to and dependent on shifts taking place in cognitive development.

Children develop in their thinking or reasoning because they abandon a way of looking at the world when it no longer works or when there is something to conflict with it. For the adolescent cultural relativism appears to be the source of growth. Recognizing the dilemma faced by young adolescents in resolving the conflict between moral relativism and black-and-white absolutism highlights the limitations of current curriculum theory and practices for elucidating if, why, and how we are to educate toward the formation of moral judgments.[138] It also highlights our limitations in translating moral judgments to actual behavior. We need to ask, "What is the price of such an increasing abstraction, such a formalization of thinking about moral issues? . . . How does abstract thought affect one's view of the particular? How does the perception of the universal affect one's attitude toward community?"[139] The answers to these questions are central to the moral implications of cognitive shifts during adolescence.[140]

Political Conceptualization

Just as Kohlberg has been the central figure in research on moral development, Adelson has been the central figure in research having to do with development of political conceptualization. Employing arguments which parallel Kohlberg's, Adelson argues that too much work in political socialization relies heavily on acquisition of knowledge, what Kohlberg calls "stamping in," and therefore has been misleading about political understanding in adolescence. "Just as the young child can count many numbers in series and yet not grasp the principle of ordination, so may the young adolescent have in his head many random bits of political information without a secure understanding of those concepts which would give order and meaning to the information."[141]

Adelson studied 450 adolescents ages eleven through eighteen in the United States, West Germany, and Great Britain in order to understand more clearly the development of political thinking during adolescence. He investigated such traditional issues of political philosophy as the scope and limits of political authority, the obligations of the citizen and the state, majority-minority relations, the nature of crime and justice, and the conflict between freedom and responsibility. Adelson found that in the growth of political concepts neither sex nor intelligence nor social class counts for much. What counts very heavily is age—the profound shift in the character of political thought occurring at the *onset* of adolescence and completed by fifteen or sixteen. "A twelve-year-old German youngster's ideas of politics are closer to those of a twelve-year-old American than to those of his fifteen-year-old brother."[142]

What Adelson is confirming here is the significance of the transition from early to middle adolescence for the achievement of formal operations. At the threshold of adolescence, unable to imagine social reality in the abstract, the young adolescent can have little concept of community, of social institutions, of their structure and functions, or of "that invisible network of norms and principles which link these institutions to each other." Also closed off to him is any substantial understanding of such concepts essential to political thought as authority, rights, liberty, equity, interests, representation.[143] As the child moves through the early years of adolescence, he achieves a more powerful sense of the future. He achieves greater astuteness about motivation. He achieves a greater skepticism about the power of law to alter the human condition.

As to modes of reasoning:

The significant transition in reasoning during the early years of adolescence involves the acquisition of a hypothetico-deductive capacity. . . .

. . . we see . . . the appearance of the *conditional mode*. . . . The youngster avoids either/or positions and thinks in terms of contingencies; the hard and fast absolutism of childhood and the first years of adolescence gives way to moral and conceptual relativism. Furthermore, the youngster begins to resist the either/or alternatives proposed by our questions. He breaks set—that is, he challenges the assumptions, tacit and otherwise, contained in the inquiry.[144]

In "Growth of Political Ideas in Adolescence: the Sense of Community," Adelson and O'Neil state that it is their impression that the most substantial shift in the cognitive basis of political discourse is found in the period between eleven and thirteen years, paralleling the change from concrete to formal operations in the work of Inhelder and Piaget. Purposely overstating the case, the authors report that the eleven-year-old has not achieved the capacity for formal operations. He has not obtained hypothetico-deductive modes of analysis. The thirteen-year-old has achieved these capacities some of the time, but displays them with inconsistent effectiveness. "The thirteen-year-olds seem to be the most labile of our subjects. Depending on the item, they may respond like those older or younger than themselves. In a sense they are on the threshold of mature modes of reasoning, just holding on, and capable of slipping back easily. Their answers are the most difficult to code, since they often involve an uneasy mixture of the concrete and the formal." In contrast, the fifteen-year-old usually has a more assured grasp of formal reasoning. He deals more easily with the abstract. The authors found only moderate differences between fifteen and eighteen-year-olds. "We do find concepts that appear suddenly between eleven and thirteen and between thirteen and fifteen, but only rarely do we find an idea substantially represented at eighteen which is not also available to a fair number of fifteen-year-olds."[145]

One of Adelson's findings with which all practitioners must deal is the young adolescent's authoritarianism. This authoritarianism affects his views on crime and punishment, on government, law, politics, social policy. It is found in both sexes and all social classes and in the three nations Adelson studied. It is, as he says, a ubiquitous feature of growing adolescents' political thought. This authoritarianism, according to Adelson, is accounted for by a lack of faith in the human capacity for self-control as well as by an ingenuous belief in the goodness and justice of authority. Another source of this authoritarian attitude is the young adolescent's inability to grasp the idea of rights. The concept is grasped only as the youngster progresses through the middle and into the later years of adolescence.

We can conclude from Adelson's work that during the years spanning the twelve-to-fifteen age range the adolescent is undergoing very significant changes in his political imagination. "The steady advance of the sense of principle is one of the most impressive phenomena of adolescent political thought."[146] During early adolescence, then, we can expect to find the anomälies, surprising gaps in knowledge, gaps between levels of understanding from one topic to another, and the discrepancies between feelings and cognition which Adelson has documented in his work.[147]

In an ingeniously contrived study, Gallatin and others (including Adelson, and deeply indebted to him) studied the development of political thinking during adolescence by interviewing 463 school children of average intelligence. The sample was drawn from equal numbers of blacks and whites, boys and girls, suburbanites and city-dwellers, in grades six, eight, ten, and twelve. Each subject was interviewed individually by means of a Piaget-type questionnaire. Gallatin found that although there were minor sex, race, and area differences, the developmental differences were by far the most striking.

Blacks were included in the study because although in the late 1960s research on the development of black youth was proliferating, there was very little that bore directly on the development of their political thinking. Black youngsters have been characterized by political researchers as "political isolates"—outside the mainstream of the American governmental system. Black high school seniors have been found to know less about government than white students and to have a weaker sense of political efficacy. Gallatin's group wondered, however, whether the growing emphasis on black pride and black power in addition to the election and appointment of blacks to government posts had begun to counteract the traditional feelings of powerlessness and political inefficacy among the young.

Gallatin was interested in researching such questions as what form of government black and white adolescents in metropolitan and suburban areas favor at various stages in their development; how ideas regarding law and order develop among these adolescents; how views regarding such issues as public welfare, minority rights, freedom of speech, and crime prevention develop; how these adolescents define the role of political parties; how they regard such pressing issues as civil disobedience and police-community relations.[148]

Gallatin found steps in the growth of political thinking which, as she says, closely parallel Kohlberg's levels. She identified three different levels of ideation: "*Level 1:* the confused, simplistic, punitive, or concretely pragmatic response. . . . *Level 2:* Transition responses: answers which express the rudiments of a political concept but remain somewhat fragmentary or personalized. . . .

Level 3: Conceptual responses: answers which are phrased in terms of some sort of political principle or ideal."[149]

The data from one of Gallatin's tables, "Level of Response by Age," call attention to the distribution across the levels among the eighth and tenth graders.

Level of Response by Age (in percentages)[150]

	Level 1	Level 2	Level 3
Sixth Graders	59	23	11
Eighth Graders	43	31	20
Tenth Graders	31	33	32
Twelfth Graders	19	29	41

Of particular interest are the implications of such findings for educational curricula. The high variability among young adolescents is problematical for traditional curricula. At the same time, it is easy, looking at a table like this one, to view the young adolescent as in a transitional stage and prepare curricula accordingly. The danger in so doing is that each individual adolescent is experiencing this age not as transitional but as one with its own integrity.

Summarizing Gallatin's results, contrary to previous research which held that political socialization is more or less complete by the end of eighth grade, the most important finding of this study is that political thinking undergoes marked changes between the sixth and twelfth grades. The adolescent experiences an increasing comprehension of the way in which the political system functions, develops more democratic and humanitarian views, the concept of government changes from restrictive to facilitative, the stance toward crime becomes less punitive and oriented more toward rehabilitation, and in general he seems to develop the perception that government is a kind of social contract. (Later in adolescence, the growth of such political ideals appears to be accompanied by an increasing pessimism or cynicism.)

Gallatin found no significant sex or area differences. On some items there were significant black-white differences, but they had more to do with attitude than with conceptualization. Blacks demonstrate a slightly less positive view of the police; whites seem to have a more cynical view of the political scene. Surprisingly, blacks were more likely to believe in the possibility of having some impact on the government of their particular city than were whites.

Most significant, however, is the comparative lack of differences between blacks and whites. On the vast majority of items there are no black-white differences at all. "It is often assumed that the two races are socialized differently, that they are in effect two separate cultures. Our own study would seem to indicate that as far as the growth of political thinking is concerned the impact of such differential socialization is relatively minor. The evolution of political ideation, if not identical, is markedly similar among the blacks and whites in our research population."[151]

As in Adelson's previous work, this particular study, with intelligence controlled, showed once again that age appears to be a more important determinant of political thinking than sex, social class, area or residence, or race. Even attitudinal differences appear to be relatively minor in comparison with age differences.

Given the similarity of findings among Kohlberg's investigations of moral development, Adelson's studies of political ideation, and Gallatin's research, Gallatin states that while it will take further time and study to construct a thoroughgoing theoretical framework, we are now on our way toward delineating a taxonomy of social thought.

Imagine the following scenario. It is late at night and a child has chosen not to go to sleep. As a diversion, he is asked to answer some of the questions in Gallatin's study. We are on a desert island. We have moved to this island because of discontent with our social system. We realize now that we must have some form of decision making. Some people suggest that everyone get together weekly and make decisions together. Others suggest that several people be chosen to represent us and to make decisions. Still others suggest that we should have one wise ruler, the wisest among us, who could be replaced in about a year were we not satisfied with his decisions. At this point, the nine-year-old insomniac chooses not to have one wise ruler because it might be possible that the community would want to dismiss him before a year had passed.

What does this answer mean? It appears to be contingency thinking well beyond the child's years, according to the research we have reported here. It exhibits a lack of faith in the benevolence of social institutions, and, given his ensuing answers, a greater faith in representative government. This inconsistency with the data from the studies we have reported is pointed out to his twelve-year-old sister, who responds, "Look at what he has seen tonight." It is August 8, 1974, the day of Nixon's resignation. As this twelve-year-old has said many times in the past years, recalling that her first social memory is of assassinations, that she has vivid recollections of heated discussions about Viet Nam, and that two years have been taken up with Watergate, "You don't know what it means to be growing up now."

It is possible that in fact we don't. It is possible that even though these studies have been conducted not about the content of political thinking but about the style, if the development of cognition is based on an interaction with one's social environment, we may need to call into question some of the data that has been presented here, especially as regards age.

Reactions to Current Research

We all want to hear that a superstage of moral development can be achieved, that the true, the good, and the beautiful are attainable. And yet it is possible that the stages beyond stage four, which Kohlberg presents as higher achievements, may be tied to particular ideological dispositions. The work of Hogan and that of Simpson have a sobering effect on research in this area. Sometimes this work is not directly about cognition; sometimes it is not about adolescence. We include a summary of their views for the implications they hold for future research about adolescence and cognition.

Hogan criticizes American moralists like Kohlberg for regarding an ethic based upon individual conscience as higher than an ethic based on conformity to cultural customs. Hogan and Dickstein, in "Moral Judgment and Perceptions of Injustice," have conceptualized moral development in terms of four dimensions considered in conjunction with the ethics of conscience and responsibility: moral knowledge, socialization, empathy, and autonomy. (Hogan later added a dimension of moral judgment.) They state that "it is impossible to equate the ethics of conscience with a developmental stage such as that referred to by Piaget's concept of autonomous morality."[152] Hogan argues that the emergence of socialization, empathy, and autonomy represents separate stages of moral development. In contrast to Kohlberg, he contends that failure of development at one point can be compensated for by successful transition to the next stage.[153]

It is Hogan's view that moral behavior consists of obeying or disobeying rules in a given social context. One form of moral behavior, obedience or conformity, is of greater significance because the most impressive aspect of everyday social life is the degree to which people obey the norms of their culture. "In the final analysis, moral behavior typically comes down to either following or disregarding a social rule of some sort; consequently a major problem for the psychology of moral conduct is to account for social compliance or noncompliance."[154]

For Hogan, to the extent that people regard the rules and values of society as personally mandatory, they may be considered socialized. To the extent that they feel estranged from these rules and values, they may be considered unsocialized. The socialization process is largely completed by the time a child enters school and results in an authoritarian ethic of conformity. What becomes critical is the individual's ability to be empathic. The development of empathy, like cognitive development generally, is probably finished by late adolescence.

There is a distinctly negative, pessimistic view of mankind that permeates the work of Hogan and of others emerging on the horizon. In contrast with Kohlberg and Piaget, Hogan assumes that moral conduct is fundamentally "irrational" and that differences even in cognitive phenomena such as moral judgments derive from personological structures.

A letter written by Hogan in reference to Kohlberg summarizes their differences:

He studies age related changes in moral judgment (i.e., how people reason about theoretical moral dilemmas)—the empirical literature suggests, however, that there is little relationship between what people think about moral issues and what they will actually do. I differ from Kohlberg secondly in that I think he drastically overemphasizes the role of reason in moral conduct–it seems to me that moral action in most cases is inspired by feelings of injustice, guilt, or moral outrage. Finally, I disagree with Kohlberg in that I think his concept of moral maturity reflects his own liberal political biases.[155]

Criticisms of equally serious import have been leveled against Kohlberg's work by Elizabeth Simpson in an article entitled "Moral Development Research: A Case Study of Scientific Cultural Bias."[156] The title itself summarizes the article. Simpson claims that in analyzing the evidence supporting Kohlberg's hierarchy of moral reasoning, the definitions of stages and the assumptions underlying them were found to be ethnocentric and culturally biased. She is also highly critical of conceptual and methodological problems of Kohlberg's cross-disciplinary and cross-cultural research. Simpson cites Bronfenbrenner's argument that class, sex, and culture are all more important determinants of moral development than are age or experience. She cites Cole's work among the Kpelle to substantiate her argument that there has not been adequate care taken in Kohlbergian cross-cultural studies. Kohlberg believes that a simple, noncomplex society implies an inability of its members to reach the highest stages of moral maturity; Cole showed that in an "ethnic" replication using materials that were familiar to the children among the Kpelle, subjects including nonliterate adults and school children from seven to fourteen years old demonstrated high levels of integrated inferential behavior.

Kohlberg sees cultural differences as relatively unimportant in the moral development of the individual. Simpson insists that the content that generalizes to build concepts is culturally derived. Highly abstract concepts such as "justice" are practically useless as cross-cultural generalizations. Concept development cannot mean the same thing from one class or from one culture to another.

There seems little doubt that even if there are methodological problems with Kohlberg's work, and even if there are conceptual problems, his work in moral development has been so stimulating to other researchers and curriculum developers that our understanding of adolescents' cognition has been greatly enriched.

We have pursued these arguments at length, through Kohlberg, Adelson, Gallatin, Hogan, and Simpson, because of core issues that are as yet unresolved. If concept development cannot mean the same thing from one class to another or from one culture to another, then a pluralistic approach to instruction towards cognitive development is mandatory in our schools. If age is the critical variable in studies of political cognition, is this generalizable to other areas of cognition? If so, then some relationship between age and class or age and culture must be determined prior to adoption of curricula. If developmental variability among young adolescents is a universal characteristic within our population, then stages of concept development, whether culture-bound or not, cannot be the determinant of school programs in our traditional grade-level school organizations. We are unable to utilize these various research studies without changing schools for young adolescents.

Aside from the "backlash" movement in the area of moral development, we see the beginning of a renewed interest in talent and creativity–giftedness–among researchers. There has been very little work in the 1960s and 1970s on the gifted, perhaps because as a society we have been concentrating our efforts on equalizing opportunity through compensatory programs.

James Gallagher contends that one of the things we know how to do with great efficiency is to identify pure intellectual power, meaning anything relying on verbal symbols. We do not know what we want to do with the verbally gifted once we have identified them. According to Gallagher, there is a certain revulsion about special programs for gifted young adolescents. These youngsters already have so much; why should we give them more? It is unequal and therefore unfair.

Gallagher agrees that it is unfair, but insists that it is a fact of life that we must rely on gifted people to make major social decisions. We need as much of their potential as possible, and that means being unfair. We change the equality argument at the point when we perceive our need for these talents–i.e., we have schools for the gifted, like medical schools and law schools. What we must acknowledge is that we need to develop these talents earlier. Our social ideologies militate against doing this. (So do our professionals: the staffs at the junior high level, for instance, are "intellectually inferior people."[157])

In 1959 Getzels and Jackson wrote that for all practical purposes, the term "gifted child" had become synonymous with the child with a high IQ. We were thus blinded to other forms of potential excellence. In addition, within the area of intellectual functions, despite work on cognition and creativity, we tended to apply the concept of creativity only to performance in one or more of the arts. The term "creative child" became synonymous with the expression, "child with artistic talents," thus hindering us from identifying and fostering cognitive abilities related to creative functioning in areas other than the arts.[158]

We have made no progress since the late 1950s. We continue to reinforce abilities in the areas of convergent thinking and evaluation and to ignore the development of divergent thinking. We continue to try to transform our divergent students into convergent students. Getzels and Jackson said, "It is our hope that the present emphasis upon research in creativity will enlarge our understanding of cognitive functioning in both the laboratory and the classroom."[159] It certainly has not in the classroom, which leads us to ask the perennial question, what is the purpose of research in education? What mechanism is needed to change practices?

At this point, Johns Hopkins University is a "hot bed" of research on precocity because it is conducting two research projects funded by the Spencer Foundation, one on scientific and mathematical precocity (Professor Julian Stanley and associates) and the other on verbal and humanistic giftedness

(Robert Hogan and associates). One aim of these research projects is to develop a systematic concept of intelligence. Another is to identify and recover wasted talent in adolescence. These researchers are working on measures of what talent is so that they can identify and reinforce adolescents' talents. If all that comes from these research efforts will be a few students who will have been helped to earn Ph.D.'s at earlier ages, then they will have indeed been very disappointing. If, on the other hand, they lead to a greater understanding of the tremendous bursts of creative energy during young adolescence, and to ways of reinforcing and harnessing those energies rather than deadening or discouraging them, we will be much the richer for such projects.

At the same time, there is a nagging sense of disturbance about the tone of some works on the gifted and the tone of some of the critiques of research in the area of moral development, compounded by recommendations for lowering the age of compulsory school attendance. One senses a certain reaction setting in in the wake of negative evaluations of the programs of the 1960s. If we "bombed out" with compensatory programs, then let us turn to the gifted; if Kohlberg's highest stage of morality represented the Berkeley free speech movement people as well as Martin Luther King, then let us research the implications of that conformity which is necessary to social cohesion. If we feel that we have been less than successful by emphasizing children's rights, then let us research once again parental rights and children's responsibility.[160] All of these are very legitimate areas of research, and we applaud them, especially the work on the gifted. There is just that nagging sense we get that on the horizon is a backlash effect which may be seen in more and more research during the 1970s.

Areas for Further Research in Cognition

Children live in social contexts, and their cognitive development is influenced by those contexts. One of these contexts is one's personal relationship with the mass media.

We need to know what the effects are on cognitive development during adolescence of the twelve to fifteen thousand hours of television that the average sixteen-year-old has watched during his lifetime.

The staff of NICHD has identified many other issues in the area of cognition that require further investigation. They see as the most obvious and general research need a concerted but varied attack on the relative ignorance that we have about changes in thinking, language, perception, learning and other cognitive functions just preceding and during adolescence. Psycholinguistic studies are needed for a thorough understanding of the use of language in the service of thinking which seems to come to fruition during adolescence. We need to know why in our society there is such great diversity in the ability to form abstractions. In order to understand the adolescents' socio-emotional concerns, we must understand the process by which they acquire or do not acquire formal thinking. An understanding of many of the social problems related to adolescence depends in part on our understanding the intellectual functioning during this period. Why do some adolescents lose the motivation for continued intellectual and creative growth? What factors in our institutions lead to this waste? We must understand the factors necessary for the development and the expression of creativity in adolescents. We must investigate creativity more diversely and develop satisfactory methodologies for measuring it. We must release ourselves from the inhibiting factors of unsophisticated instruments for measuring the subtleties of the changes in various aspects of intellectual development.[161]

Federal Funding for Research

> . . . the orientation of Federal programs is to support remedial rather than preventive efforts with a focus on cure and problem solution to a large extent.[162]

In fiscal year 1973 (FY '73), $251 million were spent by federal agencies on adolescence research; in FY '74, adolescent funding was reduced to $180.3 million; in FY '75, the amount rose to $235.7 million. In each area of research on early adolescence reviewed in this report, investigators, while pointing to the many areas that are not being researched, have summarized the highlights and emerging trends in current efforts. The funding source supporting most of the research cited is the federal government. We therefore now focus on federal support for research on early adolescence in an attempt to ascertain areas and types of research supported, levels of funding, and the outreach effect of such federal expenditures.

The most valuable source of information about federal research and programs for adolescents is the Interagency Panel for Research and Development on Adolescence. The information in this section relies heavily on the Panel's 1973 First Annual Report, 1974 Second Annual Report, and 1975 Third Annual Report, all entitled *Toward Interagency Coordination*, prepared by the Social Research Group of The George Washington University. Information has also been obtained by means of individual requests to the Social Research Group for computer runs. The following cautions are offered:

The Panel's power is the power of persuasion, and the quality of the data depends upon the information release policies of the individual agencies.[163]

The data for FY '73 and '74 represent the individual Panel member's overview of his/her agency. The collection was based, therefore, on the areas of activity judged by the individual agency representatives to be relevant. The data for

FY '75 were collected by research assistants of the Interagency Panel who studied every funded research proposal in each of the twenty-three participating agencies.

In general, the reports define adolescence as ages ten through twenty-four. The ages above eighteen are included when the target populations are college students or "others not in adult roles." (However, there is great variation, since NIMH, NIDA, and NIAAA define adolescence as ages 12-25, NICHD as 9-21, OYD and OCD as 10-17, and other agencies do not provide age specification.)

The FY '75 report is based on 2,343 research projects involving adolescents in some way, out of a total of 3,498 research projects affecting non-adults.

The FY '74 report is based on information from 3,116 projects in early childhood and adolescence; 1,964 involve adolescents. The FY '73 report is based on approximately 2,000 projects, of which 1,152 are concerned with adolescence. The data from the three reports are not directly comparable.

Because of considerable improvements in the standardization of data collection, reliable comparisons of levels of research activity between FY '75 and '74 are possible.[164] They are not possible using '73 data. We are therefore not able to conduct a trend analysis on the basis of available data. That will take several years of stable collection and classification of data. Tables are presented only as indicators of priorities.

The tables in the content areas reflect multiple classification of projects. (For example, a study on the socio-emotional development of emotionally handicapped children would appear in four or five tables.)

The degree of focus is not reflected. If a study that is heavily weighted toward physical development, for instance, has a measure designed to evaluate socio-emotional development, it is coded in both categories.

FY '73 data on juvenile delinquency came from the Social Rehabilitation Service. These projects have since been transferred to the Office of Youth Development, and from there to the Law Enforcement Assistance Administration. Given the continuing state of flux, the accuracy of the data is open to question.

Fifty-seven percent of reported research on adolescence in FY '73 related to youth with special characteristics, especially the disadvantaged and handicapped. Cognitive and socio-emotional development were studied in equal amounts (39%). The Panel's first annual report points out that this represents a departure from the recent trends in early childhood research, in which the main emphasis has been cognitive. The departure appears to be even more radical for FY '74, in which 30.54 percent related to research on special characteristics, socio-emotional development represented 19.99 percent of the total number of adolescent projects funded, and cognitive development only 12.13 percent. In FY '75, as seen in Table 1-3, the pattern is mixed, but socio-emotional development appears to be slighted in basic and applied research activity, and to be encouraged less than other areas of development in basic research funding. No reason is given for this decrease. No priorities appear to have dictated any policy calling for such a decrease. Funding patterns appear to be haphazard except in crisis areas. These figures are difficult to interpret, since much of the effort in both the cognitive and socio-emotional areas has had a narrow focus, the former on educational achievement and the latter on attitudes towards work, aspiration levels, social relations, and other affective aspects of the work experience.[165]

In FY '75, 167 adolescence projects included the physically handicapped, 170 involved the intellectually handicapped, and 162 the emotionally handicapped (Table 1-6). The most frequently mentioned target in funded projects from among the handicapped was the bilingual population ($N = 333$), and second most frequent was the "academically slow" population ($N = 210$). Given the overlapping of categories in the Panel's data and the freedom of the various agencies to define the variables of their funding efforts, one must make only qualified statements about the federal government's funding priorities over a three-year period. Nevertheless, the picture that emerges is one in which the average, nonhandicapped, nonminority adolescent receives comparatively little attention. In this sense, the "normal" youth is disadvantaged.

Keeping in mind that categories are not mutually exclusive in Figures 1-1 and 1-3, the reader is directed to Figures 1-1 through 1-4, the priorities for federal funding for FY '73 and '74 by kinds of research. We do not have comparable data for FY '75. (Figures 1-1 and 1-3 are reproduced from the Panel's first report. Figures 1-2 and 1-4 were prepared for this review by the Social Research Group. They are found at the end of this section along with Tables 1-3 through 1-13.)

Note the lack of emphasis placed on research dealing with planning and dissemination in Figures 1-1 through 1-4. Research addressing planning of policy, program, and research efforts received 1.2 percent of the total effort. Planning, evaluation, and dissemination received 19.7 percent. Dissemination received 6.5 percent of the total number of project efforts, and 4 percent of the total funding. In FY '74, dissemination appears to have fared better, receiving 8 percent of the total funding. Funding for studies of evaluation appears to have been strikingly reduced.

Planning of policy, program, and research efforts shows very low figures primarily because the data collection is based on research projects and includes only projects researching planning techniques and practices. Much of the agencies' planning does not take the form of a research project, but takes the form of intramural activity, meetings, or conferences which are not reflected in the data. Likewise, the dissemination figures underestimate the amount of dissemination that actually occurs. The percentiles cited are figures that reflect those projects that were funded for the purpose of researching new techniques of dissemination, or for the primary purpose of dissemination. The dissemination efforts normally included in most research projects are not included in these figures.

So, we cannot say how much federal commitment there actually is to planning and dissemination. Practical experience suggests an inadequate level of concern. Anyone who has been involved in preparing a proposal for federal funding knows the frustration of having no funds, indeed no time, for planning. In fact, the way in which proposals were drawn up during the 1960s for federal funds, sometimes literally overnight, makes one question the arguments now at large that the lesson of the 1960s is that money makes no difference. Money *per se* may not, but money spent only after planning, with careful evaluation, and mandatory responsible dissemination, may make a difference. The fact is that we do not know.

That digression aside, it is unreasonable to complain about lack of diffusion when such low percentages of the research projects and of the total funding directly address the ubiquitous problem of dissemination. A "lighthouse" cannot work if it has no beams.

It is not possible to ascertain with any reasonable amount of certainty how much money and how many projects serve young adolescents. We cannot account for what percentages of the projects apply or do not apply to ages twelve through fifteen. Usually the only information provided about the targeted population's age is a description such as "youth," "teenagers," or "adolescents." Therefore, it cannot be assumed that projects do not deal with youth ages twelve through fifteen. It cannot be assumed that they do. It is, as must be repeated continually throughout this review, extremely difficult to ascertain what is actually happening.

The distribution of areas of research in Tables 1-1 and 1-2 has implications that are felt throughout this report. The effects of the limited funding emphases in FY '73 and '74 in socio-emotional and cognitive research, the relatively low level of funding in health and welfare delivery systems, in the family, advocacy, nutrition, and delinquency areas have been felt by researchers and practitioners in these fields—and by adolescents. Changes in priorities are occurring, and we turn to them now, realizing that they will change almost annually.

In FY '75, the Bureau of School Systems, stressing bilingual education, supplementary services, educational technology, and environmental education accounted for 26.4 percent of all adolescence research funding. Looking in general at agencies' funding, primary research foci were upon cognitive development ($N = 165$, an increase of 26.9 percent over FY '74), upon problems of physical development ($N = 112$, an increase of 10.9 percent over FY '74), and upon health and welfare services ($N = 291$, an increase of 32.3 percent). The largest increment appears to have occurred in projects primarily focused upon law enforcement and delinquency services ($N = 66$, a doubling since FY '74).[166]

Delinquency and crisis services were low in FY '73 and '74. If federal funding is reactive, as we have argued along with many others, it also takes a long time for the reaction to set in. Public unrest about juvenile crime is slowly starting to be reflected in federal funding priorities.

The third annual report points out that in the area of adolescent social and development problems, the number of projects pertaining to sex roles and identity decreased by more than 25 percent from FY '74 to '75. Basic research on cultural and racial identity decreased by 57.1 percent, but projects in categories other than basic research increased by 15 percent. Increases of note in basic research are in employment practices (+100%), youth culture (+100%), and reading processes (+142.9%). Most noteworthy is a whopping increase to sixty-nine in research projects of all kinds having to do with adolescent legal issues (+360%).[167]

Health and welfare categories (e.g., advocacy, protective services, nutrition, delinquency, delivery systems) are reported as having risen +316.7 percent for FY '75. Funding had been lowered in FY '74, so an increase was in order. It should also be noted that while 316.7 percent looks impressive, it represents only twenty-five projects spread out over eleven agencies.

Table 1-10 indicates strong foci on alternatives to traditional education through bilingual education, TV instruction, open classrooms, team teaching, work experience, tutorial instruction, and individualized curricula. Once again, it is impossible to say how many of these projects or what levels of funding benefit young adolescents. We assume, for instance, that most or all of the work experience projects are not for young adolescents. In terms of dollars spent, relatively small amounts are going to projects involving open classrooms and nongraded schools as alternatives for adolescents, and large amounts towards work experience, team teaching, TV education and bilingual education. (Dollar figures can be found in the second annual report.)

The increases represented in Table 1-7 in federal research and development projects involving adolescent developmental problems are heartening, as are the increases in projects involving personnel (Table 1-9). Projects involving teaching techniques constitute 35.9 percent of all adolescence research and are sponsored by twenty out of twenty-three agencies represented. Parent involvement is represented in 516 projects from fifteen agencies. Note the decreases, however, in desegregation projects, represented in only eleven projects, a 76.1 percent decrease from FY '74 (Table 1-10). The decreases in the health care and community areas are distinctly disheartening and will bear close scrutiny in future funding years.

See Tables 1-11 through 1-13 for information specific to NIMH funding, highlighted here because of the Institute's excellent reputation for funding research. According to an NIMH Program Specialist, there are no obvious trends in the funding of adolescence research over the past five years. In fact, it is difficult for people within NIMH to know what their priorities are. NIMH research is most likely to focus on the preschool child, next on the adolescent, and third on the family. In May 1976, however, NIMH held a small conference on research priorities for early adolescence. It would appear that one purpose of the conference was to send out signals to the research community and within NIMH as well.

In this section we have dealt with data that are difficult to evaluate. The Interagency Panels on early childhood and on adolescence are seeking ways of encouraging researchers to use comparable methods and measures to facilitate analysis of research findings across studies. "In order for research results to add up to anything . . . there must be a capacity to compare studies; there has to be some basis for relating the findings of one study to those of another."[168] At the same time, the data from FY '73 are not reported comparably with the data reported for FY '74, there are important gaps between reporting from FY '74 to '75, and it is not possible to compare the data reported by the Panel on early childhood with that reported by the Panel on adolescence. It is a case of "physician, heal thyself," and the Panels know it.

Dissemination remains a critical problem. Efforts to coordinate research and to share information, especially among federal agencies, are taking place. The two Interagency Panels are examples. However, even the Interagency Panels have considerable difficulty gaining access to dependable information. If the agencies created for the express purpose of gathering and reporting this information have considerable problems, then the individual "research consumer," with poorer access, is understandably frustrated. The coordination and dissemination problems invariably overwhelm the "research consumer" interested in early adolescence.

According to the third annual adolescence report, the Panels have recognized the lack of a centralized source of easily accessible information from federally funded research on children and youth. The Panels therefore plan to add to their usefulness by collecting data on findings of completed projects, as well as on current projects.[169]

The dissemination of research is a serious problem for the research community itself; it is a critical but often unacknowledged problem for the various research consumers like practitioners and policy makers at the national, state, and local levels; it is virtually a disaster area in reference to the general public, or potential consumers, who have few mechanisms for utilizing the public benefits that are supposed to accrue from research efforts.

What is one to conclude from all these reported figures and charts, even keeping in mind the tentative nature of the data and the possibilities for misinterpretation? There are areas of obvious deficiency; but a great deal of money is being spent. That some of it is being spent foolishly, we can always assume. That some of it represents efforts we need to know about, we can also assume. On shelves all over this country are reports, the "dissemination" required in the funding of so many projects. We have tracked down some of these reports. Several are cited in this review. The effort required to find out what is happening remains substantial, costly, and extremely demanding of one's energies.

This is the most positive interpretation we can make of the data provided. The most negative is that a good deal of money is being spent on haphazardly ordered and/or uncoordinated and/or poorly disseminated efforts. Very little of it is spent *specifically* on young adolescents or with consideration given to adolescence in the life span. We cannot even say that the money is being wisely allocated when it is reactive, noting the areas of need under the 16 percent level of FY '73 and '74 funding and the shuffling of funding targets seen in FY '75. At best, we are troubled by the apparent priorities or lack thereof; at worst, incredulous.

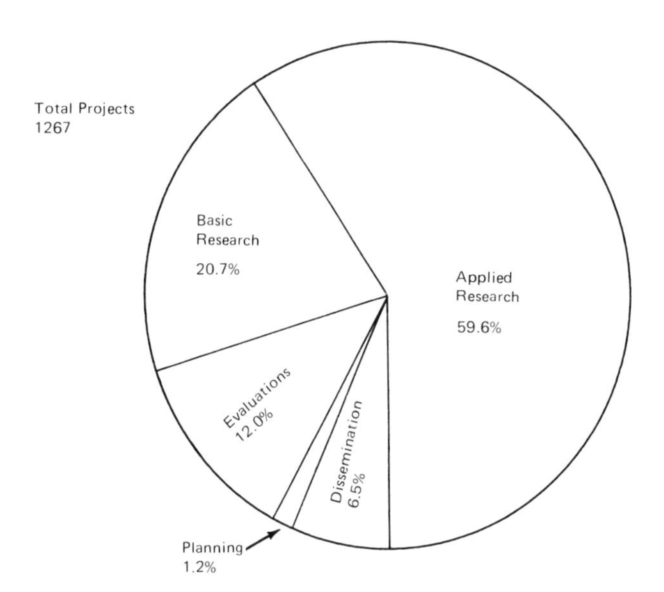

Source: *Toward Interagency Coordination* (1973), p. 90. Percentages represent non-mutually exclusive categories.

Figure 1-1. Percent of Total Number of Research Projects by Kinds of Research, FY '73.

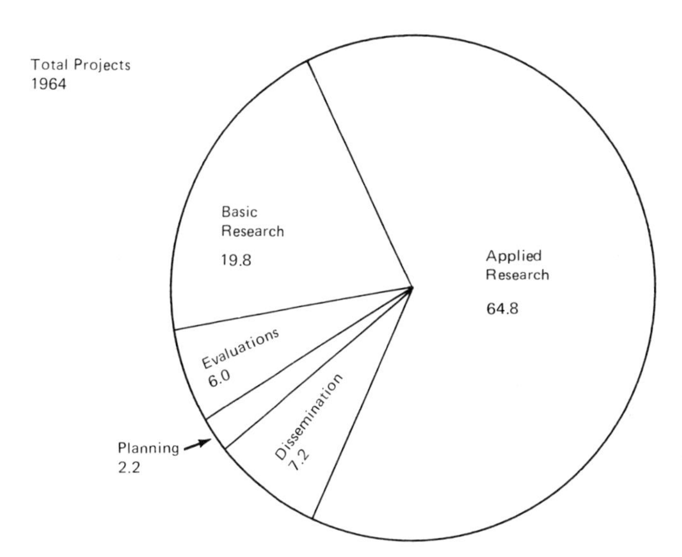

Source: Prepared by the Social Research Group for the report. Areas of research are mutually exclusive.

Figure 1-2. Percent of Total Number of Research Projects by Adolescent Research, FY '74.

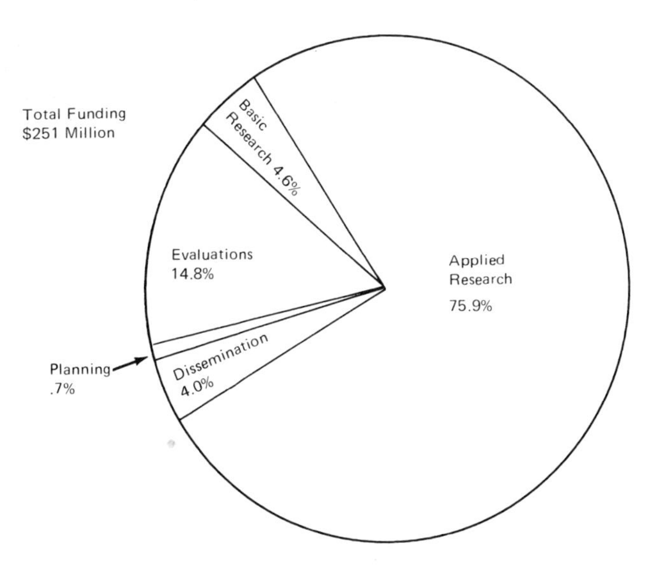

Source: *Toward Interagency Coordination* (1973), p. 90. Percentages represent non-mutually exclusive categories.

Figure 1-3. Percent of Total Funding by Kinds of Research, FY '73.

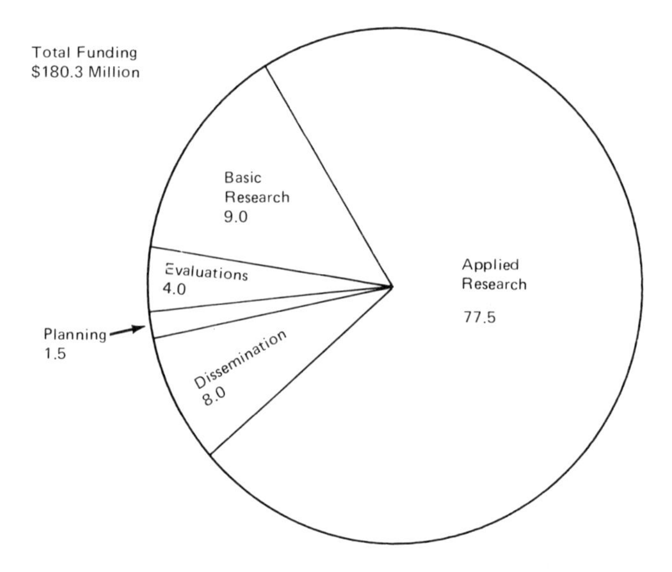

Source: Prepared by the Social Research Group for this report. Areas of research are mutually exclusive.

Figure 1-4. Percent of Total Funding by Adolescent Research, FY '74.

Table 1-1
All Agency Distribution and Rank Order (by percent) of Areas of Research, FY '73 (N = 1281)

		Percent Rank
Above 40%	–Special Characteristics	57%
26 to 40%	–Social-Emotional Development	39%
	–Cognitive Development	39%
21 to 25%	–Implementation	25%
	–Disadvantaged	25%
	–Handicapped	24%
16 to 20%	–Health and Welfare Delivery Systems	17%
	–Vocational/Technical Education	16%
11 to 15%	–Educational Innovations	14%
	–Career Education	14%
	–Physical Development	13%
	–School-Community Interface	12%
6 to 10%	–Influence of Family	10%
	–Global Approach	7%
	–Longitudinal Research	7%
1 to 5%	–Advocacy and Protective Services	5%
	–Nutrition	4%
	–Planning-Research Goals	4%
	–Methodology	3%
	–Delinquency	2%
	–Measures Development	2%

Source: *Toward Interagency Coordination* (1973), p. 81.

Table 1-2
Numbers and Percent of Areas of Adolescent Research, FY '74 (Total Adolescent Projects = 1964; Total Adolescent Funding = $180,288,409)

	N	Percent of Total N	Funding $	Percent of Total Funding
Special Characteristics	952	30.54	$84,418,778	46.8
Social-Emotional Development	623	19.99	50,146,158	27.8
Cognitive Development	378	12.13	34,706,801	19.3
Implementation	142	4.56	14,495,617	8.0
Disadvantaged	340	10.91	35,752,487	19.8
Handicapped	305	9.79	35,575,448	19.7
Health and Welfare Delivery Systems	271	8.69	23,759,710	13.2
Vocational/Technical Education	182	5.84	25,679,099	14.2
Educational Innovations	592	18.99	78,529,801	43.6
Career Education	186	5.97	30,951,547	17.2
Physical Development	239	7.67	16,957,680	9.4
School-Community Interface	462	14.82	47,725,318	26.5
Influence of Family	283	9.08	16,805,075	9.3
Global Approach	45	1.44	5,636,477	3.1
Longitudinal Research	961	30.83	86,528,445	48.0
Advocacy and Protective Services	104	3.34	11,730,393	6.5
Nutrition	30	0.96	1,574,019	0.9
Planning-Research Goals	154	4.94	11,518,063	6.4
Methodology	25	0.80	1,966,447	1.1
Delinquency	124	3.98	7,697,892	4.3
Measures Development	116	3.72	11,948,671	6.6

Source: Prepared by the Social Research Group for the author. Numbers and percentages represent non-mutually exclusive categories.

Table 1-3
Projects Focusing Primarily upon General Adolescent Development Problems by Type of Research Activity

	Basic and Applied Research and Development Activity		
	Percentage of Adolescence Projects[b] (N)	Percentage Change in (N) between FY '74 and FY '75	Number of Funding Agencies
Adolescent Development Total	19.4 (454)	+11.8	17
Physical Development[a]	4.7 (112)	+10.9	11
Cognitive Development[a]	7.0 (165)	+26.9	8
Socio-Emotional Development[a]	5.3 (123)	−20.0	10
	Basic Research Only		
	Percentage of Adolescence Projects[b] (N)	Percentage Change in (N) between FY '74 and FY '75	Number of Funding Agencies
Adolescent Development	15.5 (363)	+45.8	13
Physical Development[a]	3.9 (92)	+67.3	10
Cognitive Development[a]	5.3 (124)	+34.8	7
Socio-Emotional Development[a]	4.5 (106)	+16.5	10

[a]Mutually exclusive categories; no project was coded as applying to more than one.

[b]Total number of adolescence projects: $N = 2{,}343$.

Source: *Toward Interagency Coordination* (1975), p. 60.

Table 1-4
Projects Focusing Primarily upon Organizations That Serve Adolescents, by Type of Research Activity

Organizations Involving Adolescents[a]	Percentage of FY '75 Adolescence Projects[b] (*N*)		Percentage Change in (*N*) between FY '74 and FY '75	Number of Funding Agencies
	Basic and Applied Research and Development Activity			
Law Enforcement and Delinquency Services	2.8	(66)	+100.0	5
Health and Welfare Services	12.4	(291)	+32.3	16
Day Care	0.3	(6)	–[c]	4
Educational Institutions	55.1	(1291)	+13.2	18
Secondary	8.5	(200)	–4.3	13
Post-Secondary	3.5	(82)	–3.5	12
Special Education	5.9	(138)	–[c]	7
	Basic Research Only[d]			
Law Enforcement and Delinquency Services	0.1	(1)	–	1
Health and Welfare Services	1.1	(25)	+316.7	11
Day Care	0.1	(2)	–[c]	1
Educational Institutions	2.1	(49)	–14.0	10
Secondary	0.2	(6)	–33.3	3
Post-Secondary	0.4	(9)	–10.0	3
Special Education	0.1	(4)	–[c]	2

[a]All categories are mutually exclusive.

[b]Total number of adolescence projects: $N = 2{,}343$.

[c]No valid comparison possible.

[d]Basic and primarily focused upon organizations involving nonadults.

Source: *Toward Interagency Coordination* (1975), pp. 61-62.

Table 1-5
Adolescent Target Population: Percentage Involving the Physically Handicapped by Type of Research

	Basic and Applied Research			Basic Research Only		
Adolescent Characteristic[a]	Percentage of Adolescence Projects (N = 2,343)	Percentage of Both Adolescence and Early Childhood Projects (N = 3,498)	Number of Funding Agencies	Percentage of Adolescence Projects (N = 2,343)	Percentage of Both Adolescence and Early Childhood Projects (N = 3,498)	Number of Funding Agencies
Physically Handicapped Total	7.1 (167)[b]	4.8	13	1.6 (38)[b]	1.1	6
Aurally	2.2 (51)	1.5	8	0.5 (11)	0.3	3
Visually	1.1 (26)	0.7	7	0.1 (1)	0.1	1
Neurologically	2.8 (66)	1.9	8	0.9 (22)	0.6	5
Orthopedically	1.0 (23)	0.7	4	0.1 (4)	0.1	2
Hyperkinetic	0.7 (16)	0.5	5	0.4 (10)	0.3	3

[a]These categories are not mutually exclusive.

[b]Within the parentheses is the number of adolescence research projects currently being funded intended to affect the target group on the left.

Source: *Toward Interagency Coordination* (1975), pp. 65-66.

Table 1-6
Adolescent Target Population: Percentage Involving the Intellecually and Emotionally Handicapped and Others, by Type of Research

	Basic and Applied Research			
Adolescent Characteristic[a]	Percentage of Adolescence Projects (N = 2,343)	Percentage of Both Adolescence and Early Childhood Projects (N = 3,498)	Number of Funding Agencies	Agency Funding the Largest Number of Projects
Intellectually Handicapped Total	7.3 (170)[b]	4.9	16	BEH $N = 75$
Mentally Retarded	4.0 (103)	2.9	14	BEH $N = 36$
Learning Disabled	3.9 (92)	2.6	11	BEH $N = 52$
Emotionally Handicapped Total	6.9 (162)	4.6	13	NIMH $N = 108$
Schizophrenic	1.1 (26)	0.7	3	NIMH $N = 24$
Autistic	0.7 (17)	0.5	4	NIMH $N = 12$
Psychotic	2.1 (48)	1.4	5	NIMH $N = 41$
Drug Users	4.2 (99)	2.8	7	NIDA $N = 49$
Heroin	0.2 (4)	0.1	1	NIDA $N = 1$
Alcohol	1.6 (38)	1.1	3	NIAAA $N = 36$
Delinquents	3.3 (77)	2.2	10	NIMH $N = 39$
Abused or Neglected	2.4 (57)	1.6	7	OCD $N = 43$
Academically Slow	9.0 (210)	6.0	12	(Right-To-Read) $N = 149$
Drop-Outs	2.8 (65)	1.9	12	OTE $N = 26$
Intellectually Gifted	0.6 (14)	0.4	6	OCE $N = 6$
Runaways	2.1 (50)	1.4	7	NIMH $N = 39$
Adolescent Parents	1.1 (25)	0.7	10	NICHD $N = 8$
Bilingual	14.2 (333)	9.5	9	BSS $N = 250$

[a]These characteristics are not mutually exclusive.

[b]Within the parentheses is the number of adolescence research projects currently being funded intended to affect target groups with the characteristics listed on the left.

Source: *Toward Interagency Coordination* (1975), p. 67.

Table 1-7
Specific Adolescent Development Problems, by Type of Research Activity

Adolescent Developmental Problems[a]	Basic and Applied Research and Development Activity			Basic Research Only[d]		
	Percentage of FY '75 Adolescence Projects[b] (*N*)	Percentage Change in (*N*) between FY '74 and FY '75	Number of Funding Agencies	Percentage of FY '75 Adolescence Projects[b] (*N*)	Percentage Change in (*N*) between FY '74 and FY '75	Number of Funding Agencies
Perception of the Self	16.8 (394)	–[c]	18	1.5 (34)	–[c]	8
Cultural/Racial Identity	1.9 (46)	+15.0	8	0.1 (3)	–57.1	1
Interpersonal Relationships	6.0 (141)	+60.2	15	1.5 (36)	+20.0	6
Motivation	4.9 (116)	–5.7	13	1.1 (25)	–16.7	7
Emotional Development	7.7 (181)	+60.2	15	2.0 (47)	–[c]	6
Language Development	5.8 (136)	+65.8	15	1.8 (43)	+72.0	5
Reading Process	2.5 (59)	+5.4	8	0.7 (17)	+142.9	2
Developmental Continuity	0.9 (22)	–[c]	7	0.2 (6)	–[c]	3
Sexual Identity	0.7 (18)	–28.0	6	0.3 (7)	–	4
Attitudes	14.8 (330)	–[c]	17	2.8 (65)	–[c]	10
Coping Mechanisms	1.5 (36)	–[c]	8	0.5 (18)	–[c]	4

[a]Categories are not mutually exclusive.

[b]Total number of adolescence projects: $N = 2{,}343$.

[c]No valid comparison possible.

[d]Basic and primarily focused upon social and emotional problems.

Source: *Toward Interagency Coordination* (1975), pp. 69, 70.

Table 1-8
Projects Relating to an Adolescent's Social Environment, by Type of Research Activity

Adolescent Socioenvironmental Problems[a]	Basic and Applied Research and Development Activity			Basic Research Only[d]			
	Percentage of FY '75 Adolescence Projects[b] (*N*)	Percentage Change in (*N*) between FY '74 and FY '75	Number of Funding Agencies	Percentage of FY '75 Adolescence Projects[b] (*N*)	Percentage Change in (*N*) between FY '74 and FY '75	Number of Funding Agencies	Percentages of Projects for Basic Research Purposes
Juvenile Delinquency	1.9 (46)	–[c]	8	0.2 (6)	–[c]	3	13.0
Unemployment	0.6 (15)	+25.0	5	0.1 (1)	–50.0	1	6.7
Religious Environment	0.5 (13)	–[c]	6	0.1 (1)	–[c]	1	7.7
Status Offenses	2.0 (48)	–[c]	5	0.1 (2)	–[c]	1	4.2
Legal Issues	2.9 (69)	+360.0	9	0.1 (3)	–	1	4.3
Sex Roles	0.6 (14)	–26.4	5	0.1 (3)	–	3	21.4
Employment Practices	1.1 (26)	–16.1	6	0.3 (8)	+100.0	4	30.8
Youth Culture	0.6 (15)	+114.2	9	0.1 (2)	+100.0	2	13.3
Ethnic and Racial Culture	4.8 (113)	–[c]	12	0.3 (8)	–[c]	7	7.1
Ecological Studies	5.6 (131)	–[c]	12	2.7 (94)	–[c]	10	71.8

[a]Categories are not mutually exclusive.

[b]Total number of adolescence projects: $N = 2{,}343$.

[c]No valid comparison possible.

[d]Basic and primarily focused upon social environmental problems.

Source: *Toward Interagency Coordination* (1975), pp. 71, 72.

Table 1-9
Research Projects Involving Personnel Affecting Adolescents

Personnel in the Adolescents' Environment[a]	Percentage of FY '75 Adolescence Projects[b] (*N*)	Percentage Change in (*N*) between FY '74 and FY '75	Number of Funding Agencies
Educational Personnel	30.9 (723)	+59.2	16
Teacher Training	0.6 (13)	–45.8	8
Administrators	4.1 (96)	+284.0	11
Teachers	27.0 (632)	+68.9	14
Para-Professionals	13.9 (325)	+253.2	10
Welfare Service Personnel	0.5 (12)	–36.8	4
Police or Law Enforcement	0.3 (6)	–14.2	4
Medical or Health Care	0.15 (34)	–26.1	9
Neighborhood or Community Workers	0.4 (10)	–23.1	7
Volunteers	0.15 (35)	+2.9	8

[a]Categories are not mutually exclusive.
[b]Total number of adolescence projects: $N = 2{,}343$.
Source: *Toward Interagency Coordination* (1975), p. 73.

Table 1-10
Projects Investigating New Techniques for Influencing Adolescents

Techniques[a]	Percentage of FY '75 Adolescence Projects[b] (*N*)	Percentage Change in (*N*) between FY '74 and FY '75	Number of Funding Agencies
Teaching Techniques	35.9 (842)	+42.5	20
Bilingual Education	13.2 (309)	+451.8	10
Computer Education	0.9 (22)	–50.0	7
TV Instruction	1.6 (38)	–7.3	13
Open Classroom	2.1 (50)	+22.0	6
Non-Graded Schools	0.7 (16)	+14.3	8
Team Teaching	2.0 (47)	+62.1	10
Work Experience	3.9 (91)	–1.1	13
Tutorial Instruction	5.0 (118)	–3.4	8
Individualized Curriculum	12.0 (280)	+10.2	10
Behavior Modification	2.3 (54)	+22.7	10
Physical Therapy	0.3 (8)	+166.7	5
Speech Therapy	0.5 (11)	–[c]	4
Psychotherapy	2.9 (68)	+126.7	9
Career/Employment Counseling	5.1 (119)	–[c]	13
Deinstitutionalization	0.4 (9)	–[c]	5
Youth Involvement	2.8 (65)	–56.4	13
Desegregation	0.5 (11)	–76.1	3
Mainstreaming for Special Education	2.2 (52)	–[c]	9
Parent Involvement	22.0 (516)	+72.0	15

[a]None of the categories are exclusive of any other category.
[b]Total number of adolescence research projects: $N = 2{,}343$.
Source: *Toward Interagency Coordination* (1975), p. 74.

Table 1-11
Current NIMH Research Projects Focusing on Adolescence (August 1975)

Subject Area	Number of Early Adolescent Projects[a]	Current Funding	Number of General Adolescent Projects[b]	Current Funding	Total Projects	Total Funding
Demonstrations of innovative prevention and treatment methods for delinquent behavior	4	$456,289	7	$ 763,139	11	$1,219,428
Studies of social and emotional development, including family interactions			8	522,494	8	522,494
Studies of the development of minority adolescents	2	98,414	6	510,382	8	608,796
Studies of the causes and correlates of delinquency			5	266,689	5	266,689
Demonstrations of innovative adolescent mental health services			4	395,802	4	395,802
Investigations of the etiology and prevention of mental illness	2	130,215			2	130,215
Studies of group dynamics			2	46,076	2	46,076
Study of the legal rights of adolescents			1	86,745	1	86,745
Study of impact of television on children	1	1,342			1	1,342
Totals	9	$686,260	33	$2,591,327	42	$3,277,587

[a] Ages 12-15.

[b] Ages 16-22 or unspecified.

Source: Center for Studies of Child and Family Mental Health.

Table 1-12
Number of NIMH Adolescent Research Projects by Termination Year and Subject Area

Termination Year	Delinquency Prevention and Treatment	Social and Emotional Development	Minority Development	Causes of Delinquency	Mental Health Services	Mental Illness	Group Dynamics
1975	5	5	4	2	1	0	2
1974	3	5	0	2	3	0	0
1973	4	10	3	0	5	0	0
1972	2	5	3	1	5	1	0
1971	4	2	1	0	1	6	0
1970	5	8	2	4	4	1	0

Source: Center for Studies of Child and Family Mental Health.

Table 1-13
Funding for Adolescent Research Projects by Termination Year

Termination Year	Number of Projects	Funding during Last Active Year
1975	20	$1,228,135
1974	12	588,158
1973	24	867,889
1972	18	950,218
1971	14	472,850
1970	27	838,762

Source: Center for Studies of Child and Family Mental Health.

Research Recommendations

Scattered throughout these pages reviewing research on early adolescence have been specific recommendations for research. It is our purpose here to summarize these recommendations in such a way as to provide a sense of their scope.

Research is badly needed on basic issues of adolescent development in the biological, socio-emotional, and cognitive areas. Such research depends upon the elaboration (or further elaboration) of a theory or theories of adolescent development. Such theory is essential if we are to make comprehensible the phenomena of adolescence. It is also essential if we are to outline what we do not yet know. This is the major conclusion of a meeting held by the Interagency Panel with John Hill and Robert Grinder. It is representative of the views of all the researchers cited in this study.

Almost all researchers agree that we need to know more about adolescents from various socioeconomic levels and ethnic groups. At the same time, some investigators point out that all youth, not only special minority groups, must be included in our research allocations. As we have said, the "average" adolescent should not be "disadvantaged." We need especially, as Robert Grinder says, to study "the broad question of socialization for living in a culturally pluralistic society."[170]

Everyone can provide a list of areas to be researched. The recommendations made by John Hill are the most comprehensive and eclectic of any we have seen, and so we record them at length. The range and variety of research issues summarize most of what we hear investigators suggesting:

1. *Foster basic programmatic research which relates directly to the major issues in psycho-social development during adolescence.* Much of the presently available information about development during adolescence is only incidentally related to the period, focuses on males instead of females, is cross-sectional rather than longitudinal, does not take seriously the diversity of adolescent setting and experiences, and is done in discrete and unrelated "chunks" rather than programmatically . . .

2. *Foster basic and applied (demonstration, action, policy, and evaluation) research on the effects of organizations on adolescent behavior and development.* Of the three social networks within which adolescents function most of the time, most is probably known about peer groups, next most about the family, and least about larger organizations. The impacts of school, of church, of the military, of voluntary organizations and of job settings on adolescent behavior and development is minimal . . .
3. *Foster basic and applied (demonstration, action, policy, and evaluation) research on various kinds of "health" education.* [Here, Hill is taking on the research component of such programs as sex and drug education programs, but the argument applies across the board.] . . . They often are not helpful about better ways of delivering educational services because they are not designed to contrast them. They do not reveal much about what kinds of adolescents benefit from given kinds of methods because they are not consciously designed to do so. The techniques used are more the most primitive ones behavioral science has to offer rather than better-developed ones: many times ratings are used which have few practical advantages over the old-fashioned testimonial. . . .
4. *Foster research on socialization for work and family roles.* [Here, Hill is most concerned with the role of women in our society.] Particularly needed in relation to social and educational policy would be studies of occupational modeling–the effect on girls of exposure to occupational models whose characteristics represent reversals of the usual "feminine" occupational choices and stereotypes. . . . Some programs of socialization for the world of work must be coordinated with or deal with issues on socialization for family roles as well. . . .

   Similarly, the role of males in this socialization process requires elucidation. . . .
5. *Foster research on the social perception of adolescence and its determinants.* Ambivalence toward adolescents in Western society has been remarked by many students of the period and social commentators. What are the sources of adolescent-inspired fear and anxiety in parents and nonparents alike? What accounts for the perpetuation of adolescent stereotypes and the preoccupation with strategies of control in dealing with adolescents? What are the consequences for adolescent development of variations in social perceptions of them? Are there differential rates of success for programs dealing with adolescents and youth as a function of adult attitudes and stereotypes? Can changes be effected in such social perceptions . . . ?
6. *Foster the establishment of at least four university-based, regional centers of excellence in the study of adolescence* [for building visible and strong research and doctoral training efforts]. The centers and their programs should be formally associated with a strong program in developmental or social psychology or in sociology lest the present tendency to set the period apart from the remainder of the life-cycle prevail.

   The needs of the field suggest that high priority should be given to developing centers which would develop programs of: policy-related research; bio-behavioral research; and research on the impact of organizations on adolescents and adolescence. Each of the centers should have a balanced program of instruction but the research thrusts should be relatively few in number.
7. *Foster the establishment of at least one, and preferably two, major research institutions devoted to programmatic, longitudinal studies of adolescence.*

> Many of the most important problems of adolescent growth require short- and long-range longitudinal research strategies to attain solution. . . . The exigencies of the publication and tenure system and the autonomy ethic in the typical university department suggest that it is not suitable for this task. An independent research institute established expressly for the purpose would be more suitable. . . . fellowship opportunities should be arranged for senior scholars and pre- and post-doctoral research internships for junior scholars; in this way, the Institute would serve a training function as well. . . .[171]

One recommendation that Hill makes indirectly is that we must attract and train new kinds of youth workers. This is an argument that predominates the literature on teacher education, perhaps because we "prepare" so many teachers in our society. It is, however, an issue underlying every area of this report. It is our opinion that we constantly fight an obvious fact: we know that programs succeed if a charismatic and dedicated person provides leadership over a sustained period of time; we know that in all research about teacher effectiveness, it is the particular personality factors of the teacher (which elude statements of "competencies") that make the greatest differences, and not particular packages or techniques. We could extend this argument to every area. Why do we always fight this obvious resource? Instead of bemoaning our inability to become people-proof, we should be developing training programs that insist upon the personological factors first and foremost.

And such people should inform our research efforts. The perspective of such practitioners is invaluable.

The recommendations already summarized have moved from substantive issues that demand further study to several mechanisms for setting such study in motion. In this line, Konopka asks that data be gathered on youth uniformly throughout the United States and be reported periodically for each state. This recommendation underscores the frustration of every investigator who has attempted to gather what one would presume to be fundamental data on adolescents.

Konopka then recommends that such data be analyzed for implications and national trends. We see this as a necessary precursor to informed policy formulation at the national level.

Finally, Konopka goes beyond the recommendations made by Hill for establishing research mechanisms by calling for the formation of a major office in the federal government with specific reference to youth development. This office would have total responsibility for coordinating and facilitating research and experimental programs concerned with adolescents. Bureaus and agencies charged with overseeing research and programs for all youth have placed their major focus on young children. Konopka concludes that an office for youth affairs is needed in order to insure that attention be turned to research and experimental efforts concerned with adolescent development.[172] We see no movement in this direction; in fact, we see movement away from it. This recommendation demands careful consideration and review. As the Interagency Panel staff argues, long-term research is necessary in order to ascertain long-term effects of influences from the natural environment and from planned programs. Short-term funding, or the discontinuance of support of productive research, has often resulted in the loss of data, which is cost-ineffective at best. Less benefit is derived from research dollars when short-term funding is mandated inappropriately.[173]

One final doubt needs to be aired. In the section of this chapter entitled "Research on Early Adolescence" we described several recommendations which, when looked at together, emerge as a trend in our approaches to young adolescents. We refer here to adolescence-in-the-life-cycle research, to calls for interdisciplinary and ecological approaches, and for age-integration. In the sections on juvenile justice and handicapping conditions, we discuss a strong trend toward the inclusion of as many youngsters as possible into the mainstream. This "holism" has become, we think, something of a *weltanschauung* and may become a fad. Age-integration, life-span and ecological approaches, and interdisciplinary research are more than overdue reactions to the fragmented approaches we have taken in other areas of research like early childhood and later adolescence.

Our concern is that whereas, for instance, there is now a substantial body of research information and program data on early childhood ready to be integrated in a holistic approach, there is no such body of fragmented data on early adolescence. There is nothing to be reactive about. It is possible that, lagging behind as it is, early adolescence may once again be "overlooked" in these integrative approaches because so much more existing knowledge and talent will be on standby for other age groups. This age group is in danger of being, if not overpowered, then blurred over.

An Apology

This review of research on early adolescence, always spilling over into adolescence in general, has been long and tedious. We regret that, since it is a wide-open field, in some cases on the threshold of very exciting breakthroughs, in others so untouched that fine adventures await us in those undiscovered territories to the west of early childhood.

Part II:
The Young Adolescent and Social Institutions

Introduction to Part II

. . . the greatest significance of the total community. . . lies in the fact that many of the problems the child faces, and the possibilities for their solution, are rooted in the community as a whole and are therefore beyond the reach of segmental efforts at the level of the neighborhood, the school, or the home. We have in mind such problems as housing, welfare services, medical care, community recreation programs, sanitation, police services, and television programming.

Given this state of affairs, it is a sobering fact that, neither in our communities nor in the nation as a whole, is there a single agency that is charged with the responsibility of assessing and improving the situation of the child in his total environment. As it stands, the needs of children are parcelled out among a hopeless confusion of agencies with diverse objectives, conflicting jurisdictions, and imperfect channels of communication. The school, the health department, the churches, welfare services, youth organizations, the medical profession, libraries, the police, recreation programs—all of these see the children of the community at one time or another, but no one of them is concerned with the total pattern of life for children in the community: where, how, and with whom they spend their waking hours and what may be the impact of these experiences on the development of the child as an individual and as a member of society. . . .

—Urie Bronfenbrenner
Two Worlds of Childhood

Part I of this overview of research and programs for young adolescents deals with biological, socio-emotional, and cognitive research. We have noted with concern the lack of a coordinated effort in adolescence research. We have suggested that such an effort cannot be launched without a holistic view of the adolescent living through a particular period in the total life span.

In Part II we look at some of the social institutions that serve young adolescents: the school, the various service institutions for the handicapped, family, voluntary youth-serving agencies, and the juvenile justice system.

In looking at these institutions, we are seeking to find out how they cope with and serve young adolescents. Research does not tell us what the daily lives of young adolescents are like. It does not touch them directly. Social institutions do. Most adolescents are deeply involved in at least two, the family and the school. Some are served by additional, positive social structures like youth organizations and health-serving institutions, some by negative social structures like correctional institutions.

Every adolescent deals simultaneously with at least two or three layers of socially structured institutions; and yet, because of the ways in which society sets up its service boundaries, each institution usually copes in a vacuum with these adolescents.

Thus, whatever coherence has been achieved in Part II of this report is editorial in nature, having been imposed on the "hopeless confusion" that Bronfenbrenner derides.

The coherence is editorial because of another, more intractable problem, which underlies the often conflictual, competing, or inadequate service boundaries. Social institutions that serve young adolescents can be no more coherent than the purposes that undergird them. Unsure of who these young adolescents are, unsure of ways in which other domains affect their lives, unsure of who we want these young people to be, we lack as a society the integrative purposefulness needed to provide for them coherently.

2 Schools and the Young Adolescent

Introduction

Many schools are dreary, unimaginative, and routinized places; schools for young adolescents are particularly so. The lack of talent of school personnel for this age group has not been exaggerated by critics; the lack of training has been underestimated.

The least fortunate students are those who have been segregated by age in those junior high schools which are exactly what their name denotes–smaller or younger or less developed versions of senior high schools. Next are those who are considered "elementary" students beyond their years or "secondary" students prematurely; they at least partake of the comparative largesse of talent, training, and good will found in some elementary and senior high schools. Most fortunate are those young adolescents who are placed first in middle schools and then in senior high schools as a result of local concern for the many meanings of adolescence.

There is considerable lack of fit between what we know about young adolescents and what we do to them five days a week in schools. According to Don Wells, Headmaster of the Carolina Friends School and member of the Task Force on Middle Schools (National Association of Independent Schools):

> When attempting to construct a program for the early adolescent, one is immediately struck by the wide disparity between the data we have on the early adolescent and the programmatic response we devise. . . . 1) FACT: Early adolescents need to try on a wide variety of roles. RESPONSE: We class them in . . . few roles to make them a manageable lot. 2) FACT: Early adolescents vary enormously . . . in physical, mental and emotional maturity and capability. RESPONSE: In schools chronologic age is still the overwhelming factor used in grouping students. 3) FACT: During early adolescence the development of control over one's own life through conscious decision making is crucial. RESPONSE: Adults make all meaningful decisions for almost all early adolescents almost all the time, but do give the early adolescent the "freedom" to make the "safe" . . . decisions. 4) FACT: Early adolescence is an age where all natural forces (muscular, intellectual, glandular, emotional, etc.) are causing precipitous peaks and troughs in their entire being. RESPONSE: We demand internal consistency of the early adolescent, and in schools even punish some for not achieving this consistent state despite the fact that it is totally impossible for many to achieve at this point in development. 5) FACT: Early adolescents need space and experience to "be" different persons at different times. RESPONSE: We expect them to "be" what they said they were last week because otherwise we cannot do *to* them with forethought. 6) FACT: Early adolescents are

preoccupied by physical and sexual concerns, frightened by their perceived inadequacy. RESPONSE: We operate with them each day *not* as though this were a minor matter in their lives, but as though such concerns did not exist at all. 7) FACT: Early adolescents need a distinct feeling of present importance, a present relevancy of their own lives now. RESPONSE: We place them in institutions called "junior high schools" which out-of-hand stress their subordinate status to their next maturational stage, and then feed them a diet of watered down "real stuff". . . .[1]

This review seeks to find out who is doing what, where, for young adolescents. In the context of schooling, we are concerned with who is struggling creatively with adolescent development–with changing bodies, emotions, intellect, social relations with peers and adults, family interactions, values. This does not mean that schools are *responsible for* all these aspects of development, but that they must be *responsive to* the individuals experiencing this time in their lives.

We have found very little. We do not intend to document one school here or one research report there which appears promising. Rather, we will attempt to provide an overview of the issues troubling people who are responsive to young adolescents in schools. The state of schooling for this age is so messy because so few people are concerned with the issues raised in earlier sections of this report. We have asked what it means to become an adolescent. Were school people to become engaged in this question, the implications for schooling would be radical.

What do people talk about when they talk about schools? Buildings, budgets, busses (the three "b's" principals worry about), course requirements and electives, scheduling, counseling, administration, sometimes teachers, parents, students–bricks, bodies, books. We have found the following: very few talented people talk about any of these in reference to young adolescents; there is more talk about buildings and books than about students; there is little talk about learning; the research that could be called "research on schools" usually lacks the sophistication of the biological, cognitive and socio-emotional research we have reviewed; practitioners read almost none of the research, anyway; a good teacher or principal knows in his innards from daily sensitivities what researchers are verifying piecemeal; there are excruciatingly few good teachers and principals for young adolescents.

This chapter on schools is a great disappointment to us. The moment one begins to review research on programs in schools, one is in the realm of bombast, ideology, defensiveness, ignorance, emotionalism. Our recommendation to the reader is to read the previous chapter on research and to draw implications from it for schooling young adolescents. There is nothing here than can equal the overwhelming, quiet evidence in that chapter of our failure to start with people instead of with buildings and books.

It is not our purpose to write a position paper on schooling, but rather to report on the informed positions others are taking. This section is disappointing to us because we learned so little. It is spotty because we refuse to give it a false coherence. It is a failure, because we are left with our rhetoric and little more.

The Purpose of Schooling

If civilization is to be coherent and confident it must be *known* in that civilization what its ideals are. There must exist in the form of clearly available ideas an understanding of what the fulfillment of the promise of that civilization might mean, an imaginative conception of the good at which it might, and, if it is to flourish, at which it must aim.

—Walter Lippmann
A Preface to Morals

Schools are society's mechanism for socialization. At one time, they shared that function with the family and the church. Now they share it also with the media and an increasingly powerful peer society. We are told by some social observers that the school remains the one major vehicle for socialization as the influence of family and church diminish. We are told by other observers that the role of the school has diminished as the media and ethnic subcultures become more powerful.

There is a traditional tension between the Jeffersonian view and the egalitarian view of schools. In the former, schools are instruments for preserving "the heritage" by defining an aristocracy of talent for leadership. In the latter, schools are the melting pot wherein all may learn so as to partake equally of America's dreams. This tension is now history. There is a goodly amount of well-documented literature disclaiming the myth that schools were ever meant to be an equalizing social agent.[2]

It is possible that the emerging tension now is between those people who would like to return to the Jeffersonian ideal and those who want to preserve cultural differences through the schools. The egalitarian dream lies, for the moment at least, drowned by the tomes of research data overflowing with our alleged "failures" of the 1960s.

Greenbaum says, "The primary function of schooling is socialization, whether the school is viewed from the perspective of the society, the community, the parents, or the child; and the primary question underlying the present malaise in education is socialization toward what?"[3] Since we do not know what our social ideals are, we cannot, as Lippmann would hope, be either coherent or confident as a civilization, or in the institutions which promote that civilization.

What a society values determines the priorities of its allocation of resources. In times of external crisis schools function smoothly. The society has a coherent set of purposes in educating its young. So, during the Sputnik era various philosophical and theoretical approaches could coalesce into "structure of the discipline" curricula. Now, during a time of shrinking resources, it is possible that cost-effectiveness and accountability as to outcomes may take precedence over the process-oriented approaches of the past decade. We may be entering a period parallel to Henry Higgins's judgment of the French: "The French don't care what they do, actually, as long as they pronounce it properly." Those programs for which we lack measures of "pronunciation" will suffer when competing for the limited resources available against those programs that have objectives we know how to measure. Given the relatively primitive state of educational evaluation methodologies, we can expect substantial discontent a decade from now if we gear our programs to those outcomes we can measure (i.e., hold ourselves numerically accountable for). In other words, we are in a period in which we lack an underlying coherent set of purposes, no matter what the apparent surface gloss is. We will be busily pursuing objectives based on expedient goals rather than on deeply held convictions about the value of schooling.

In *Decade of Experiment: The Fund for the Advancement of Education, 1951-1961*, the following questions were posed for the 1960s:

1. Can the function of schools be clarified?
2. Can the curriculum be designed anew to reflect all we know and still have to find out about the learning process?
3. Will the teacher shortage be solved?
4. Will it be possible to develop schools that challenge and capture the interests of youth in the depressed neighborhoods of large cities?
5. Can we work out a better basis of financial support for our schools (to equalize educational opportunities)?
6. Building on the experience of the fifties, will we find ways to bring all sound new ideas and techniques together to achieve not just a patchwork of improvement but a coherent design of advancement?
7. Can we improve our educational programs to make the most of human talent?[4]

We have the answer to question number three, and only a partial answer at that, since we have solved the quantitative shortage only. We might want to rephrase some of the other questions, or add and delete some. The first question remains the unsolved and central dilemma of schooling in America. We have not clarified the function of schools.

We have especially not clarified the function of schools for young adolescents. The articles that have hit the mass media about the growing dismay over "liberalized education" are noteworthy for what is missing: any indication that change took place in junior high schools in the 1960s that might trigger a backlash in the 1970s. We emphasize time and again the acquisition of basic skills in the primary grades and then the status of high school juniors and seniors (our "products") as they prepare to enter the job market or higher education. We have no societal sensitivity to the developmental importance of early adolescence. We lack even the pragmatic, if less sensitive, vision to see this age group as at least pivotal in the schooling process. It is our "missing link."

We see two themes emerging from the morass of rhetoric about schools. One is that we must severely limit the goals of schooling to what schools can deliver: training in the "essentials" or "basics" like reading, writing, arithmetic, and communications. The other is that we must revive in schools their original purpose of educating, and education is a moral endeavor. The proponents of these approaches to schooling often appear to be at diametrically opposing ends of a continuum, but schools are attempting to incorporate the entire continuum from training to education into their statements of purpose.

The recent work of Carl Bereiter exemplifies the schools-as-training-sites position. In *Must We Educate?* (the answer is an emphatic NO) he argues that the "three R's" can be taught by a well-organized program that leaves "as little as possible to the cleverness and determination of the child," implemented by teachers who "concentrate on mastery rather than providing experiences or stimulating personal growth."[5]

Bereiter argues that schools are attempting both training and child care functions, but that good training and good child care have almost nothing in common. Training is authoritarian, judgmental, and highly focused, whereas child care allows maximum reasonable freedom, is not judgmental, and is indefinitely broad in scope. "With such differences it stands to reason that training and child care should be separated; different kinds of people should provide them, under different circumstances. The child should know when he is in one and when he is in the other."[6]

Schools, according to Bereiter, should get out of the business of child care and get into the business of training, so as to free children (an interesting critique of the "free school" concept).

> . . . one thing does seem clear and reasonable: teaching people skills renders them potentially more powerful, and wider distribution of personal power is bound in the long run to work in the interests of freedom. What is more questionable is the effect of education beyond skill training, for when it comes to the development of personality and values it would seem that education can work as easily against as in favor of freedom.[7]

Thus, Bereiter disagrees with the Supreme Court that "no one can question the State's duty to protect children from ignorance." Such a duty, and thereby a right, is highly questionable since it infringes upon the individual's liberty in the personal areas of value formation and personality development.

The view of schooling as a moral process is exemplified by Charity James in her work with schools and in such books as *Young Lives at Stake* and *Beyond Customs*. Silberman, in his introduction to *Young Lives at Stake*, says of Charity James that "she recognizes, with Dewey, that education is inescapably a moral enterprise," and "with Socrates, that education 'is not about something casual, but about the proper way to live.' "[8]

Can the function of the schools be clarified? Probably the closest we come to a comprehensive societal view of schooling is in Bronfenbrenner's *Two Worlds of Childhood*, a book with which James would be more comfortable than would Bereiter. Bronfenbrenner warns that during the past decade schools have become breeding grounds of alienation because of their segregation from the rest of society. Education in America "emphasizes subject matter to the exclusion of another moral aspect of the child's development–what the Russians call *vospitanie*–the development of the child's qualities as a person–his values, motives, and patterns of social response. . . ."[9] It is of crucial importance that American schools be reintegrated into the life of the community. If radical changes are not introduced so that the young are exposed to modes of behavior for living in a cooperative society, it will not be primarily the needs of the disadvantaged or the "problem children" that will be unmet; ". . . it will be all children who will be culturally deprived–not of cognitive stimulation, but of their humanity."[10]

Implementing programs oriented toward the so-called basic skills is a relatively easy enterprise. It is easier to lower than to raise our sights. As a matter of fact, we are masterful at lowering our objectives while heightening our rhetoric. The debilitating sense of failure from the 1960s is merging with a narrow management-by-objectives accountability mentality, motivated by limited evaluation techniques. This merger may determine a mindset in education that will bypass confronting the central issue without which we cannot know what schools are for: "If civilization is to be coherent and confident it must be *known* in that civilization what the ideals are."

Historical Development of the Junior High School

The junior high school movement began in a laboratory school in Berkeley in 1909, quickly followed in 1910 by a similar school in Los Angeles. By the end of the second decade of the twentieth century, what now appear to be quaint period pieces were being written about the junior high experiment.

For instance, G. Vernon Bennett, the City Superintendent of Schools of Pomona, California, also a lecturer in education at the University of Southern California, wrote *The Junior High School* (1919) as a guide for the study of the "movement."

Demands were made by society upon schools to solve problems which, according to Bennett, were impossible to cope with under an 8-4 organization, thereby leading to the junior high movement:

(1) That the enormous leakage from school in the seventh, eighth, ninth and tenth grades cease;
(2) That an effort be made to destroy the influences of schools which tend to send young men and women into unsuitable and worthless vocations and

that a positive effort be made to guide them into suitable and worthy occupations;
(3) That the modern tendency to lengthen the period of preparation for skilled vocations be checked and some method be found for shortening the period so that men may become self-supporting and society-supporting at an earlier age; and, finally
(4) That the school system check the physical, mental and moral evils that accompany and grow out of adolescence.[11]

The "leakage" was a serious problem. According to Bennett, statistics from Los Angeles between 1896 and 1911 indicated a dropout rate before the end of the first year of high school (ninth grade) of 54 percent; before the end of tenth grade, 45 percent of those remaining dropped out. Minneapolis reported similar figures. Taking various accounts as a whole, it was assumed that 60 percent of elementary school graduates failed to reach the third year of high school.[12]

We can see emerging from the early literature on the junior high school a concern that as more students were included in the public educational processes, schools were failing to meet varying needs. Special emphasis, from the start, was therefore placed on the vocationally oriented, nonacademic student. By beginning secondary education earlier, in a watered-down version ("the senior high school student does as much in one fourth a year as a junior high school pupil does in one third of a year"),[13] students could find and be prepared for that vocation for which they were best adapted, at an earlier age and without school failure.

The vocational and social class emphases were openly expressed in rhetoric different only in vocabulary from present rhetoric about school dropouts and welfare rolls.[14]

As for the fourth cause cited by Bennett for the change to a 6-3-3 organization, the need for the school system to check the evils of adolescence, Bennett warns us about arrested development caused by overstudy, fright, "perverted sex habits as self-abuse," and others ranging from "looseness" to "shamelessness," improper actions by girls "at delicate bodily periods," exercising adult desires, lying, disobedience to parents, reading "trashy" novels, and "frequenting moving picture houses."[15] The vocabulary is different from ours today, as are some of the concerns. What is familiar is the idea that the schools, indeed school organization *per se*, are called upon to be the cure-all for changing social mores among the young.

By 1920, when Thomas Briggs wrote yet another book entitled *The Junior High School*, hundreds of junior highs were being established, often without real reorganization or an underlying rationale. Briggs verbalizes concerns similar to Bennett's, although now with slightly more hindsight and sophistication.

At the end of the period of elementary compulsory education, he reports, there are three distinct groups of students for whom schools must provide: those who can and will persist at least through secondary education, those who intend to leave school for work as soon as the law allows them to, and those whose length of stay in school is highly uncertain.[16] The American ambition "to secure for the next generation a better lot than that of their parents" makes this both a land of opportunity and a land with schools that are institutions of "amazing waste." All three categories of students are placed in college preparatory curricula, given the usual school offerings. The alternatives are to restrict academic preparatory courses to students with good grades and mental ability (a restriction that would be "inaccurate") or to leave it, "as at present," up to the individual and the parents. This latter option leads to large losses in finances to the community, in spirit and self-confidence among students who fail, in progress to those who do have the ability to succeed, "and in faith in the schools to parents and other taxpayers."[17] (Once again, we can hear the past ringing through to the present.)

The solution to the dilemma is the junior high concept, an intermediate institution in which schools can "explore by means of material in itself worthwhile the interests, aptitudes, and capacities of pupils," reveal to students the major fields of learning and careers, and "start each pupil in the career which, as a result of the exploratory courses, he, his parents, and the school are convinced is most likely to be of profit to him and to the State."[18] After this, the student is to be released from compulsory school attendance.

Briggs is not unmindful of what Bennett called "the evils of adolescence." A further argument set forward by advocates of separately organized junior high schools, he reports, is that this more homogeneous grouping of pupils "in age, interests, and social maturity" makes teaching better and discipline easier. Advocates feel, he says, "that it is especially desirable that early adolescents, who are neither children nor youth, should be segregated in order that adequate provision may be made for their peculiarities of disposition." Further, he adds, it is argued "that the influence of early adolescents on small children is frequently bad, and that if kept by themselves during the transition to youth they will be less influenced to imitate the undesirable traits of older pupils."[19]

Arguments were also made on the basis of what would now be called "cost effectiveness"–the more economical utilization of plants and special teachers, the use of outgrown high school buildings too good to destroy but unsuited for elementary programs, the growth of population in sections of cities remote from existing schools, and so forth. Chief reasons given by administrators for establishing junior highs included the by now familiar assortment: to provide educational opportunity, to relieve congestion, to utilize an old high school building, to provide better education for grades seven through nine, to increase retention, to bridge the gap between elementary and high schools, to provide earlier differentiation, to introduce prevocational work earlier.[20]

In the main, however, the arguments highlight the fact that junior highs served to segregate young adolescents from younger children and older adolescents while they passed through their "peculiarities," and while there was time for the sorting-out process to beat out the end of compulsory attendance. (The 8-4 organization, it was also argued, caused unjustifiable leakage, causing a break exactly at the time when the law released pupils from attendance.) These arguments–segregation, sorting-out, and eliminating leakage–emerge strongly in the rhetoric of the period.

By 1937, Ralph W. Pringle's book, *The Junior High School*, has a subtitle: *A Psychological Approach*. Pringle looks at the sociological demands made upon the schools at the start of the "movement." From a purely practical standpoint, he says the "most potent" factor in the growth of the junior high school movement was "the unprecedented increase in the number of young people from twelve to eighteen years of age who were seeking an education; provision had to be made for them and without delay."[21] Also, our "theory of secondary education," unlike the Europeans', demanded that pupils must not fail, rather than that only the brightest shall pass. "The American junior high school thus became the foremost institutional expression of the theory of secondary education for all the people, as opposed to the older European doctrine of secondary education for the selection of an intellectual elite."[22]

The junior high school thereby becomes the instrument of the democratic belief in equal opportunity, at the same time that it is acknowledged by Pringle as placing its strongest emphasis on "vocational guidance."

Pringle emphasizes what he sees as the greatest weakness of the 8-4 organization: it does not meet the needs of preadolescents and early adolescents, who present schools with more heterogeneous and rapidly changing behavior than do any other combinations of pupils. This fundamental weakness, he insists, was never discussed by critics of the 8-4 system. It is the thesis of his book that the junior high school is a unique unit whose functions will be realized by constant adaptation of methods and materials to the changing nature of pupils as they pass from prepubescence through pubescence to postpubescence.

How much has the junior high school developed since these early works? The "leakage" problem is not so severe as it was in 1911, but it has certainly never been claimed that the junior high school was the instrument of change that lowered the dropout rate. The career education movement of the past few years highlights the failure of the schools to provide the prevocational and preprofessional preparation that was central to what was new in the curricula of the junior highs. Complaints about the lack of coordination between elementary and secondary schooling still abound. Students are now seen as having to make two adjustments rather than one. No one will come out as openly as did the early observers to applaud the separation of young adolescents, their "peculiarities" and "evils," from elementary students; we can still find observers who appreciate the protection of young adolescents from the influences of older students in senior highs. It would be difficult to find anyone who would applaud the junior high as a sorting-out agency.

These observations present us with some of the ironies inherent in schooling for young adolescents today. What was once concern over "leakage" is now a debate over lowering the compulsory attendance age back to where it was in the early part of the century, when its timing was seen as being so unfortunate for youth and for society. The "new" career education is defined as being "exploratory" in the junior high school, exactly the definition that Briggs, in 1920, saw as the only viable one for junior highs. The hitch now is that, unlike earlier in the century, child labor laws prevent this "exploration" from leading to the meaningful activity which, as Bennett said in 1919, is so strong a desire "in the breast of the adolescent." The separation of young adolescents from the influences of older students continues despite all the data that tell us that it is the younger adolescent, if any, who is "rebellious," that it is in the junior high years that drug abuse and illegitimate pregnancy rates peak, and most important, that these years do not present us with a homogeneous group. Rarely met are the hopes of people like Pringle that the heterogeneity of the students in grades seven through nine would be well served by this instructional unit through diverse and changing materials and methods.

Finally, the one "merit" of the junior high unit cited in early works that has lasted through the years is a bitter heritage for this institution: secondary education is begun earlier, in a watered-down version. The junior high is a *junior* high school. That is its one pervasive and lasting characteristic.

One of the concepts propelling the "junior high movement," starting secondary education earlier, should have meshed exactly with the demands made upon schooling by the earlier maturation of adolescents. It is the unkindest cut of all, the greatest irony of current schooling for young adolescents, that the junior high school has not developed a separate definition, the trained administrators and staff, the organizational patterns, the curricula, or even the sophisticated awareness of who its students are, to allow for this meshing to take place. The lack of fit between institution and client is more painfully obvious at this level than at any other in our public education system.

Junior High Schools Today—The Reformers

In 1920 when Briggs wrote, there were hundreds of junior high schools being established. For the most part, however, young adolescents were still attending elementary schools and then either going on to high school or entering the labor force. Where are they today?

People wake up every day and pursue their daily course. A myriad of statistical compilations tell us what they do and where. There are over sixteen million people in the United States between the ages of twelve and fifteen. Between 98 and 99 percent receive some kind of schooling. Approximately 16,000 ten- to fourteen-year-olds are in training schools, and 4,000 ten- to fourteen-year-olds are in detention homes (figures are for 1970). Where are the rest?

We cannot say. From data available in 1976 we can say that in school year 1973-74, there were 2,629 middle schools, 58,755 "other elementary schools," 7,462 junior high schools, 4,445 junior-senior high schools, 2,321 combined elementary-secondary schools, 11,205 senior high schools, and 1,365 one-teacher schools. In 1972-73, of the twenty-eight states reporting a division of seventh and eighth grades into elementary and secondary enrollment, 35.3 percent of the seventh graders were in elementary schools, and 64.7 percent in secondary schools. For eighth graders, the percentages were 32.2 and 67.8, respectively. We have no idea what the figures are for the ninth graders, our lost tribe, statistically speaking. We cannot say what the ratio of the young adolescent students in junior highs is to those in "other elementary schools," since no one knows exactly what this category means.

At this point, it is impossible to say where young adolescents are. For instance, researchers for the Federal Reserve Bank study of Philadelphia schools say, "We looked at 627 students in 103 elementary schools between the end of the third and the sixth grades, 553 students in 42 schools between the end of the sixth and the eighth grades, and 716 students in five senior high schools between the ninth and twelfth grades." In a note accompanying this statement, they add, "The 42 schools included elementary, junior high and middle schools. All of these schools in the sample have seventh and eighth grades."[23]

If it is impossible to say where young adolescents are, there is also no consensus about where they should be. They are, for the most part, where it is practical to house them, and it is practical to house them in the junior high buildings already standing.

Because of our failure to research adequately the various and interrelated changes that occur during early adolescence, and because we have failed to conceptualize adequately this time in the life span, we have been hampered in designing effective educational programs for young adolescents. Our absence of knowledge and our failure to utilize the knowledge we have acquired have had a profound impact on our educational system.

Various efforts at reform have been attempted, or at least called for. The most widespread has to do with school organization as to grade level: the middle school movement.

The Middle School Movement

. . . following a steady, if erratic, pattern of development, (the) new junior high program was so influential that by 1960 76 percent of all the junior and senior high schools in the country were in systems whose organizational pattern was something other than the 8-4 plan (6-3-3, 6-2-4, 6-6). These "reorganized schools" enrolled 82 percent of the students in grades seven through twelve. And then came the Middle School!

—Maurice McGlasson
The Middle School: Whence? What? Whither?

The exclamation mark at the end of McGlasson's statement connotes dynamic change in the organization pattern of schools for young adolescents. Nevertheless, there are far too few people concerned with grades seven through nine and yet it is our greatest problem area. The tacit assumption seems to be that problems emanate from elementary schools and will clear up miraculously in senior high.

There are few proponents of junior high schools these days. They are seen for what they usually are: ill-conceived, watered-down high schools plagued by a lack of fit between the schools' organization and their students.

On the other hand, considerable excitement has been generated among educators by the so-called "middle school movement." The Midwest Middle School Association became a nation-wide organization in 1973—the National Association of Middle Schools—and publishes its own journal, the *Middle School Journal*. Entire issues of such journals as *Educational Leadership, National Elementary Principal* and the *NASSP Bulletin* have been devoted to middle schools. Surveys of research and programs concerned with middle schools have been and are being conducted.[24]

Whether one sees middle schools as having grown geometrically in the past few years or as having been a movement that never quite got going depends upon one's definition of "middle school." A grade definition (middle school equals seventh, eighth, and at least one grade below) leads to conclusions of tremendous growth. A qualitative definition in terms of curriculum and school organization leads to conclusions that not much has changed.

According to McGlasson, we are concerned here with more than 8,000 schools, about three-fourths of which are known as "junior high schools" (considered to include grades seven to nine) and one-fourth as "middle schools" (including grades six, or five, to eight). There are many variations in organizational pattern among these schools, resulting from "influences other than the educational program, usually building facilities and enrollments."[25] And court orders.

Nevertheless, some observers are willing to generalize about trends in middle schools which differentiate them from junior highs. Thomas Gatewood of Central Michigan University, editor of *Middle School Journal*, feels that middle schools are beginning to move now at the grass roots level toward new instructional philosophies and school organization (away from departmental structures, and toward interdisciplinary instruction).[26] McGlasson writes that middle school administration seems to differ, being somewhat more flexible with respect to use of time and personnel, with greater emphasis on methods and media and somewhat less on content.[27]

John Henry Martin, in his introduction to the *Report of the National Panel on High Schools and Adolescent Education*, says, "Surprisingly, we found no research with significant findings to substantiate one organizational pattern over another. Four year high schools versus three year schools, junior high schools, middle schools, six year schools or three-three schools, all lack a validating research base."[28] Lloyd Trump reported the same lack of conclusive evidence about the superiority of any particular type of grade distribution among schools, probably since the differences in programs within the junior high, middle, and intermediate schools are greater than the differences among the three types of schools.

McGlasson says that research studies have indicated "that in most cases the listing of offerings in a Middle School is essentially the same as the junior high school which preceded it, with the possible exception of introducing home-making and technical arts earlier."[29] At the same time, he also says that the middle school, "perhaps" more than the junior high, "has tended to feature mini-courses, learning packets, so-called independent or directed study, team teaching, continuous progress, individualized instruction, and variations on the humanities theme and organization."[30]

Trump summarized it all by saying that no one has analyzed the problem since the 1920s—at which time Leonard V. Koos found that provisions for youth (ages 12-14) were actually better in six-year schools. "One might argue very well that the criteria he used were wrong, but the burden of proof then lies upon the persons who would develop better criterion-referenced instruments."[31]

There is a growing consensus about one thing: school size. "Think small." Many middle school people have been saying this for several years. John Henry Martin reinforces the consensus: "Operating plants that house upward of a thousand students are not in our judgment an optimal setting for improving intergroup and interpersonal relations. . . . The institutional imperatives of orderly movement and peaceful custody that result from sheer mass of numbers make efforts toward humane considerations of individuals difficult."[32] Institutional rigidity is inherent in bigness. "We have lived for a generation with the paradox that increasing size was a necessary precondition to economically justify a diversity of school offerings, while size itself became a strong limitation of the flexibility needed to establish variable learning modes."[33]

No matter what the size or school grade organization, if the principals cannot be the "instructional leaders" they are supposed to be, we will be wasting our time over the great middle school controversy and in many others as well. A study of elementary principals subtitled "Beacons of Brilliance and Potholes of Pestilence" found that "most of the elementary principals interviewed said they felt inadequate to improve the education in their schools." Some cited lack of qualifications to judge innovations.[34] Given the lack of teacher preparation programs for the middle grades and this lack of administrative skill, the outcomes of our decisions about configuration of grades will be severely limited.

Does it matter what school organization as to grade level is selected? The obvious answer is that it does not. Rather, what seems crucial are the rationales for and process of selection. Those middle schools that are generated because educators are concerned about making the system fit "transescent" young people are going to be better places for learning. Sal DiFranco, principal of MacDonald Middle School in East Lansing, Michigan, says that the two basic assumptions of the middle school movement are that young people learn at different rates, in different ways. Designing programs based on these assumptions leads to the creation of options within schools.[35] We would suggest that it matters less that the grades are six through eight at the MacDonald Middle School in East Lansing, Michigan, or five through eight at the Carolina Friends School in Durham, North Carolina, or seven through eight in Quincy, Illinois, than that the decisions are made for educational reasons based on what practitioners and researchers know about pre- and young adolescents.

There are, however, less than obvious answers about whether all this matters or not. Based on the earlier physiological maturation of young adolescents, there are people who argue strongly against the junior high school. Middle schools allow younger students to enter a more mature environment and ninth-graders to reclaim their places in high schools. Rose Frisch of Harvard University's Center for Population Studies argues that educators and policy makers for education have not yet caught on to the accelerated pubescent growth changes.[36] This issue is confused by the rationale for junior high schools based precisely on the effort to introduce a more "mature" curriculum into the so-called "junior" years. There seems, however, to be nothing in the structure of the junior high organization that takes into account the earlier and extreme variability of growth.

There may be arguments based on social and emotional needs in favor of one or another school organization. According to Roberta G. Simmons, sociologist at the University of Minnesota, the move from grades six to seven is a difficult one, especially for white girls. An article by Simmons, Rosenberg, and Rosenberg, "Disturbance in the Self-Image at Adolescence," reports the findings of a cross-sectional study of self-image development in urban school children in grades three through twelve. "A definite disturbance of the self-image has been shown to occur in adolescence, particularly early adolescence. . . . In many areas, a particular rise in disturbance appears to occur when the child is twelve, that is, between the twelfth and thirteenth birthdays. . . . It seems to increase, if at all, after age thirteen or fourteen."[37] The researchers found that twelve-year-olds who had entered junior high school had lower self-esteem, higher self-consciousness, and greater instability of self-image than twelve-year-olds in elementary school. "The transition into junior high school seems to represent a significant stress along several dimensions of the child's self-image, while aging from eleven to twelve and twelve to thirteen does not in itself appear stressful. Within the same school class, age makes little difference; but within the same age group, school class makes a great difference."[38] The transition from junior to senior high school does not show a parallel effect on self-image.

And so, we must argue, against anticipated data to the contrary, that school organization as to grade level does matter. The data probably will not support this argument partly because the measures in many studies will be inadequate, partly because content is more important than form, given the diversity of the students, and mostly because many of the schools will be the same crushingly boring and utterly mediocre environments for young adolescents, whatever the age organization. Given a school environment that matches young adolescents in their vitality, creativity, and sensitivity to change (and not in their egocentrism and defensiveness), any organization will look beautiful. But given two schools equally open to the variability and energies of this age group, school organization based on differing choices about age-integration and the implications of adolescent development should produce some differing outcomes. We don't know what these will be.

In any event, those people who appear to be most responsive to the issues of adolescent development are found mostly in the "middle school movement."

Were all students in middle schools during grades six or seven through eight, that would still leave out around 50 percent of the young adolescents with whom we are concerned. As Hickson says, too few people care.

Alternative Schools

Increasing expenditures on traditional educational practices is not likely to improve educational outcomes substantially.

—Harvey Averch *et al.*
Rand Corporation,
How Effective is Schooling?

Considerable activity in school reform has been and is being devoted to alternative schooling, or the creation of public options for students and parents. Fantini summarizes eight types of "typical" optional schools in *Public Schools of Choice*: traditional or standard; nontraditional, nongraded; special talent development; technique oriented; total community school; Montessori environment; multicultural; and subcontracted.[39] These options are rarely discussed and even more rarely provided for young adolescents.

We have seen research studies investigating what happens to students from "open" elementary schools when they get to "closed" junior high schools. We have seen studies investigating student adjustment and gains in alternative high schools after completing "traditional" junior high schools. Where are the options in the middle? What is happening in junior high, rather than before and after? We have found one study that is researching these questions on a broad scale. Researchers at the Johns Hopkins Center for Social Organization of Schools are involved in a study of the effect of school organization on 7,000 students in grades four, five, six, eight, and eleven in thirty-four schools. The study investigates the effects of open environment schools on such variables as student reactions to school, self-reliance, decision making, and academic achievement on standard tests. (Five components are used to define "open environment": variety of activities permitted, individualization of tasks, sharing of responsibility for selecting assignments, sharing of responsibility for supervising progress, and sharing of responsibility for setting goals.)

The researchers' analysis for grade eight is particularly provocative, since the findings do not necessarily hold for grade six, yet many more "open" programs are devised for grade six than for grade eight. These findings were that (1) there is a significant positive overall effect of open schools on students, (2) the overall effects are generally strengthened by duration, and (3) students from open families gain more from attending open schools, although all students react positively.[40] The strongest effects of open school attendance on student self-reliance, however, are for those who have *not* had similar experiences at home.

As McPartland and Epstein point out, research in schools has been limited by the remarkable similarity of tasks, rewards, and authority systems from school to school. Useful research has been hampered by the lack of contrasts in school organization. As Vito Perrone, Dean of The Center for Teaching and Learning at the University of North Dakota says, "There's clearly not enough."

Perrone feels that many attempts like Metro and Parkway would be useful for young adolescents. They would be given more fundamental learning experiences utilizing their enormously high energy levels. High school students can sit down again; many junior high-aged students need to be up and out of school. But things are "awfully quiet."[41]

As recently as 1970, we were reading Carl Rogers, Abraham Maslow, and others, who were telling us, as Weinstein and Fantini did, "Significant contact with pupils is most effectively established and maintained when the content and method of instruction have an affective basis."[42] We don't hear much of this now, especially not at the junior high level.

We do see a base of talent and experience built during the 1960s and early 1970s from the support given to alternatives and options. This pool of talent and experience is not being drawn upon for young adolescents. There are those, like Vito Perrone, who feel that now is the time for massive support of alternative programs, including "open education," for this age group. Vernon Smith of the National Consortium for Options in Public Education (NCOPE) estimates that there are between two and three thousand alternative schools. Most are high schools, next numerous are elementary schools. Very few are middle or junior high schools. This group is least being served at the present time by alternative schools. We cannot see what the source will be for stimulating dialogue about viable options or strategies for developing them. As Tom Wilson of the Center for New Schools says, "I have a basic problem about whether schools for kids this age make sense. It's such a crazy age. Who is thinking about what makes sense? The talent in this country is not involved with this age group."[43]

One person who is involved is Pauline M. Leet, Director of the Bureau of

Curriculum Services in Pennsylvania's Department of Education. In a paper entitled, "Socialization and the 'Middle' Child: A Twentieth Century Model for a Seventeenth Century Process," Leet suggests an alternative to the "zoo keeper" model of junior high instruction in which "control is the magic word," control more rigid than any in prior schooling, enforced during a physically vigorous time of life.[44] Leet's suggestion is to offer an option for junior high students. She proposes to abolish the standard junior high school for some students and establish three years of real work experiences. Work does not become a substitute for schooling, but an integral part of education. Seventh graders would be divided into work teams of no more than six people, working under the direction of a team leader or mentor. There would be four nine-week terms, each containing six weeks of work and three of intellectual, aesthetic, and physical education. Work experiences would include community projects and work with the very young and the very old. Problems perceived as a result of the work experience would provide the basic content for the home-base three weeks. In eighth grade, business, industry, and public agencies would be optional work sites. In the ninth grade, students would work alone in a work experience of their choosing.

This is not "career education," in the sense that there is no career choice emphasis. Work would be engaged in and studied for the data it provides about oneself, one's family, and one's society.

If young adolescents can contribute something of value to their community, perhaps it can change their perceptions of themselves and communitys' perceptions of youth. The program acknowledges that we can choose not to be a part of a school structure in which teacher morale is extremely low, students are restless and anxious, and "the concepts, the strategies, the complexly beautiful balances of science or of language, all the elements that might have made a person love a field enough to want to teach it, are wrung of significance by the indifference of this crude, clamoring, free and unfree, uncertain and defenseless aggregate.[45]

The emphases on meaningful work, the arts, basic skills, peer cooperation, and age-integration are all *au courant*. What is novel in this proposal is seeing them included in one viable program that abolishes the junior high school.

Another person deeply concerned with education for eleven- to sixteen-year-olds is Charity James. James identifies the educational needs of young adolescents, as against their psychosocial needs, in order to help schools articulate new programs. For instance, schools may not be able to do much about a student's need for a "good self-concept," but they can do something about adolescents' "need to be needed."

In *Beyond Customs* James identifies several such needs: the needs for myth and legend and fact; the needs for physical activity and stillness; the need to explore and affect one's outer environment; the need to match inner and outer realities (the "conscious search for consciousness" which begins earlier than schools recognize), the needs for intensity and routine; the need to need, and the need to be needed. The fourfold curriculum she proposes in *Young Lives at Stake* evolves from a recognition of these needs and consists of interdisciplinary studies, autonomous studies (intradisciplinary), remedial education (related to special needs, for everyone), and special interest or "orbital" studies. The emphases are strongly on the arts, personal exploration, group activity, and meaningful work.

We have selected Leet and James as examples of two different approaches to alternatives (1) because they are representative of two thrusts, towards work experiences and towards the arts, which we see usually at the senior high level, and (2) because they are articulate but infrequently cited critics of schooling for young adolescents. Other people might just as well have been chosen.

The call for alternative schooling for adolescents continues from responsible sources, whatever the faddism in certain regions of the country. The National Panel on High Schools and Adolescent Education recommends the establishment of alternative schools with racial, ethnic, bilingual or multicultural emphases. In "Requirements for Healthy Development of Adolescent Youth," Gisela Konopka recommends the creation of options and alternatives within and outside of existing school systems. "The deliberate promotion of pluralistic learning environments staffed by adults from a variety of backgrounds would provide far greater learning experiences and participation by a larger segment of teen-agers."[46] "Coleman II," *Youth: Transition to Adulthood*, suggests increased specialization among the nation's high schools.

The first annual report of the Interagency Panel for Research and Development on Adolescence states that educational innovations received 14 percent of the federal education budget, including individualized instruction, television instruction, and cross-age tutoring, with over 50 percent of the total accounted for by television instruction. "Except insofar as television instruction provided for education outside the school system, little research was reported on educational alternatives to the present school system."[47] Comparable data are not available in the second and third annual Panel reports, but there appears to be a shift towards a higher percentage of federal funding of open classrooms and nongraded schools, and a shift away from funding work experiences and youth involvement projects. The first annual report states, "If additional research continues to verify the findings of the Youth in Transition study (and the earlier Coleman study) that school programs have little differential effect on the achievement of students, then research on alternatives and complements to the traditional school experience must be conducted and their effect on individual students assessed.[48]

The recommendations of major reports are for senior high schools. No one is calling for options for young adolescents. They are as overlooked in this area as in all others.

Reform through Compensatory Education

Our present strategy, if it can be called such, has failed to make major inroads on the educational problems of disadvantaged adolescents, and a new plan is urgently required.

—Larson and Dittmann

Compensatory education as a concept of social intervention is controversial. The programs guided by the concept are often equally controversial. The results are ambiguous. Given the amount of energy spent nationally on compensatory schooling, a review of programs for young adolescents is in order.

The Educational Policy Research Center (EPRC) of the Stanford Research Institute has been the major source of evaluation of ESEA Title I programs for adolescents. *Adolescence: Alternative Strategies for Compensatory Education*, by Meredith A. Larson and Freya E. Dittmann, was widely circulated in draft form. Usually EPRC's studies end up on a shelf in Washington. This one, partly by design and partly because of its controversial nature, received considerable publicity. It is available to the public, in revised form, as *Compensatory Education and Early Adolescence: Reviewing our National Strategy.*[49]

Adolescence: Alternative Strategies for Compensatory Education is based on over 130 ESEA Title I state reports from 47 states over a five-year period. The authors conclude that disadvantaged students in intermediate and secondary grades are seriously neglected as a result of our national policy of compensatory education. A small and declining percent of federal money for compensatory education is spent on basic learning skills for children beyond the age of ten. The report recommends the formulation of a new strategy for providing equal, age-appropriate efforts throughout all grade levels.

Larson and Dittmann's work is based on the standard definition of "disadvantaged": pupil achievement at or below 0.7 of the norm, or about eighteenth percentile. A total of $1.6 billion has been spent annually, with more proposed for the future for the "disadvantaged," sums that would represent underfunding, according to the authors, were they to reach even all eligible *young* children.

The authors are in strong disagreement with the present federal strategy, which is premised on expectations that money spent on preschool and primary aged children obviates the need for special attention in later years. Many children do not attend or do not benefit from early programs; in addition, even those who do benefit regress to previous levels by the time they enter junior high school. Most important, adolescents have learning needs specific to adolescence which cannot be met by earlier intervention.[50]

The effective difference between disadvantaged and middle-class environments widens during adolescence as the intellectually less rich environment becomes a greater handicap for the adolescent. Therefore, "the school must play a broadened role in providing compensations for the lack of special resources in the student's environment." The authors are not claiming that the adolescent's higher cognitive capacities do not develop, "but only that they are tested and fulfilled by the informal political learning which is abundantly at hand, rather than by involvement in the intellectual pursuits associated with secondary schooling—or even in achieving more basic academic skills. Thus the developmentally effective environmental differences between lower- and middle-class adolescents can be seen as becoming greater in adolescence instead of smaller, in sharp contrast to the prevailing logic of early intervention."[51] *Sic transit* the dreams of the 1960s.

The authors argue that special programs should end at grade three only if the goal is to provide disadvantaged students with third grade skills. "If our goal is indeed to provide students with eighth grade skills, then we must provide assistance with teaching and learning these skills *at least* up to and through the eighth grade."[52] The logic seems irrefutable. It leads to the following acidic comment:

> The consequences of casting such students loose and denying their importance both in rhetoric and in practice seems oddly to have escaped the planners of most compensatory education programs. The effects of many prior years of expensive and maybe even successful compensatory attention can be negated so easily at this juncture that it would seem at the very least a clever expedient to continue compensatory attention through the period of early adolescence.[53]

There are less cynical reasons than expediency for continuing attention to adolescents, reasons based on the increasing cognitive and psychosocial potentials discussed earlier. Larson and Dittmann see developmental changes such as adolescents' growing capacity to deal with conceptual systems, to take an objective viewpoint, and to reconsider their relationship with school and society as providing motivational paths to learning basic and applied skills. These changing abilities specific to adolescence create enormous learning potential if we will become willing to view adolescent clients of compensatory education as active (not passively thankful), evaluating (not uncritical) partners (not recipients).

The bulk of Larson and Dittmann's report is based on answering the following assertions about the effectiveness of compensatory education for adolescents:

> Grade equivalent (g.e.) gains are smaller in secondary programs than in primary programs.
> Adolescent programs are less effective at moving disadvantaged students toward national norms.
> The gap between normal achievement and the achievement of disadvantaged students is so large by adolescence that students cannot change their learning patterns enough to make a difference.[54]

Contrary to arguments that secondary programs achieve lower average g.e. gains, the pattern is one of steadily increasing gains.

As far as moving disadvantaged students towards national norms is concerned, the authors make a cogent argument against current measurements while meeting Congressional critics on their own terms. Even though they maintain that "demonstrated competence . . . and similar measures of total outcome" would be preferable to testing month-for-month gains, they found that compensatory programs achieved about a five percentile net increase in each grade level.[55]

In reference to the argument about the increasing gap between "normal" achievement and the achievement of disadvantaged students, the data show that the grade-equivalent effects of the compensatory programs tend to increase rapidly over the grades, and are about twice as great at the junior high levels than at the primary grade level.[56]

These results were reported by the states despite the obstacles that the structure of junior and senior high schools' contexts pose. The organization of elementary schools lends itself to the introduction of compensatory programs in basic skills. Reading and computing form the central focus of the curriculum. It is not necessary to create "special time" for reading instruction by "cannibalizing" other subjects. Fewer instructional materials are needed because there is less range in the absolute levels of skills in any single class. Elementary teachers have training in teaching basic skills and in teaching them to children with disparate abilities. At the junior-senior high levels, there are fewer developed materials and a greater need, caused by the greater absolute range among skill abilities. Teachers are subject-matter oriented, lacking a vested interest in promoting basic skills. The administrative structure reinforces this subject-matter orientation through departmental organization structures. Administrators place little pressure on the teachers to acquire skills in teaching reading.[57] Indeed, according to Larson and Dittmann, "That secondary programs should have even occasionally been successful under these circumstances would have been surprising. That they have as good a track record as programs in the primary grades is amazing."[58]

Adolescents receive far less compensatory education than do young children. Larson and Dittmann concluded, from evaluating the state reports, that "in no state was participation of Title I programs allocated equally among elementary and secondary levels; in only one state had participation of secondary students risen over time (Rhode Island); across the nation, the proportion of secondary students receiving Title I assistance has dropped steadily over the five-year period under study. From approximately 32 percent of the total in 1969, the secondary students accounted for only an estimated 18 percent in 1973."[59]

It is difficult to justify this trend when state reports yield data showing that compensatory education programs in grades seven through twelve are at least as effective as those in grades one through six in moving disadvantaged students toward national reading test norms. We may question the quality of the state reports—and we do—but we assume that discrepancies, evasiveness, tunnel vision, and the like are common to evaluation procedures and reporting across grade levels, leaving the *comparative* findings relatively unchanged.

Adolescence: Alternative Strategies For Compensatory Education is an important document for the questions it raises and cannot answer:

What we would really like to know is whether any programs result in a change in acquisition rate that is more than temporary, and whether such changes are more lasting when made at certain age levels. Until such time as careful longitudinal study is done we will have no answer to this central issue in compensatory education.[60]

Larson and Dittmann launch an attack on the measures of evaluation used in the reports, an attack which takes its rightful place in the growing body of criticism of educational evaluation:

Our present data tell us nothing . . . about how well students are learning to use the increasingly sophisticated and powerful cognitive abilities which they acquire as they grow up. It does not tell us how well adolescent students can solve tasks of logic and generalization, or how creatively they can recombine the bits of knowledge they have at their disposal. We do not know whether they are interested in or satisfied by their own learning experiences, or whether they are learning the personal and social skills which can ultimately allow them to assume better jobs and better lives than would otherwise have been their lot. All we really know is that they have acquired five or twenty or two hundred new vocabulary words each year, and this is minimal information indeed.[61]

The standardized tests are irrelevant to the long-term goals of the projects evaluated. "The central problem is that we have not defined what such goals mean in operation, nor have we developed any broadly valid measurements against which the progress of students and schools toward such goals can be evaluated."[62]

One gets the growing sense of having passed through Alice's looking glass. This report is telling us that compensatory education "works" for adolescents, based on evaluative measurements that do not tell us what we need to know, because we have not adequately defined what we want to do.

In 1973 California identified fifteen programs in twenty-four different junior high grade groups, with gains ranging between 1.5 and 3.8 month-per-month grade equivalents. California is a special case, since its special program, AB 938, was designed by the state legislature to develop cost-effective models of basic skills education for junior high students. Nevertheless, similar projects can be found in some other states, although no other state legislation is aimed specifically at their development: for instance the Remedial Reading Laboratory Project in El Paso, Texas, Junior High Learning Resources Center in Stoughton, Massachusetts, the High Horizons programs in Connecticut, and isolated projects with Right-to-Read.[63] The authors experienced great difficulty in finding out about many of the programs for adolescents; programs for young children are more widely disseminated and are more accessible to researchers. There are materials in Title I and Right-to-Read files and on shelves about effective compensatory education for adolescents which are difficult to obtain. The bureaucratic hindrances are impressive. One has to "oil" one's way in to gain access to them. ERIC and the Interagency Panel's data are considerably limited for policy makers who want the facts about particular programs. Virtually no dissemination exists for programs for adolescents.

More controversial documents like Larson and Dittmann's need to achieve broader circulation so that more people will reinvestigate the questionable basic tenets that undergird many entrenched educational policy decisions.

Major Reports on the Reform of Secondary Education

National panels on the reform of secondary education have captured a good deal of professional and lay attention. Panel documents include *Youth: Transition to Adulthood* (the *Report of the Panel on Youth of the President's Science Advisory Committee*, popularly referred to as "Coleman II"); I/D/E/A's *Reform of Secondary Education* (the report of a panel chaired by Frank Brown); the National Society for the Study of Education's *Yearbook on Youth*; the *Report of the National Panel on High Schools and Adolescent Education*, chaired by John Henry Martin; and *The Greening of the American High School.*

These reports reflect a general rethinking of the role of schooling in our lives. They are an amalgamation of often conflicting positions.[64]

For instance, the *Report of the National Panel on High Schools and Adolescent Education* recommends "that we reemphasize the basic role of the high school as society's only universal institution for the education of the intellect." The Panel advocates casting off those activities that have accrued uncritically to the schools (specifically, high schools), reducing the global goals of secondary education, and focusing on the "essential skills susceptible to training."[65]

At the same time, the Panel's report, similar to the work of such people as Charity James, advocates strongly the integration of the arts into the schools. Recommendations include mini-schools in the various arts, contracts between artists and schools so that students may attend classes taught by professional artists in their natural environments (cf. the Urban Arts Program of the Minneapolis Public Schools), helping teachers to express themselves creatively and thereby to encourage the artistic in their students (cf. IMPACT, Interdisciplinary Model Program in the Arts for Children and Teachers, funded by the Office of Education, involving administrators, teachers, parents and artists), and programs similar to the Artists-in-the-Schools program.

According to the Panel on High Schools and Adolescent Education, only 12 percent of high school students in this country have meaningful contact with the arts. The arts are treated as ornamental, not as processes whereby people become aware of their individuality. Despite our rhetoric, the Panel concludes, arts are isolated from school business.[66]

In addition, the Panel places a great deal of emphasis on "meaningful work." Career education has been interpreted as a way in which society can socialize its young into "the world of work." "Meaningful work" is based on a recognition that adolescents need to and want to contribute their energies to the community, but lack access routes for doing this. We therefore need to socialize the community to recognize the valuable resource which is being wasted. The Panel calls for such opportunities. (So does Konopka; so does Hill; so does James; so does Bronfenbrenner: ". . . surely, the most needed innovation in the American classroom is the involvement of pupils in responsible tasks on behalf of others within the classroom, the school, the neighborhood, and the community.")[67]

It is difficult to conceptualize a school that both limits its goals to the acquisition of "trainable skills" and also creates environments in which the arts flourish and in which students move without a sense of inner contradiction from school work to community work. James says, ". . . the first steps in a new direction will be to enrich and humanize living in schools. Out of this will come a new openness between a school and the wider community of which it is a part, and to talk of living in schools will no longer seem to suggest a special kind of living."[68] Others say that the first step is a kind of consolidation of forces, focusing the schools' energies on the so-called basic skills and jettisoning other goals. The Panel's report recommends both tactics at once.

There is, then, a certain lack of coherence among, and sometimes within, the various recommendations being made. It must be stressed, also, that even when the various panel documents purport to be discussing schooling for younger as well as older adolescents, the focus is decidedly, usually exclusively, on the senior high school (and sometimes beyond).

Two reports, neither of them national in scope, specifically address the needs of the junior high school. The first is a research report sponsored by the Federal Reserve Bank of Philadelphia, a study of the effects of school resources on student learning. It was not the purpose of this study to recommend reforms for particular levels of schooling. Rather, its purpose was to analyze what school resources can have an important impact on which students, since few school inputs benefit all students. The averaged data of most studies may, the researchers argue, disguise the true impact of certain resources. "The preferable data are the experience levels of specific teachers confronting specific pupils."[69]

The researchers conclude that specific reallocation of school resources so that they are targeted to those students who benefit most from those resources can increase learning.

What is of interest for this report is that one can ferret out from among the cited data results of importance to policy makers concerned with schooling for young adolescents. For instance, when looking at the impact of school size, the researchers found that increased learning at the elementary and senior levels takes place in smaller schools, especially for black elementary students and low achievers in senior highs. "At the junior high level, school size seems inconsequential over the range examined. It seems, however, much more beneficial to be in an eighth grade that is part of an elementary school than in one that is not."[70]

The special vulnerability of junior high-aged students emerges from the data: "In junior high school, the impact of the racial balance on blacks and nonblacks varied. In general, junior high students seem to be more sensitive to a number of factors in their surroundings that don't influence their elementary and senior high counterparts. For example, they respond, in terms of learning, to whether they have moved about more or less frequently and whether they and their parents are native born."[71]

This vulnerability, especially to social conditions, is highlighted in data on racial balance. For black and nonblack students in the junior high sample, there is a slight positive effect reported from attending schools that are up to 50 percent black. After 50 percent, however, and in contradiction to findings for other age groups, "Blacks experience significant learning growth as the proportion of Blacks in the school increases (all other factors remaining the same)."[72]

The Federal Reserve Bank report constantly cites data for junior high students that differ from data for other age levels. Since its purpose is not to recommend policy as to grade level, one must find this material for oneself in the report. Nevertheless, it is clear from the report that "something is going on" during the early adolescent years which shows up in the data, but which is not being faced squarely even by many reformers, let alone researchers.

The second report which involves young adolescents, but is not national in scope, is the *Report of the California Commission for Reform of Intermediate and Secondary Education*, a group of thirty-six Commission members known by the acronym RISE. The RISE *Report* presents a separate, short section on early adolescence, stressing reliance upon demonstrated proficiency in reading, writing, and computation for educational progress at the intermediate as well as senior high levels. The Commission calls for gradual transition to greater decision making responsibility, more options in programs and learning styles, learning at various locations closely linked with and supervised by schools, and a smaller school setting for young adolescents who are learning to live with others. The curricular emphases are on exploration of careers, performing arts, and on mastery of essential skills.

The RISE *Report* argues that, according to studies, early adolescence should be a time of rapid learning. The myths that militate against recognizing this–emotional turbulence, "social enslavement," lack of cognitive changes, generational conflict–do so to the detriment of schooling for young adolescents.

In addition, the *Report* stresses that this age is a time of breaking out of egocentrism.[73] In other words, the *Report* takes into account the relationships between cognitive and socio-emotional changes discussed in Chapter 1.

Unfortunately, although the authors of the *Report* see clearly the need for changes in a system of intermediate education that has had no comprehensive plan of reform in more than sixty years, "the Commission has no intention of prescribing *how* these programs should be developed and carried out."[74] We are therefore left, for reasons of internal school politics, with several needed insights and no suggested mechanism for change. Nevertheless, the RISE *Report* represents a major step toward recognizing that the reform of schooling must include intermediate education. In 1973-74, a record number of approximately 45 percent of entering freshmen at the University of California failed the College Entrance Examination Board's English Competency Test—and entering U.C. students represent the top 12 percent of California's high school classes.[75] Challenging early childhood educators and senior high school personnel will not be enough for comprehensive reform. For once, at least on paper, the middle is not left out.

In general, the national and regional reports are disappointing in their failure to grapple openly with the reform of intermediate education. It may well be time for the establishment of what John Hill has called "a blue-ribbon national commission" to evaluate the concept and workings of American junior high schools.[76]

Schooling for Minority Youth

There is a White part of me and a Native part of me. The White part of me has no childhood and no parents. But the Native part of me has no adult.

—Anonymous Alaskan College Student[77]

John Taborn, taking part in a seminar on meeting the needs of Youth at Minnesota's Center for Youth Development and Research, argues that black youth historically have been aware that goal-setting is a futile endeavor. Now, changes are occurring. Young adolescents, like minorities in America, are moving from subordination and dependency to autonomy. Adolescence for minority youth, therefore, can be extremely difficult. The struggle is twofold: finding both personal and racial or ethnic identity.[78]

We have often expressed personal concern that minority students of junior high school age have a tendency to ascribe to black (or Chicano or Puerto Rican, etc.) identity problems issues that every adolescent must cope with. When problems are written off to "dealing with Whitey," one wonders how and when the adolescent deals with himself or herself. What does "adolescence" mean, then, for such members of subcultures in America?

We have not found answers to this question. What we have found is that schools seem relatively tangential to the process of identity formation among minority youth. This may be because earlier years of damage in schooling have established the schools' irrelevance to their personal lives (a defense, in part). It may be because the expectations of the subcultures for adolescents are in conflict with the assumptions of the schools.

America has historically depended on its schools as its main socializing institution, and in the long years of immigration, has expected public education to initiate and integrate its newcomers into the mainstream society. William Greenbaum's article, "America in Search of a New Ideal: An Essay on the Rise of Pluralism," describes that process as the attempt of the Protestant Anglo-Saxon society, considering itself superior, to impose its value system and culture upon minority societies. The newcomers in the nineteenth century were looked upon as dirty, ill-kempt, inferior specimens, who somehow had to be cleansed and lifted to Anglo-Saxon standards. *Putnam's Monthly* reported, "Our readers will agree with us that for the effectual defecation of the stream of life in a great city there is but one rectifying agent–one infallible filter–the SCHOOL."[79]

The degree to which this system of education has "worked" with immigrant groups and ethnic minorities has depended in general on the degree to which the value systems and/or physical appearances of the minorities were already similar to the predominant culture. There remain in our country millions of native and immigrant Americans who have not found the schools to be an aid to entering the mainstream society. There is practically no point upon which our society agrees more strongly than in the recognition of the schools' poor record in educating these groups, and almost no point upon which we disagree more strongly than on the reasons for this record. Puerto Ricans, Mexican-Americans, native Americans, and blacks, in large numbers, are not being educated in our schools. Large numbers drop out of school at the legal age or before; the ones who remain often discover that their years spent in school result in only scant preparation for competition in a tight or closed job market.

The dropout rate is frequently used as a measure of school failure, the assumption being that if the schools are offering a child what he needs or perceives that he needs, he will remain to reap the benefits. This question is of particular relevance to professionals studying the period of early adolescence, since it is during this time span that the decision to leave school is usually made. Studying the dropout pattern of minorities is extremely difficult because of record-keeping practices of school districts. Richard Rivera points out that the Board of Education in New York City does not offer "scientific data" on the dropout rate itself, much less on the reasons for dropping out.[80] In addition, what is often overlooked in these studies is that even the high dropout rates are inadequate indicators of the amount of schooling being received by minority youth. There is evidence that the schools have no chance to educate some minority children because they are never enrolled. A study in Boston revealed that despite mandatory attendance laws, 31.2 percent of Spanish speaking children were not attending school and 26.4 percent were not even enrolled. "The highest proportion of out-of-school children with this group is the twelve through fifteen age bracket, where 34 percent were not enrolled."[81] In Philadelphia, only about 67 percent of eligible Puerto Rican children are enrolled in school.

Finally, even if we had accurate statistics about numbers of school dropouts and numbers who do not enroll at all, it would be necessary for us to interpret these numbers. Although we consistently make the assumption that dropping out (or nonenrollment) is solely a dysfunctional phenomenon—the failure of the mainstream society to acculturate minority youth, or the failure of the minority culture to take advantage of the access route provided by schools—we might also explore the functional relationship between the various values of American subcultures and being independent of the school system.

Investigations into racial and cultural differences and deficiencies in the late sixties and early seventies turned the schools into a political battleground from which the smoke is only beginning to clear. Research and programs in this field have been somewhat stymied. Each recommendation has met with such vociferous denunciation from various interest groups that many scholars have hesitated to publish their findings.

In this section we are not covering new ground. The arguments have all been heard before. There are shelves of books and articles, and hundreds of programs addressing themselves to improving schooling for numbers of subsegments of our population. We see no breakthroughs in sight. It is our aim here to clarify the arguments as they apply to young adolescents. We are ultimately concerned with ways in which schools are or are not structured to deal with identity issues of minority youth, and with subcultural values in general.

We begin with the premise that many begin with: large numbers of these young people are not learning in our schools. The arguments as to cause fall into three often overlapping categories: (1) there are aspects of the subculture that militate against these students' doing well and/or staying in school; (2) there are aspects of our schools that militate against these students doing well and/or staying in school; (3) there are aspects of society at large that militate against these students doing well and/or staying in school. While adherents of each of these arguments might favor such programs as ethnic studies and bilingual classes, they begin with different premises and proceed with different orientations as to the causes of the high dropout and failure rates among minority youth.

These issues are of particular significance for young adolescents for several reasons. Since it is during early adolescence that the decision to drop out is usually made, the nature of the "fit" between the subculture and the school is especially important at this time. It is also during early adolescence that vocation becomes a serious issue for many young people. (Puerto Ricans, for instance, make life choices very early.)[82] Whether or not the school plays a role in such choices, and what the nature of that role is, are important issues for minority youth. Most important and most elusive, during early adolescence the definitions of the self as separate from and a part of one's culture become central tasks. Schools can play a facilitative role in these tasks, a negative role, or become irrelevant to them.

Aspects of the Subculture and Schooling

There has been considerable effort on the part of sociologists, anthropologists, and educators to examine the cultures of minority groups to determine what characteristics and value systems may be most strongly in conflict with mainstream American society. These studies are numerous, but they all share a common problem: the difficulty and danger of generalizing across class divisions about a culture that is daily altering under the impact of the particular American experience of the minority group.

There are, however, a number of fairly safe generalizations upon which many sociologists agree.

In the Spanish speaking minorities, both Mexican-American and Puerto Rican, there is an emphasis on family solidarity and structure that permeates the relationships of these groups with the outside world. The major components are male superiority ("machismo") and holding family responsibility above personal considerations. The emphasis on generosity and personal sacrifice for the good of the larger group has been interpreted as destructive of academic and occupational competition. (One example is the occasional practice among Mexican-Americans of keeping a daughter at home from school if she is needed to care for a younger child.[83]) Although "machismo" still plays an important role in Spanish-speaking minorities, it is beginning to fade as a deterrent to female educational and occupational advancement.

It still may play a role, however, in the difficulty adolescent males have in adapting to the American educational environment. "The village boys have especially suffered. Regarding themselves as adults at the age of puberty, they find it difficult to accept female dominance by mothers and teachers."[84] Machismo "may be one reason why so many Mexican-American boys drop out of school early: a boy is *macho* if he is working, earning money, and standing on his own two feet."[85]

Although the concept of "machismo" may have lost some of its force in these societies, the idea of the father authority figure and his close control over his children remains rather strong. Educators see this as clinging to a traditionalism that may jeopardize the independent, personal achievement goals of the children. A study conducted in Los Angeles and San Antonio in 1966 showed that Mexican-American parents were more interested in discipline being taught in the schools than in academic instruction, and that parents' ideal of the model child was one who showed respect, knew his place, and did not trespass in areas not his business.[86] One researcher points out that the schools are sometimes seen by Chicano parents as a force seeking to destroy family ties: "Actually you are not going to affect the dropout rate as long as the school stands as a symbol of Anglo-Saxon superiority. The Mexican community doesn't trust the schools. The schools threaten to take away the patriarchal rule in the families. . . . There is a good deal of paternal pressure on the kids to drop out of school."[87]

Other factors of Spanish-speaking minorities that may affect academic performance are spiritualism (emphasis on ultimate good rather than material necessity), fatalism ("Dios dirá"), and a sense of hierarchy that fosters class rigidity.

Various elements of American Indian culture are also seen as counter-productive in a competitive school situation: emphasis on freedom, generosity, and orientation toward the present rather than the future (some tribes have only present tense verbs), concern for harmony with nature rather than control over it, and a value system that judges men by who they are rather than by what they have.[88]

Some researchers have pointed out a small cultural difference that seems superficial, but apparently has an impact on the school situation: eye contact. Jacquetta Hill Burnett noticed in her study of Puerto Rican young adolescents in Chicago, that whereas the teachers depend on eye signal for recognition, the Puerto Ricans "come to school with a somewhat different coding which says it is rude to stare a person in the eye for too long. Moreover if one is in a particularly formal situation with the teacher, or is being corrected, then one is careful not to look the teacher or adult in the eye since it may signal defiance."[89] The same is true for other cultures. Teaching an Indian child to smile and nod his head at the teacher in a classroom immediately affects the teacher's assessment of the child's willingness to learn. "Neither smiling nor nodding was part of the little boy's culture, but until he was taught to behave in ways that signaled his desire to learn, he was abandoned."[90]

Researchers investigating aspects of black culture signify that it is not so much a conflict of values that separates blacks from the mainstream but a conflict of methods. Blacks are seen to hold similar values to white society—family loyalty, compassion, hard work, piety, desire for financial security and leisure time.[91] However, the vehicle of academic performance has not become a secondary value for achieving primary goals.

Aspects of the Schools

We are making a distinction within the groups of researchers and educators who have joined in an attack on the existing school systems in America. Those in favor of "pluralism" ask the schools to change to meet the differing needs of its minority groups. There is an implication in such recommendations that there is a "differentness" about the subculture that must be accepted and coped with. There is another view, however, that denies cultural differences as an impediment to education *in a humanistic environment*. The contention of these critics is that minority groups could perform well in school situations if the schools were structured to give them a fair chance.[92]

Daniel Levine sees the "ineffectiveness of the school in teaching lower class youth as deriving not so much from its commitment to values which are foreign to the youth, as from its failure to provide the type of environment which would reinforce their groping and half-hearted attempts to live up to these goals."[93]

The major elements in the school system today that work against ethnic minorities are seen to be (1) racism, (2) lack of models, and (3) isolation from the community that the schools are to serve.

(1) Racism: "However well-meaning whites may be, they lack the social perception to penetrate the mass of white racism that permeates the American school but is almost imperceptible to them. . . . Nowhere is the effect of white supremacy more pervasive and debilitating than in the American school."[94]

This racism is most often attacked at the level of the classroom teacher; primarily, it is the teacher who through stereotyping and low expectations forces the child to poor performance (the familiar "self-fulfilling prophecy"). Although the teacher may exhibit no overt racism, her low demand functions as a debilitator.[95]

Of course, learning is a considerable problem when school children are totally unable to communicate with their teachers. One wonders why an adolescent should not drop out after having gone through a school system in which, for instance, there is roughly one Puerto Rican teacher for every three hundred students (in New York District 1), "isolating the Puerto Rican child from his own culture, background and language."[96] (It is estimated that only 2.7 percent of Chicanos are in bilingual programs.[97])

Racism is also seen as functioning in the tracking system of many schools, whereby higher percentages of minority students are placed into vocational programs. Guidance counselors also come under attack for almost automatically discouraging minorities from high academic aspirations. The effects are felt keenly during young adolescence.

The advocates of this view hold that another evidence of racism in the schools is the paucity of educational resources available in the inner-city schools. "The greatest percentage of least experienced teachers (29-41 percent had from one to three years of experience) work in poverty areas where books, supplies, and advanced teaching materials are hardest to find. So the children who are achieving at the lowest level are being 'taught' by relatively inexperienced personnel" in schools with the highest rate of overcrowding.[98] It is not clear what aspects of experience should be included to define "experience" for a teacher of inner-city young adolescents. Longevity does not seem to be the key.

What is clear is that if the least talent is found at the junior high level, inner-city junior high schools have more than their fair share of "the least."

(2) Models: A major complaint of minorities is that the personnel of the schools are predominantly white Anglos. This prevents the children from sharing a cultural compatability with the teacher as well as convincing them that education as a profession is out of their sphere. There are widespread and urgent requests for more hiring of minority teachers and superintendents to direct the education of their young. In some areas this is seen as an urgent pedagogical necessity. In New York City, for instance, one out of seven school children speaks no English.

In the Southwest, the area of heaviest Chicano concentration, 17 percent of school enrollment is Chicano, but only 4 percent of the teachers are Mexican-American;[99] in New York 22 percent of the children are Puerto Rican but only 0.6 percent of the teachers;[100] and in Philadephia, which has over 7,000 Puerto Rican children in school, as of 1974 there were no Puerto Rican principals or vice-principals.[101]

Aside from linguistic problems, minorities feel that as long as their children have no models with whom they can identify and who understand the particular circumstances from which these children come, school can have little relevance to their lives. Given the importance of role models during early adolescence, it is little wonder that minority youth feel schools to be irrelevant to their present concerns, to say nothing about their future.

(3) Isolation of Schools from Community: The idea of the community center, only one of whose services is schooling, is the only breakthrough we have seen in restructuring the school organization to fit the mores and needs of the subculture. In so doing, it speaks to the arguments both of those critics who stress the subculture and those who stress the school organization in accounting for school failure and dropouts. The concept, however, has no champions serving as advocates for adolescents.

Meanwhile, the isolation of schools from the community can be seen in case after case like the following: in the schools included in the survey of Southwest Chicano education, four million families identified Spanish as their mother tongue, but 89 percent of the schools sent notices home written only in English. The report also showed that little attempt was made to set up liaisons with social services in the barrios and little use was made of Mexican-American educational consultants to solve problems in the schools.[102]

There is also growing fear among parents in ethnic subgroups of cultural schizophrenia in their children. For young adolescents who are facing the identity confusions of being American and a member of a proud subgroup, schools must be facilitative or they will be rejected. School systems like the ones described above place adolescents in an untenable situation.

Jacquetta Hill Burnett's study of Puerto Rican adolescents in Chicago reveals the way in which faulty institutions can compound and create disadvantages for minority groups. "We found that the disadvantages of being culturally different often were as attributable to inadequate provisions on the part of institutions that presumably offered services, to the disadvantaged among others, as to deficient abilities and cultural characteristics."[103]

Aspects of the Society at Large and Schooling

A final component of this discussion of the schooling of minority youths is the consideration of whether the schools, after all, are the main source of the failure of these groups to function in our industrial society. Is our society, in fact, placing an unrealistic demand on our school systems to handle a problem that has deep and wide roots throughout the structure of our society?

Several aspects of minority cultures may contribute to unsuccessful school participation ("machismo," "Dios dirá") but many sociologists, anthropologists, and educators who have studied these groups assert that these cultural elements are less a deterrent than is the structure of the society into which they are trying to enter. This is to say, the discrimination and the lack of job opportunities that these groups have faced have created a sense of futility that affects their job orientation and attitudes toward education, and they have passed many of these attitudes to their children. In other words, there is a consensus among many social observers that neither cultural differences nor school organization are critical factors, even though they may militate against the individual's easy adaptation to schooling. The problems are rooted in the feeling of futility caused by the lack of economic security in the future. This feeling is passed on from one generation to the next.

We suggest that at exactly the time in one's life when one begins to look at the future as being a part of one's destiny, such an inheritance is disabling. It is bound to affect one's relationship with the social institution which, it was hoped, would equalize opportunity.

Until the impoverished minorities can see that educational efforts on their part will result in the kind of advancement they seek, in the form of real job opportunities and real equality with the majority culture, schools, and especially schools for adolescents, will continue to be an institution fraught with frustration and failure.

Emerging Trends

Emerging trends are few and weak, but they do present themselves. The first, and potentially most important, is a growing dialogue about adolescence in general.

There are several signs that the interest in the larger age group of adolescence includes concern for early adolescence. These signs can be seen in California's Commission for the Reform of Intermediate and Secondary Education (RISE), already referred to. Even should legislation not support the Commission's recommendations, the project represents an important step in recognizing that intermediate education must be carefully scrutinized. Looking only at senior high schools is an incomplete strategy.

In a smaller but noteworthy effort, the National Association of Independent Schools (NAIS) has appointed a Task Force on Middle Schools. The Task Force is conducting a review of the educational experiences of the middle school-aged student. Its members are then committed to supporting programs that respond to the problems and strengths of eleven- to fourteen-year-olds.

The Educational Policy Research Center (EPRC) of the Stanford Research Institute continues to work on a series of shorter papers on aspects of adolescent education, including the availability of specially trained teachers and of programs and materials in the basic skills area for adolescents.

Also, John Hill, in his program recommendations to the Office of Child Development, recommends the establishment of a "blue ribbon" national committee to review the junior high school's ability to meet the needs of early adolescents.[104] These reports–John Hill's, Project RISE's, and prospective ones from NAIS and EPRC–address schooling for young adolescents directly. They lead us to conclude that the growing national dialogue on adolescence will not overlook early adolescence completely.

A second trend, the community school, is barely discernible at the junior high level, but is appearing, interestingly, from various diverse sources.

Alan Green of Educational Facilities Laboratory says that there is a growing tendency to reconnect the school to the community when planning school facilities. The community school or community center combines schools with other social services, like recreation, day care, the arts, libraries, health, and job training. Green cites The Whitmer Human Resources Center in Pontiac, Michigan, the John F. Kennedy Center in Atlanta, the Dunbar School in Baltimore, and the Thomas Jefferson Center in Arlington, Virginia, as examples. "The objective is to reintegrate the social services of a community while bringing greater efficiency to the use of capital and operating dollars by sharing space, overhead, personnel, and services."[105]

Architectural changes referred to by Green, made in planning for declining school enrollments, can lead to the kind of *interrelationships* among schools and other community services that precede the *integration* of school life and community life we have discussed.

Given the critical role of schools in the lives of adolescents, "unless they are supportive of programs aimed at reform in other areas, those programs are likely to fall short."[106] The educational system is in a pivotal position. We have already had much to say about the implications of physiological development for school organization. We are deeply concerned about the lack of integration of services among health care and educational agencies. Bronfenbrenner says, "The success of any program designed to foster the development of children requires as its first ingredient an intact child."[107] We would argue in addition that health care does not stop with intervention at the prenatal and early childhood levels. Given the velocity and intensity of the adolescent growth spurt, developmental disorders may have their source in adolescence. Schools remain aloof from the physiological demands of early adolescence. They thereby abdicate their responsibility to design programs for young people who are "intact" and can participate to their full potential in those programs.

Hill points out that the problems of variability in biological and psychological maturity are particularly acute during the transition from middle childhood into adolescence.[108] There are precious few schools in the public sector that are struggling with the implications of such observations. The community school concept is one viable approach.

The demands for getting the kids out of the schools into the community and for getting the community into the schools are becoming more prevalent. We do not see any movement anywhere to provide appropriate, comprehensive services to the critical developmental age of early adolescence. As yet, the holistic approach as represented by community schools has no delivery system in the multiple institutions affecting adolescents.

A third trend involves two ripples in the area of teacher education. The first of these has to do with accreditation; the second has to do with alternative approaches to teacher education.

It is generally agreed that the least talented of our teachers are attracted to the junior high schools. In part, this is caused by the lack of prestige associated with this level. It is a non-area. No noteworthy programs of teacher preparation have been designed for junior high school teachers. Preparation is usually either elementary or secondary (that is, senior high).

Our absence of knowledge about young adolescents once again has its impact on the educational system, here seen in the area of teacher preparation. A cycle of mediocrity results that is difficult to break into. Teachers, inadequately prepared, enter the classroom and quickly take as their models those more experienced teachers who seem to be surviving. Departments of education wishing to break out of the traditional elementary or secondary programs for future junior high teachers find few classrooms where their student teachers can practice alternate methods of teaching young adolescents. The practicum experience is less than successful. Also, there are usually no courses offered, much less required, in adolescent growth and development. Learning theory courses are oriented toward younger children. Future teachers choose between preparation for secondary certification, which is highly subject-oriented, and preparation for elementary certification, which is highly student-oriented but lacks the depth of commitment to a discipline that can enrich classroom experiences for adolescents. Teachers, inadequately prepared, enter the classroom. . . .

Without the classrooms appropriate for young adolescents already established as training sites, teacher preparation is very difficult. Without adequate training of teachers, such classrooms cannot be established. Meanwhile, graduate degrees are not offered for teachers of teachers at this level, since there are no courses and no faculty members to stimulate and supervise masters and doctoral students.

This vicious cycle has previously been ignored. There is now movement in the credentialing of teachers at the state level. The North Central Association of Colleges and Secondary Schools tends to classify junior high schools and middle schools as secondary schools. The Southern Association of Colleges and Schools tends to classify them as elementary.[109] Some states have begun to seek new certification patterns. According to the Middle School Resource and Research Center in Indianapolis, there is or has been action in close to twenty states for establishing certification for teaching in middle schools.[110] Several universities are implementing teacher-training programs for the middle years. (According to Perrone, middle schools are kept from being better and different from junior highs by the inability of teachers to cope, given their prior training and lack of support in the field.)[111]

Even if teacher preparation became superb overnight, the situation would barely improve, given the present job market. In-service training has become critical if change is to occur. Hill points out that the impact of Piaget's work on curriculum and instruction at the junior high level has been negligible. Understanding the nature of formal operations has not been a part of teacher training. "Thus, the role where one might expect the greatest impact of cognitive change has rarely been defined in such a way that the impact could be exercised."[112] Otto and Healy are concerned with the devaluing, negative attitudes of adults towards adolescents. "There is some evidence that these attitudes are particularly deeply entrenched among teachers. . . . It would . . . seem both logical and necessary that during a period of maximal growth and stress such as adolescence, a series of strongly ego supportive experiences be built into the educational sequence."[113] Charity James works with teachers to help them discover the artist in themselves and in their students. Larson and Dittmann call for the in-service retraining of secondary teachers in a variety of content areas to facilitate greater coordination between students' new and changing basic skills and the rest of their school experience. An essential aspect of the success of special programs (in this case, compensatory) is the climate created by the attitudes and interest of a school's entire professional staff.[114] Joan Goldsmith, co-director of the Institute of Open Education in Cambridge, Mass. (affiliated with the Antioch Graduate School of Education), is convinced that "most adults . . . carry with them conflicts which first emerged during the years twelve to fifteen which they have not successfully resolved. These conflicts have to do with individuation and separation from family of origin, competency in the world of work, loss and death, and intimacy with another person. . . . Our work with middle school teachers has shown us the importance of helping teachers in these concerns in their own lives. They are then able to help their students."[115]

In each case cited, the concern is with in-service training and retraining of experienced teachers and administrators. The stress is not on changing to a particular type of learning environment so much as it is on becoming a more effective educator, whether in an open or a comparatively traditional setting.

It has been said that the fastest vehicle in a vacuum is a bandwagon. Teachers' centers have been that vehicle. They have been there on a day-to-day basis, in the field, while universities have stood aloof. They have provided alternative in-service experiences which state departments of education and universities have not. The effective centers have been more sensitive to the implications for schools of the biological, socio-emotional, and cognitive research we have discussed than have many university teacher education programs. State and local in-service training is usually of poor quality and derided by the teachers involved. Teacher centers are the major alternative for training after certification, and there are not many teacher centers for teachers of adolescents.

There are many educators who believe that teaching is an art. Many others believe that the source of teaching is science, our knowledge of the learning processes. It is not necessary to take sides in this issue to see that we prepare neither artists nor applied scientists for the classroom. Artists "enrich" the school experience through programs like Artists-in-the-Schools. Clinicians (applied scientists) are called in for special problem areas. Who are the teachers? What is their professional identity? We cannot know, unless we know what schools are. We always end where we begin. We do not know what we want our teachers to be because we lack an underlying coherent set of purposes for schooling. Nowhere is this felt more keenly than in teacher preparation in schooling for young adolescents.

Finally, a fourth trend involves accountability and the courts. Marian Wright Edelman, a lawyer who has been in the forefront in the area of children's rights, says that "lawyers over the last ten to twenty years have made a whole lot of decisions that educators should have made."[116] Decisions about mainstreaming handicapped children into the regular classroom and about the responsibility of schools to non-English-speaking students are not at all peripheral to the learning process itself. The *Peter Doe* case can change the nature of schooling for adolescents.[117]

This well-publicized case involves an action brought by the parents of a graduate of the San Francisco School System who, as a result of extensive testing, after graduation, was classified as a functional illiterate. As a result, plaintiffs contend that the school system has not met its basic obligations either to "Peter Doe" as a student or to his parents as taxpayers. Such an obligation, it is asserted, is inherent in a compulsory attendance scheme. Plaintiffs analogized their situation to that of a mental patient who was involuntarily committed by a court order. In such cases the courts have not been reluctant to establish a right to some minimum level of treatment for such patients.[118] Though plaintiffs do not contend that there exists an absolute right to an education,[119] they do contend that the school system must provide some minimum level of education as a "*quid pro quo*" of the compulsory attendance statutes.

By holding schools accountable to students and taxpayers because of the compulsion they exercise over the lives of those who are required to attend, a tool for improving the basic level of education may be developed. The rationale advanced in *Peter Doe* has not yet been adopted by any court and it is much too early to decide whether such an approach will succeed. Nevertheless, in the absence of clarified goals, society may once again receive the definition of schooling from the courts. Lawyers will have decided what educators could not.

The effect on schooling for young adolescents may be dramatic. If schools are held accountable for teaching "basic skills" to everyone who is required to attend, the aims of schooling may be determined by an even narrower definition of the learner than we now have. Schools will be closer to Bereiter's vision than we might now expect. It will be easier for states to lower the age of compulsory attendance than to meet law suits, easier to flunk students out than to try harder to teach them, easier to crack down on them than to seek alternate ways of reaching them, easier to see them only in terms of the minimal standards of performance schools will be held measurably accountable for. It will be difficult to convince school systems to consider the holistic view in relating to a young adolescent when they know that they have only one or two more years to make good on society's investment. The pressure that will be on schools housing young adolescents, and therefore on the students in them, may be as wasteful as is the current lack of accountability. The sanction for noncompliance in practice may remain against the students.

On the other hand, as Sugarman argues in "Accountability through the Courts," "Perhaps through education malpractice suits the courts will provide a forum for addressing the difficult questions of the causes of learning and nonlearning." Also, such suits will force schools to define their limitations. "A heightened realism about what schools can and cannot do could be a valuable result in such litigation. . . ."[120]

It is not our purpose to advocate one position or another, but to call attention to the lack of vision and colloquy among educators about an issue critical to the nature of their profession. It is unclear to us whether society needs or wants to be relieved of the responsibility for making such decisions. Certainly, society as a whole is ambivalent about the role of schooling, and if educators cannot lead, then the courts must. This is a trend we see discussed within the legal profession. Its implications for adolescents remain unexplored by educators.

The Abyss

Given the ills and vulnerabilities of a mass society, the first great task of education is to develop a sense of the core of identity in oneself and of the authentic in whatever one's life touches.

—Max Lerner
Education and A Radical Humanism

In an attempt to get minimal information about the types of activity and change occurring at the junior high level, we sent a questionnaire to all fifty states and to twenty municipalities. The response astounded us. Record keeping is uniformly spotty about this age group. Questions that could have been answered with ease about six-year-olds could not be answered about twelve-to fifteen-year-olds—even where they are, absentee rates, and the percentages continuing to receive special services beyond elementary schools. All we can conclude is that no one cares enough to compile or to process such data. Beyond this, in only two or three states could there be said to be a firm, conscious, state-directed effort at revision. We asked, "What program and research efforts are being sponsored at the state level specific to this age group?" and in most cases received the answer, "None." No profile could be derived from the information, just another corroboration of the lack of commitment to young adolescents.

In this section on schooling we have attempted to highlight areas being considered by people involved with schools. We have reserved our discussion about schooling for young adolescents with handicapping conditions for a separate section. There are several curricular areas to which we might have devoted a great deal of time, especially reading.[121]

One of several surveys in 1974 found that one in twenty people between twelve and seventeen could not read at the *fourth*-grade level, with an even higher rate among the poor and inner-city youth.[122]

HEW's report, *Literacy Among Youths 12-17 Years*, states that approximately 4.8 percent, or one million of the 22.7 million youngsters who would be in grades six through twelve, cannot read materials intended for a fourth-grader, i.e., cannot read at the *beginning* fourth-grade level. Illiteracy is most prevalent among boys, especially blacks from low-income families with little or no formal education. Illiteracy rates were as follows: 4.7 percent white males, 1.7 percent white females, 20.5 percent black males, 9.6 percent black females; 27.4 percent among youths whose parents had no formal education; 8.9 percent among youths whose parents had at least an elementary school education; from families with incomes of less than $2,000, 8.8 percent white, 22.1 percent black; incomes of $5,000-6,999, 3.5 percent white and 12.6 percent black; incomes of over $10,000, 0.8 percent white and 4.7 percent black were judged illiterate.[123]

The Louis Harris Survey suggests that seven million people under the age of sixteen will become functionally illiterate adults.[124]

We have decided not to pursue this issue despite the imperative nature of social concerns about illiteracy. We believe strongly that the failure to read with ease and enjoyment is an inestimable personal loss, and that illiteracy is a shameful social loss. "Reading" is an emerging trend, and will certainly be everyone's specialty if cases like the *Peter Doe* case are decided in favor of the plaintiffs. But we do not believe that reading programs can be much more effective than they now are in the school situations in which most young adolescents are placed.

We have therefore decided not to discuss any particular curricular issues. It will be time to discuss curriculum when the following blatant voids in schooling for young adolescents are attended to.

First, there is no linkage between the junior high school as a social structure and the young adolescent whom we know from personal, research, and theoretical knowledge. The tasks of adolescence include separation, including the capacity to function on one's own; individuation, including the establishment of an inner sense of uniqueness and continuity; and commitment, including the capacity to interact with others so as to contribute to social cohesion. At present, there are few aspects of schooling for young adolescents that foster the accomplishment of these tasks.

Instead, junior high schools appear to be obsessed with issues of control, as if assuming the inevitability of adolescent conflict caused by intrapsychic forces. These expectations of conflict may be self-fulfilling prophecies; or they may exaggerate aspects of behavior which, as we have seen, are not inevitable. Educational policies based on the aforementioned adolescent tasks rather than on institutional expectations of rebelliousness would alter schooling dramatically.

Adolescence is a time when one integrates one's past experiences and forms a growing awareness of a personal destiny. It is also, as Konopka points out, a time when one becomes part of one's own generation. Therefore, "friends are the lifeblood of adolescence," people to be trusted, to listen, and to understand feelings. Loneliness becomes a new personal experience.[125] Schools remove adolescents from their friends. Approximately 70 percent of the girls in Konopka's sample expressed a positive attitude toward school: it is a place to meet and be with friends. Schools either militate against this, or at best see it as a by-product of the real business of schooling. "It cannot be stressed enough that this function is the most significant one to the young people themselves and has a deep impact on their whole attitude towards people as well as learning."[126]

During a time of life where social interaction is so critical, it is difficult to be considered special or different. The race picture is better, Konopka reports, when the varied populations are equal enough that no one has to struggle for friendships (cf. the Federal Reserve Bank of Philadelphia findings) and when schools make a conscious effort to include social life as part of its educational purpose.[127]

It would seem patently obvious, from all the research data on the inter- and intra-individual variability among young adolescents, that a variety of school styles is demanded for this age group, which now receives the fewest options.

American schools are designed for a long, slow, steady maturing process. There is nothing in the research data to support such a design; quite the contrary. The junior high school, which was originally expected to speed the process of schooling, has evolved as an intermediate structure which puts the adolescent on "hold" during years when we wait for him or her to grow up, feeling unsure or even helpless about our instructive purposes.

Early adolescence is a time during which life-changing cognitive growth may occur. The individual's cognitive behavior is extended at this time, if it is ever going to be, to the capacity for hypothetical, abstract thought. Such an extension makes possible, among other activities, the formulation of personal values. Schools for young adolescents appear to proceed from day to day totally unaware of this transformation, yet it is of such import that it can determine the tenor of one's future life.

Instruction in most junior high schools proceeds on the assumption that learning is cumulative and sequential, that small increments in specific skills are integrated hierarchically. The research that dominates the field of cognition indicates that learning is dependent on stage acquisition, the *stages* being sequential. Abilities differ among young adolescents not only in degree, but in type. It is as wasteful to present abstract material prematurely as it is to remain oblivious to new mental capacities.

The implication for junior high curricula is that they must be based on a relationship between presentation of subject matter and the cognitive stage of development of the students, rather than between subject matter and chronological age in combination with reward structures.

The second blatant void, implied in the first, is the failure of schools for young adolescents to acknowledge differential growth spurts. We have repeatedly noted research data that indicate the extensive range of differences in growth along several dimensions among young adolescents of the same chronological age and within individual adolescents. A school structure that assumes, through grade organization and age segregation, homogeneity of growth among its students functions in the dark, and in the dark ages of school organization.

Third, there is a serious lack of integration among other service communities and schools for young adolescents. This void has been noted often in the field of compensatory education. Schooling alone cannot solve the educational problems of the poor. A comprehensive effort is usually called for by social critics, one which includes attention to housing, health, nutrition, and needless to say, poverty. Birch and Gussow cite data showing that from among eighty adolescents referred to a New York hospital by Job Corps recruiters, 24 percent were found to have health problems so serious as to require immediate treatment. These problems ranged from tuberculosis to severe cardiac conditions. The U.S. House of Representatives' Subcommittee on the War of Poverty held hearings during 1965 for which Job Corps applicants' records were reviewed. Fifty percent of these sixteen- to twenty-one-year-olds had never been to a physician before applying to the Job Corps. Ninety-eight out of 159 school dropouts in Boston who were examined for the Job Corps had pathologic conditions including asthma, disorders of the central nervous system, of hearing, and of vision.[128] It is patently absurd to hold one social institution, the schools, accountable for the failure to retain these adolescents and to instruct them successfully. It is equally absurd to hold no one accountable for integrating the service structures that are supposed to provide for the health, education, and welfare of these minors.

The case is easily stated when such glaring statistics are available. They are not available for the adolescent population at large, which is relatively unstudied and where the effects of lack of service integration (and lack of services) are more subtle. We have already quoted Bronfenbrenner on the need for the reintegration of children into the adult community. What we cannot present is the synthesis necessary for such integration. No one has asked the necessary questions or produced some viable answers, let alone come up with workable delivery mechanisms. The dialogue has not begun.

Fourth, there has been no recent examination on a national basis of the disjuncture between ideology and structure in schooling for young adolescents. Instead, there is a confusion of recommendations calling for everything at once–fewer demands, more demands, early end to schooling, dropout prevention of older students, the retreat of schools to "the basics," the inclusion of schooling in the larger society. Schools face inwards and outwards, reacting to external forces and setting forces in motion. Given the confusion of demands, schools for young adolescents can be expected to remain unchanged by these external forces. There can be no substantial changes without greater coherence of societal demands, and there can be no such coherence without greater and more widespread knowledge about adolescents.

It is the misfortune of young adolescents that two areas of confusion and ignorance converge at this time in their lives and in such an important social institution: confusion about the purposes of schooling and ignorance about early adolescence as a critical developmental stage in the life span.

If, as Max Lerner says, the first task of education in a mass society is to develop a sense of "the core of identity in oneself and of the authentic in whatever one's life touches," then we have yet to begin to approach the first step in educating young adolescents.

3 Service Institutions and the Handicapped Young Adolescent

Introduction

> . . . handicapped youth broadly include those with a significant physical or mental impairment that results in the need for special services not required by "normal" youth . . . of the 83.8 million aged 0 to 21 youth in the United States in 1970, over 9 million are handicapped. Even taking into account the difficulties of making precise estimates without a comprehensive census of the handicapped population, the figures indicate clearly the tragic proportions of the problem.[1]

> The exceptional (handicapped) child is the child who deviates from the normal or average child 1) in mental characteristics, 2) in sensory abilities, 3) in neuromuscular or physical characteristics, 4) in social or emotional behavior, 5) in communication abilities, or 6) in multiple handicaps to such an extent that he requires a modification of school practices, or special education services in order to develop to his maximum capacity.[2]

Handicapped youngsters comprise between 9 and 10 percent of the school-age population. Although handicapped young adolescents experience many of the same problems confronting handicapped citizens of all ages, they also have special needs related to their particular developmental stage and their particular position in our society's institutions. In this section we discuss adolescents who are (1) physically, (2) emotionally, and (3) mentally handicapped and offer an appraisal of services available to them. First, however, we present an overview of general problems in serving handicapped children and youth.

The issues involved in classifying children are complex and often heated. Nicholas Hobbs, editor of *Issues in the Classification of Children*, argues that while a dozen or more categories have acquired legitimacy in the classification of exceptional children, serious problems are caused by lack of sophistication in taxonomy, professional biases, neglect of determinants of problems, and the use of classification to legitimize social control of the individual.[3]

The social and political contexts of classification bear continuous scrutiny, as do the methods of identifying the population of concern and the rationale of treatment programs. Labeling "is in continual danger of being reified by those who employ it conceptually, simplified by those who use it practically in empirical investigation, and vulgarized into a tautology by those who reduce a point of view to a definition."[4]

These implicit cautions pertain to all ages and all handicaps. We bear them in mind, aware that the pitfalls are ubiquitous.

Services For Handicapped Youth: A Program Overview (Rand Report R-1220) points out that there is a "bewildering maze" of agencies, services and programs for handicapped youth. The direction needed to match individual needs and local capabilities has been no one's prime responsibility. The handicapped, their parents, and professionals like doctors, teachers, social workers, and counselors, are often unaware of resources which do in fact exist. The effort required to master the maze and to gain access to services is often extraordinary, given the lack of comprehensive information generally available. Thus the quality of services becomes limited.[5]

The report (R-1220) describes problems in five major classes: (1) inequity, (2) gaps in services, (3) insufficient knowledge, (4) inadequate or deficient control, and (5) insufficiency of resources.

By inequity, the authors are referring to unevenness in accessibility to services and unevenness of quality of services across states and among categories of handicapping conditions. Within states, the authors are particularly concerned with the inequity of services for preschool children, rural youth, and certain classes of urban children.

Gaps in services include neglect and underdevelopment of prevention, identification of those needing services, and referral. The report also points to the inadequacy of institutions that emphasize single types of services for handicapped persons who have complex and multiple changing needs.

Insufficient knowledge refers to low quality or nonexistent planning and evaluation. The underlying problem is the failure to establish methods of obtaining high quality data. "In some programs no one really knows who is doing what for whom or with what effect."[6]

In discussing the problem of inadequate control, the authors survey the "vast system" of "varied, fragmented, uncoordinated" services for handicapped children. "The sheer number of institutions dispensing funds and services under many enabling legislations contributes to a situation in which no one individual or group of individuals plans, monitors or controls the handicapped service system in any comprehensive fashion. Policymaking, funding, and operating decisions are often made by entirely different groups of people, based in each case on an almost total lack of data about program effectiveness; and as a result, accountability is generally very weak."[7]

Finally, the authors state that current resources are insufficient if our criterion is to be the provision of services to each handicapped person in need. At the same time, improving services and delivery systems is possible at present funding levels.[8]

The authors of *Services for Handicapped Youth* report that three points emerged repeatedly during the course of their investigation: (1) agencies do not serve a significant portion of the population in need; (2) agencies generally do not know approximately how many unserved people there are; (3) very few agencies have outreach programs to identify the population in need.[9]

The discussion that follows concerns the handicapped young adolescent. Some of the problems to be explored apply to other age groups as well. Certainly all of the issues summarized from the Rand report apply to young adolescents. Problems of the handicapped ante- and postdate school experience; they are pervasive during the school years. We do not argue that as a period of development early adolescence should be served preferentially. We do argue that this period of development is poorly attended in terms of resources, programs, and especially understanding. Our area of concern focuses on those issues the handicapped child faces when approaching and experiencing the years of early adolescence.

We have had to depend frequently on what people in the field say rather than on "hard" data. No central agency reports information according to ages. The only medical service that collects and provides age breakdowns is the Crippled Children's Service. The authors of Rand Report R-1220 were interested in age only in terms of inequity of services across states, and particularly in terms of preschoolers and eighteen- to twenty-one-year-olds. Therefore, a great deal of the information reported in this section is "hearsay," based on self-reporting from practitioners, researchers, and agency administrators. The data are not otherwise available.

Physically Handicapped

This section will be concerned primarily with the state of services for physically handicapped young adolescents, although the problems of physical, emotional, and mental impairment are often intertwined, particularly in the field of education. We deal here with two major areas of concern: medical care, and social and emotional development.

Medical Care

The physically handicapped young adolescent generally has access to the same quality of medical care that is available to handicapped people of all ages. Relative to other services, access to quality medical care is generally good. The adolescent can receive medical attention for a specific physical need, whether one is suffering from a long term handicap or whether one is a recent victim of the frequent accidents that befall children and adolescents. However, like people of all ages, if one is multiply handicapped, there will probably be difficulty securing the coordinated and multifaceted services necessary for amelioration of the condition. Medical care in America is highly specialized, as are the various national handicap societies.

The adolescent, whether singly or multiply handicapped, however, faces an additional problem: the securing of medical care that takes into consideration the important developmental changes of early adolescence. The relatively small number of physicians who work primarily with adolescents, and the even smaller number who work with physically handicapped adolescents, are in general agreement that medical services for this age group are severely hampered by a serious lack of medical knowledge of the important and various physical changes of adolescence. "In general, the teenagers get lumped with either the children or the adults. The relatively small number of physicians working in Adolescent Medicine together with a limited interest in teenagers by psychiatrists has produced little information about this particular age group and constitutes a major gap in medical knowledge."[10] Dr. Robert Deisher, Professor of Pediatrics and Director of Adolescent Medicine at the University of Washington, and Dr. Michael Cohen, Professor at Montefiore Hospital, Bronx, report that there is proportionally less help for this area of medicine than for almost any other.

There are only 500 members of the Society for Adolescent Medicine. Dr. Adele Hofmann, who conducted a survey of fellowships in adolescent medicine in 1973 under the aegis of the Society for Adolescent Medicine, writes that there were, as of 1975, approximately fifty available fellowship slots in the United States and Canada in some thirty institutions. (There appears to be a greater press toward some form of certification in the field, according to Dr. Hofmann.) These few fellowships may be a source for training future trainers and researchers, but cannot be a viable source of health care providers. Therefore, since only 5 percent of generalists practicing family medicine, internal medicine, or pediatrics have received training in adolescent health care, many doctors like Dr. Hofmann feel that undergraduate and house staff training must include adolescent medicine. As is, "the vast preponderance of teen-agers in our country now receive care from those who deal with them out of self-taught experience or, barring that, frank ignorance."[11]

There is a serious lack of medical information on the effect developmental changes may have on handicapping conditions. Medical services to adolescents are also limited by a lack of understanding of the emotional problems involved. Dr. William A. Daniel, Jr., Chief of the Adolescent Unit of the University of Alabama Medical Center and past President of the Society for Adolescent Medicine, writes:

> I know of no other problems that are greater than those related to physical and mental handicaps of adolescents. Nor do I know of any conditions where less is being done. . . . I believe that the greatest lack in the handling of physical handicaps in young adolescents is an all too frequent neglect of psychological factors. In other words, physicians and others tend to treat the disease or disorder of the body and not the patient, they do not help the person.[12]

Dr. Harris Faigel suggests that there is not only a lack of understanding of the severe emotional stress of the adolescent but also an unwillingness on the part of many doctors and professional personnel to become involved on this level. "The most common compensatory mechanisms we see used by professionals to cope with the personal horror of being confronted with the handicapped teenager are withdrawal, denial and omniscience."[13] He also sees psychological understanding as a primary force in bringing about rehabilitation and insists that a coordinated approach is essential. "It is the team approach, whether the handicap is congenital or acquired and whether it is acquired early or late, with the team moving in early and developing a comprehensive medical, surgical, social, educational and psychological plan involving the patient, his extended family and his environment, which permits maximum rehabilitation."[14]

Seeing the patient as a whole person is a valid medical practice regardless of the age or developmental stage of the patient being treated. What makes it more difficult when working with adolescents is that most professionals haven't the resources at hand to deal with the particularly complex physical and emotional changes taking place in this age group. Dr. Evelyn Ayrault, while researching a book on handicapped teenagers, reported that she was unable to find any important study in the field and quoted a neurologist at New York University as saying, ". . . it is much easier to treat and habilitate the handicapped child and the aged than the handicapped teenager and adult. Teenagers and young adults create too many problems and as a group are not yet fully understood. Their group is one of the most difficult to get rehabilitation personnel to handle, evaluate, and train."[15]

Federal aid for medical services to handicapped youth is mandated primarily through Medicaid, Maternal and Child Health Service (MCHS), and Crippled Children's Services (CCS).

Federal, state, and local governments expend about $315 million annually for health services for handicapped youth; this comprises 6.7 percent of the total amount spent for all services for this group. The largest portion of this money is expended through Medicaid ($185 million) to poor and medically needy handicapped youth.[16]

As records under Medicaid are not kept separately by age or handicapping condition, statistics on care of age groups are not available, and it is impossible to assess with accuracy the exact role that Medicaid plays in serving the handicapped. There is no evidence that one age or one handicapping condition is being better cared for than another.

Evidence of national concern for early intervention resulted in the passage of an amendment in 1967 to establish Medicaid's EPSDT, providing for mandatory Early and Periodic Screening, Diagnosis and Treatment of all Medicaid eligible children. Although there are no reliable data on the evaluation of this program, all indications are that it is not being implemented with any consistency across the states.

The remaining government programs, however effective or ineffective they may be, do tend to concentrate their resources on prevention, early diagnosis, and treatment of young children. The interest in prevention, while relatively high in these *health* services, nevertheless represents a small percentage of the total expenditures for *all* types of services for handicapped youth. Rand report R-1220 states that of the $4.7 billion spent annually on handicapped youth (ages 0-21) less than $50 million have been targeted specifically for prevention activities.[17]

The emphasis of MCHS is on prevention of handicaps by (rubella) immunization, maternity care, well baby clinics and other services for young children. Most MCHS funds are not expended on handicapped youth, but rather are targeted toward screening and early intervention so as to promote health and prevent physical and mental handicaps.[18]

MCHS is considered by most observers to be very troubled at best, providing uneven services across states and resting on uneasy funding. In any event, the $25 million expended by MCHS represents a small proportion of the $1.110 billion total federal resources going to handicapped children and youth, and the $315 million for health services.

CCS furnishes quality medical care for a wide range of handicaps and is considered "a bright spot in services to handicapped generally," because "planning for the total needs of the individual handicapped child is a hallmark function of the CCS program."[19] The CCS program accounts for only eighty-eight million dollars, and also expends the largest portion of its money and energy on the very young. Twenty-nine and five-tenths percent of all handicapped youths (ages 0-21) treated in 1970 were under four years old, 59.6 percent were under ten. This is a nationwide mean. There is considerable inequity across states. At the same time, 22.9 percent were ten- to fourteen-year-olds. It is noteworthy that the one agency that is widely considered to be relatively successful does not overlook the young adolescent.

It is estimated that there are nine and one-half million handicapped persons under twenty-one years old in the United States. CCS services around 500,000 yearly, of whom 112,595 are ten- to fifteen-year-olds. This is a small percentage of the handicapped youth who could benefit from its services.

One exception to the general lack of interest in adolescents as a target group is the Veteran's Administration's program for handicapped children of disabled veterans. Rand report R-1220 states that benefits begin when the child reaches age fourteen, and include diagnostic and rehabilitative services, with major emphasis on occupational objectives. Approximately 200,000 adolescents have received benefits under this service through the years.[20]

There is no carefully formulated and coordinated program for handicapped youth in our country. R-1220 notes that the bulk of government spending for handicapped youth is targeted toward the poor (since it is expended primarily through welfare-associated programs such as Medicaid). As the rich can generally afford the best of private medical care, the middle income families may make up the poorest served portion of the population.[21] In addition, although the general pattern of federal funding for health services stresses the younger child, and though medical services for young children seem to be improving in the area of identification, careful referral and follow-up treatment seem sadly lacking.

Given the lack of organization and general ineffectiveness of many high priority programs serving the very young handicapped child, it is not realistic to assume that health services for young adolescents, who do not constitute a target age for any major health program, are likely to improve in the near future.

And yet, in speaking of physically handicapped adolescents as opposed to handicapped children, we are not talking about two different groups of young people with competing demands for medical services. We are talking frequently about the same people, whose need for services vary at different ages of their lives and whose handicapping conditions frequently call for a therapeutic approach geared to their developmental stage.

There are at least three groups of adolescents who require services specialized to their needs differentiated from those of early childhood: (1) those adolescents whose physical handicaps predated adolescence, but which might be affected by the complicated biological changes of this age; (2) young people who had apparently normal childhoods, but who experience developmental problems at the age of puberty; and (3) adolescent victims of accidents.

Rand report R-1220 mentions that there is "relatively little hard information on the many crucial biological and behavioral changes taking place during the adolescent years."[22] We have already summarized the state of research on "normal" adolescents; research on handicapped adolescents is even more scant. Without financial support and encouragement for research in the complicated area of adolescent development and without a sizable body of professionals trained and engaged in treating adolescents, there can be little hope of alleviating the severe trauma that faces these young people. They must handle the anxieties common to most "normal" youth while at the same time struggling with the frequently overwhelming obstacles caused by their particular abnormalities.

Social and Emotional Development of the Physically Handicapped Adolescent

Adolescence involves crucial self-examination, the first self-conscious effort of an individual to identify "selfness" and evaluate it against the other "selfs." The difficulty that a handicapped adolescent has in developing a sense of self-worth is inestimable. The body consciousness that is painful enough for the normal youth becomes excruciating to one already aware of limitations.[23] Ayrault points out that physical changes of adolescence are often more disturbing and threatening to the handicapped, that such changes may frighten them and emphasize their feelings of inadequacy.[24] It is more difficult for youths with physical disabilities to develop feelings of masculinity or femininity, and the question of a normal sex life causes considerable anxiety.

In addition to the pressures brought about by physical development, handicapped teenagers are also feeling, for perhaps the first time, the pressure of competition in the outside world. They are leaving the cocoon of the home and the child-centered classroom, and within the limitations of their particular handicap are beginning to participate in social and community activities. Their venture out of childhood is complicated by the fact that they may differ in various age levels—social, emotional, and learning—from their peers.[25] Most early adolescents are seeking and achieving a higher level of detachment from adults, but the handicapped are frequently still under the close protection of anxious parents. This overprotection prevents maturing and makes them even less acceptable to their peers.

As part of their growing consciousness of the community, physically handicapped adolescents begin to think of the future and wonder how they will be able to perform in a society that demands a high degree of self-sufficiency. Will they be able to care for themselves eventually? acquire an education? find and hold a job? marry? raise children?

At the same time that they are becoming more aware of the world around them, the world, unfortunately, is becoming more destructively aware of them. Some handicaps that pass almost unnoticed in young children become only too obvious in the teenager. Seizures or acts of violence of brain-damaged children will be a cause of concern for those around them, but will not arouse fear the way a teenager out of control will. "The teenage handicapped person *scares* people,"[26] and he or she is only too aware of the revulsion evoked. Not only do they have to cope with this rejection; they have to depend on less supportiveness than do younger children. (In a report of a reading program in a Wisconsin school system the director noted that the young blind children got considerably more instruction in mobility than the teenagers because they appealed to the maternal instincts of the professionals working with them.)

It is no surprise, then, that handicapped teenagers have a high incidence of personality problems: anxiety, depression, guilt, self-abasement, hostility, self-deception[27] and generalized fears. "Any handicap delays the orderly progression of maturation from one stage to the next, and tends to prolong or make adolescence permanent with its emotionally unsatisfactory imbalance between dependence and its aspiration of independence."[28]

If these young teenagers are to avoid "permanent adolescence," they are going to need considerable help—particularly in the form of enlightened counseling from parents, teachers, doctors, social workers, and indeed as much contact as possible with adolescent psychologists. They will need help in making a satisfactory adjustment to living day by day; they will need someone to answer questions about sex; someone to assess realistically the probable limits of their achievements; someone to encourage independence and suggest ways they can contribute to their world. They must be helped to avoid both fantasy and despair in forming a realistic self-concept and a real sense of self-worth.

At present in our society, only a small minority is receiving this help. The specialists in adolescent medicine and psychology are too few, and as we have pointed out, the knowledge doctors have is often too limited. The agencies that work with the handicapped center their efforts on the medical and educational needs of the young child and on the vocational training of the older adolescent and adult.

Dr. Richard Israel, Director of Professional Programs and Services of the Alexander Graham Bell Association of the Deaf, has remarked that their Parent Organization is composed mainly of parents of young children, because the advice and information the organization has concerning teenagers is scant. When parents have requested counseling for adolescent problems (dating, sex, etc.), the Association has been unable to find any specialists in the field with enough expertise to handle the questions.[29]

Dr. Henry Cobb, a member of the President's Committee on Mental Retardation and the editor of the Committee's final report, has stated that researchers have in general not been noticeably interested in the effects of handicapping conditions on personality formation. A small body of research does exist, but it tends for the most part to examine the more extreme deviations of behavior and psychopathology.[30]

The coordinated approach advocated by doctors of adolescent medicine seems essential. Research about adolescent development and its impact on handicapping conditions is the first requirement. There should be active support and encouragement for doctors and psychologists to specialize in adolescent development. There should be greater emphasis on the inclusion of adolescent medicine in undergraduate and house-staff medical training for all doctors. Medical knowledge should be effectively disseminated to teachers, parents, and counselors. Without this coordinated approach there will be more and more handicapped who remain in a permanent state of adolescence, incapable of reaching their full potential and inadequate to meet the demands of the adult world.

Emotionally Handicapped

Prevalence and Manifestation of Emotional Disturbance

In a sense we have a tendency to regard *all* adolescents as "handicapped"—awkward, untrustworthy, immature, inconsistent—and we are therefore inclined to ignore teenagers who have *real* problems.[31]

. . . a majority of young people live more or less uneventfully with the help of parents and peers through the hazards of puberty and adolescence, and eventually come into some degree of conformity with adult standards. A highly visible and significant number do not, however. Increasing attention must be paid to the psychology and sociological problems of youth in modern society. . . . I seriously doubt that we have a more important problem.[32]

Normative studies of adolescents indicate that emotional development of many adolescents is continuous and undisturbed. "The *normative* or *modal* adolescent appears also to be a psychologically *normal* adolescent."[33]

Masterson et al. compared symptom patterns in nonpatient adolescents and adults with adolescents being evaluated at the Payne Whitney Clinic. Symptom patterns were defined as including even mild anxiety or depression. Researchers found 17 percent of the nonpatient adolescents to be completely free from symptoms; 20 percent experienced moderate to severe impairments of school and/or social functioning.[34] As Weiner points out, the 20 percent parallels the incidence for adults found in other studies, as does the 17 percent figure. We can conclude that adolescents are no more likely than adults to suffer from psychological maladjustment.

Nevertheless, if approximately 20 percent of nonpatient adolescents are moderately or severely impaired psychologically, extreme care must be exercised in assuming that such symptom formation is merely transient, something to be outgrown, even normal. To view normative adolescence as a disturbed state is to run the risk of ignoring marked turmoil which is in fact deviant adjustment or psychopathology warranting professional attention. Masterson, conducting a follow-up study, "The Symptomatic Adolescent Five Years Later: He Didn't Grow Out of It," concluded that "Adolescence was but a way station in a long history of psychiatric illness. . . ."[35]

Many psychiatrists and other specialists take exception to this viewpoint, arguing that pejorative labeling of disturbances in adolescents is extremely harmful and unnecessary, since the observed disturbances are very often transient.[36]

Nevertheless, data from investigators like Masterson and others indicate the need for studying the causes and prevention of mental illness in adolescents, in order to help prevent permanent personality deterioration.

In 1965, investigators reported that one-fourth of all persons served by psychiatric outpatient clinics in the United States were ages ten to nineteen. Adolescents constituted between 30 and 40 percent of all patients seen in the psychiatric units of eastern United States general hospitals.[37]

Data reported in 1969 in Rand Report R-1220 (see Table 3-1) indicates that ten-to nineteen-year-olds represent approximately 28 percent of total terminations from outpatient psychiatric clinics. Fourteen percent are ten-to fourteen-year-olds.

Such figures reflect two polar issues in adolescent mental health referrals. On the one hand, many adolescents are not treated because their aberrant behavior is seen as normative. Thus, the figures may be unrepresentatively low. On the other hand, the sudden jump from the five-to-nine age group to the

Estimated Number of Total Terminations from Outpatient Psychiatric Clinics by Mental Disorder and Age, 1969

Diagnosis	All Ages	5	5-9	10-14	15-17	18-19	20-24	25-34	35-44	45-54	55-64	65-74	75+
Total	818,865	15,426	80,049	113,751	79,959	37,220	95,307	153,142	115,843	70,567	34,786	14,635	8180
Mental retardation	29,879	2,900	8,180	7,931	3,183	1,186	1,755	2,042	1,211	836	451	113	91
Organic brain syndromes associated with alcoholism	4,833	---	---	13	35	45	227	726	1,186	1,352	890	278	81
Organic brain syndromes associated with syphilis	552	---	13	82	20	7	13	53	57	84	138	52	33
Organic brain syndromes associated with drug or poison intoxication	2,770	2	20	94	371	357	765	486	283	182	123	52	35
Organic brain syndromes associated with cerebral arteriosclerosis and senile brain disease	5,388	---	3	5	4	2	5	35	61	229	1,002	2,165	1877
Other organic brain syndromes	16,746	904	3,598	2,552	981	474	1,141	1,664	1,488	1,386	1,234	762	562
Schizophrenia	100,784	480	1,717	2,897	3,880	4,331	14,333	27,158	23,381	14,189	6,000	1,777	641
Major affective disorders	12,519	7	13	25	69	70	443	1,045	2,043	3,834	3,466	1,218	286
Psychotic depressive reaction	5,470	6	23	85	141	128	477	1,021	1,185	1,001	847	390	166
Other psychoses	3,371	17	47	85	90	112	352	575	636	657	520	217	63
Depressive neuroses	70,340	89	507	1,967	2,584	2,854	10,626	19,504	14,682	9,467	5,410	1,983	667
Other neuroses	56,060	218	2,679	4,581	2,685	2,562	9,108	15,865	10,056	4,892	2,237	694	483
Personality disorders	124,455	420	4,914	13,769	12,996	7,281	22,192	31,441	18,980	8,608	2,477	840	537
Alcohol addiction	17,188	3	2	22	64	91	566	3,373	5,696	4,861	2,074	347	89
Drug dependence	7,558	---	2	122	648	867	2,127	2,134	1,013	401	152	65	27
Psychophysiologic disorders	5,319	35	317	502	372	207	616	1,126	1,018	614	345	128	39
Transient situational disturbance and adjustment reaction to infancy	144,089	3,115	27,610	41,326	29,822	7,924	9,262	11,154	7,337	3,545	1,453	833	708
Other	211,544	7,230	30,404	37,693	22,014	8,722	21,299	33,740	25,530	14,429	5,967	2,721	1795

Source: *Mental Retardation Sourcebook of the Department of Health, Education and Welfare*, DHEW Publication No. (05) 73-81, Sept. 1972, p. 91, as reported by James S. Kakalik et al., eds., *Services for Handicapped Youth: A Program Overview*, R-1220 (Santa Monica, Cal.: Rand Corporation, 1973), p. 255.

ten-to-fourteen age group reported in Table 3-1 may reflect communities' and parents' tolerance levels. As Cohen et al. point out, behavior tolerated in childhood is no longer acceptable as children approach adulthood and are judged according to standards of adult behavior. Thus, a number of quite disturbed children are ignored until they have grown well into adolescence. What has been accepted as childishness or immaturity in the child suddenly becomes cause for alarm in the adolescent.

Acting-out adolescents are therefore more likely to be referred to help than are the depressed or withdrawn. Some secondary symptom, like school failure, is usually required before the depressed adolescent is perceived as needing help. Anorectic adolescents often suffer severe physical debilitation before referral is deemed appropriate.[38] Society appears to be much more deeply concerned, even preoccupied, with antisocial behavior, especially when related to sex, drugs, and delinquency.[39]

This is where federal and state allocations are found most heavily, both for research and for programs. The level of funding for programs and services for unwed mothers and drug abuse follows the expected pattern of being reactive to perceived social crises.

Rand report R-1220 states that the population and cost data of programs primarily intended for the mentally handicapped (the authors lump together the mentally retarded and ill) are not well known, "even by those having direct operational responsibility for programs." Quality evaluation is almost nonexistent. Coordination among "the baffling array" of programs is more rhetorical than real. Research is not large-scale, nor is it child-specific. The authors characterize the systems model appropriate to describing federal programs for the mentally handicapped as a "disorganization" model.[40]

In the following pages we will discuss the dilemma of the adolescent whose problems result in sex-related problems, in suicide (the unacknowledged adolescent crisis), or in drug dependence. Since antisocial behavior or delinquency is discussed in a separate section, we will not deal with it here, even though such behavior is often linked to emotional disturbance in some form.

Sex-Related Problems

One of the most personally perplexing changes occurring during puberty is sexual maturation. Suddenly the unknown, taboo-ridden world of adults applies to one's own experiences. The biological upheaval is difficult enough to cope with strictly on that level, but the overlay of anxieties can lead to socially unacceptable behavior in the young adolescent. Even more serious, the behavior may ultimately be personally unacceptable but entrapping.

In their report *Normal Adolescence: Its Dynamics and Impact*, the Group for the Advancement of Psychiatry state that in the years of early adolescence, the greatest preoccupation is with the physical aspects of sex rather than with an emotional relationship. They report that the surge of sexual and aggressive tendencies leads not uncommonly to group masturbation and homosexual activities. "At this age homosexual behavior more appropriately should be viewed as a temporary defense against the fears associated with the move toward full heterosexual relationship." Another defense, temporary or permanent, against the fears of puberty is asceticism, but the Group feels that "as his ego begins to cope with, assimilate, and integrate the changes brought by puberty, the adolescent turns increasingly toward the opposite sex."[41] They view late adolescence as a period of greater stability of the biological process, permitting a shift of love interest and real emotional involvement.

In her study of adolescent girls, Konopka found no great "sex revolution" but more openness in discussing sex. Premarital sex past age fourteen is considered acceptable by most of the respondents, so long as it occurs in a loving context. Casual sex is usually rejected as demeaning. Many would consider these findings indicative of a "revolution."

A watershed age appears around fourteen years. Sexual intercourse before fourteen is seen as too early, alarming. Above fourteen or fifteen, it is accepted as more usual. Experiences before fourteen are usually disagreeable, often forced, taking place in the home or while running away.[42]

Dr. Lucie Rudd, Chief of Roosevelt Hospital's Adolescent Clinic in New York City, testified before a Senate committee about the speed with which increased activity is affecting younger adolescents: "You know and I know that the federal law requires a welfare recipient, who has had a baby, to be given, without charge, contraceptive advice. But do you know the age range of the pregnant girls today? Three years ago they were seventeen and eighteen. In 1971, they are fourteen or fifteen. . . ."[43]

The psychological aspects behind pregnancy are complicated by varying subcultural norms. It must be determined on an individual basis whether pregnancy in a young adolescent is a symptom of emotional disturbance. Counseling and guidance are required to sort out the facts and circumstances leading to the pregnancy. If a girl has become pregnant for reasons other than carelessness, investigation into the cause is indicated so that motives that might require professional intervention may be unearthed.

The emotional and social needs of young unwed mothers have been recognized in recent years, and some fine services are available. While it is true that many schools still require dismissal of the pregnant school girl, some do not, and some districts have established special schools for unwed mothers. Her education more or less uninterrupted, the young mother also has the advantage of being with other girls experiencing the same problems.

The federal government funds many programs for unwed pregnant teenagers, such as the Children and Youth Projects of the Maternal and Child Health Service. The rationale underlying programs may in some cases have nothing to do with the needs of young adolescents. Many are geared solely to assuring the health of the newborn baby. Some are motivated by desires to diminish welfare rolls, or to reduce school dropout rates and concomitant problems. Nevertheless, it is noteworthy that when the federal government, even in its "disorganization" model, assigns priority to an area for intervention, programs spring up at state and local levels that have the potential for diminishing stress and even for enriching the lives of young adolescents.

Abortion is a different issue. With relaxed abortion laws becoming more prevalent, abortion has become more acceptable as an alternative to pregnancy, but retains antisocial connotations. What this means, psychologically, should be considered. Counseling must be provided.[44] A more positive approach to unwanted pregnancy is sex education, including social information about contraception for adolescents.[45]

The pregnant adolescent girl has more options today, and social institutions have become more responsive, but further educative processes in pregnancy prevention are needed for the *young* adolescent girl. This will not happen until we can accept the statistics confirming earlier sexual activity. (Konopka found girls reporting that sex information, although more available than heretofore in the schools, is often late and inadequate.[46])

In addition, since sexual acting out is socially acceptable in young males, societal intervention is deemed appropriate only when such acts as rape or child molesting are apprehended. Programs that deal with pregnant adolescents usually ignore the adolescent male participant.[47] Changes are required to give young boys the care they require.

And all of this will not be adequate if we deal only with those manifestations of sexual development that we find socially abhorrent—teenage pregnancy and abortion. Other manifestations of sexual maladjustment, for instance the growing incidence of anorexia nervosa in young adolescent girls, require societal attention in the form of funding for research and for psychiatric/medical care. One can only hope that such psychological problems as anorexia need not become as epidemic in proportions as abortions and drug misuse before they receive such funding.

Suicide

Although sexual acting out is openly acknowledged as an adolescent problem, and one receiving considerable federal funding, suicide is not. Vital statistics of the United States for 1965 reported suicide as the fifth leading cause of death among fifteen- to nineteen-year-olds in the United States (the first four causes being accidents, malignant neoplasms, major cardiovascular-renal disease, and homicide). In 1975, Cohen et al. reported that statistics show the peak time for suicide attempts as being between ages fifteen and nineteen, with the incidence of suicide now having increased to the fourth most common cause of death for this age group.[48]

Weiner reports that while there are six to ten suicide attempts for every suicide in the general population, various studies of adolescents (10-19 year olds) report attempt-to-completion ratios of 50:1, 100:1, and even 120:1. In addition, given parental attempts to conceal attempts and professionals' inclination to disguise them as accidents, any such figures are at best rough estimates, and perhaps gross underestimations.[49]

Adolescent boys differ from girls in the frequency with which they attempt and complete suicide. Weiner reports a 3.4:1 ratio of boys to girls in completed suicides, and a reversed 3.5:1 ratio of girls to boys in attempts. Both boys and girls prefer hanging and shooting as means for completed suicides, ingestion as a means for attempts. These choices parallel adult patterns.

Family disorganization, escalating problems, behavior indicating alienation from "significant others," and the failure of previous suicide attempts to alleviate stressful situations are factors repeatedly reported as preceding adolescent suicide attempts. The importance of what Weiner calls "communicative and manipulative intent" to adolescent suicidal behavior is underscored by the statistic from one study that 89 percent of adolescent suicide attempters make their first attempt at home.[50]

No one suggests that one should consider every depressed, irritable, withdrawn, or rebellious adolescent as potentially self-destructive. At the same time, since depressive behavior, including disrupted eating, sleeping, social, and academic patterns usually precede adolescent suicidal behavior, it has been suggested that recognition of this "syndrome of adaptive decompensation" would help detect 70 percent of impending suicide attempts.[51]

There is widespread failure to recognize the seriousness of an adolescent's suicide attempt when the physical consequences are negligible. Instead, even the most seemingly manipulative or offhand attempt must be seen as a distressed gesture of communication. Suicide kills. Attempted suicide destroys. It is one of the major areas of acting out to emerge in adolescence, one whose incidence has been increasing.

Drug and Alcohol Abuse

In some communities drug abuse among school children reaches a peak when they are in the seventh and eighth grades, or when they are thirteen and fourteen years old. The abuse levels off as early as the ninth grade and may decline in later high school years.

An incredible amount of literature has emerged in an effort to analyze the effects drugs have on adolescents. Crisis centers and drug abuse programs have sprung up all over the country. Parents have been shown the drugs at PTA meetings; major newspapers have given vivid descriptions of the "high" of particular drugs; television programs have been devoted to all aspects of the problem. This emphasis on drugs by the media has done a great deal to enhance the value of drug use as a status device, especially among the younger, junior high-aged student.

Konopka found that when girls take drugs, they may often start around ages twelve or thirteen, but also earlier. No girl reported starting later than age seventeen. One-half reported never having used drugs, but most are tolerant of those who do.

The largest number of girls in Konopka's sample have experimented only a few times. The overwhelming majority who have tried hard drugs consider their effects negative.

What is most important in Konopka's report is not numbers of users, but the meaning that drugs and alcohol have for adolescent girls. Drugs and alcohol are considered a very important personal issue with deep and private significance, whether the girl is a user or a nonuser.[52]

Experimenting with drugs is not necessarily an indication of emotional disturbance, and young adolescents who are occasional users are not the youths who end up in a crisis clinic. They are vulnerable, however, to the "halo effect" mentioned earlier; that is, the more drugs are talked about and taught about, the more likely they are to use them. Many observers therefore conclude that the antidrug campaigns in the classroom have had a boomerang effect. This conclusion should be borne in mind as alcohol programs become more numerous.

Many psychiatrists regard alcohol and drug abuse as a cry for help. The abuse can be responsible in early adolescence for delaying maturation–the youth is able to postpone coping with physical and emotional realities. Proper treatment and counseling are then essential for continued healthy development.

Some researchers claim that alcohol and drug abuse has to be attacked as a group problem, not as individual deviant behavior. "There seems to be nothing that sets [the adolescent drug user] apart from his peers physically, mentally, or emotionally, nor does he seem to be different from his counterparts of previous generations in these respects. Rather he seems to be a normal adolescent that is behaving in a normal manner to a group that exhibits deviant behavior. This is exactly the opposite of the position of the adult addict, who operates outside of the commonly accepted behavior patterns of his peer group. This, then, is properly a problem of group pathology, and an adequate treatment modality must concentrate on the group in order to help the individual."[53]

There is little reason to restate all of the societal ills and pressures that have been cited as major factors in drug use. It is more important to ask what is being done–what services a young person can utilize in a drug, alcohol, or any other crisis.

Intervention and Treatment

Clinics do not receive handsome funding allocations, and yet an important service available to the troubled adolescent is the accessibility of an adolescent clinic. Minnesota Systems Research conducted a survey of adolescent health care provisions. They were able to analyze the services of forty-three clinics, and found, among other characteristics, that only 35 percent of the programs provide or have access to hotline or crisis telephone services. If the program is associated with a children's hospital, a private practice, or the military, it is less likely to provide this service than is any other type of program. They also found that 65 percent of the programs provide rap or peer group sessions as a method for information and problem sharing, and for group counseling. Ninety-eight percent of the programs provide psychological counseling, 84 percent provide treatment.[54]

At this point, aside from the few hospital-based adolescent clinics in existence, the other available services for emotionally troubled adolescents, besides private treatment, are free clinics, hotlines, and school guidance counselors. These are limited, controversial, sometimes priceless and sometimes dangerous sources of help.[55]

The Joint Commission on Mental Health of Children, a nongovernmental, multidisciplinary, nonprofit organization, conducted a study of mental health services in this country for all children and youth, authorized by Congress and largely funded through grants from the National Institute for Mental Health. In their report they evaluated the state of services for adolescents. They summarize, "To put it briefly, insofar as our mental health care is concerned, as a society we fail our teen-agers at almost every level."[56] The Clinical Committee of the Joint Commission, in making its final recommendations, names two priorities in development of services, preschool children and adolescents, and stresses the importance of gearing mental health services to the developmental age of the patient.[57]

Members of the Joint Commission found that children under fifteen are the only age group that has recently shown an increase in first admission rates to mental hospitals. Most of these are adolescents. Approximately 13 percent of these hospitals provide separate units for children; 26 percent provide services but not separate units.[58]

In noting that facilities treating adolescents are presently taxed beyond capacity because of the recent upsurge of numbers applying for treatment and because of community pressure to remove deviants from circulation, the Committee admits that resources to meet the needs of this group in a one-to-one therapy situation simply do not exist. Their recommendations include the conversion of large, ineffective institutions into small residential treatment centers, with boys and girls on the same campus, receiving intensive care. For youth who are not dangerously disturbed, the recommended treatment would take place in outpatient clinics and in small residential community treatment homes. They report that given the limited resources of money and manpower, community mental health programs that attack social problems and prevent serious mental illness may be the most effective economic effort our society can make.

In fact, very little is known about the services available to disturbed adolescents. We do not know to what extent treatment is offered in community mental health centers, by free clinics, hotlines, etc., or what the general quality of such treatment is. It remains an area for investigation.

What we do know is that adolescents do not seek treatment easily. "Anxious to be like his peers, he is not likely to declare himself deviant and seek correction. Aware of physical changes as well as emotional turmoil, he is not well able to sort out warning signals which indicate a need for help. He is particularly unwilling to seek help from the adult world, which is often uncompromising, demanding control and performance at a time when these are difficult to achieve."[59] In addition, the adult world may be unwilling to recognize the adolescent's age-appropriate right to make decisions for himself. Therefore, as Cohen et al. conclude, the less structured programs run by young people themselves are so attractive, whatever their successes and failures. They meet the two preconditions that the adolescent may well set if he is to seek help: confidentiality and personal control over the limits of participation and investigation.[60]

(A study of adolescent health attitudes of 5,600 youths from the Twin City Metropolitan Area indicates, however, that 41.9 percent of adolescents turned to parents or guardians when seeking help with health problems. Their medical choices are traditional even in an area rich in alternative resources.[61])

In describing the adolescent's pathway through the mental health system, Cohen et al. discuss the mutual distrust between adolescent and therapist. The adolescent who has not sought treatment himself and is generally wary of adults resists establishing a trusting relationship with the therapist. The therapist is aware that "the developmentally fragmented personality of the early adolescent often is not up to the rigors of in-depth treatment. Until recently, and even now in many settings, there has been hesitation . . . about taking on the emotionally disturbed younger adolescent. Even mental health professionals often find the seethings of adolescence too contagious to deal with at close quarters."[62] While the older adolescent can engage in in-depth treatment, the younger adolescent finds himself without a place in the system, too old for child-appropriate play therapy techniques and too young for the verbal interplay of adult treatment.[63]

Psychotherapy for the adolescent who is integrating new biological, social, and emotional experiences, and experimenting temporarily with various coping styles, requires different techniques from psychotherapy that involves reconstruction of personality style. The young adolescent is not developmentally prepared to have defenses stripped away to rework previous experience or to achieve deep insights. The present is too much with him.[64]

When the comparatively superficial crisis intervention from open-door clinics, the adolescent crisis unit, and the neighborhood-based, nonprofessional drop-in crisis unit proves insufficient, few resources are available for ongoing treatment. The chronically troubled adolescent may be extruded without adequate treatment from the mental health system and become engaged in the one ever-present institution, the courts.[65] In Connecticut, for instance, the peak ages of referral to the juvenile court system are from thirteen to fifteen, but only 10 to 15 percent of the referrals are accused of delinquent behavior that is threatening harm to society.

Whether the referral is made to the mental health system or to the juvenile courts depends in large measure on the race and financial status of the adolescent. It also depends on parental motivation, which may be based on the fear and anger aroused by the evocative behavior of maturing adolescents, recalling for many parents the discomforts of their own adolescence and leading to loss of control.[66] When control is the motivating force, referral to the courts as against the mental health system depends on parental sophistication. In any event, the motive is not lost on the adolescent. The adolescent learns too often that "the aim of the mental health system . . . is to control his behavior, not to help him develop as an individual."[67]

Several observers note that clinical neglect of disturbed adolescents stems not only from parental and personal assumptions and biases but from the reluctance of clinicians to accept adolescents as patients. As a result, there is relatively limited clinical information about young adolescents. There are, as not only clinicians but any practitioner working with this age group will attest, fewer people as interesting to work with, but there are certainly easier ways to make a living.[68]

Adolescents are the largest users of psychiatric clinics in the United States; however, only one-third actually receive treatment. There are, then, "many lost opportunities to help young people avert subsequent, more serious psychological breakdown."[69]

Mentally Handicapped

Mental Retardation

The mentally retarded adolescent faces problems different from the normal adolescent during the stressful period of the onset of puberty. These problems are summarized by Hutt and Gibby:

From the psychological standpoint there are important problems during puberty. The increased sexual drives and the great importance attached by society to the development of secondary sexual characteristics make unusually difficult the readjustment of the mentally retarded child, whose capacity for understanding and dealing with these phenomena is limited.

The gap between the retarded child and other children of his own age widens during puberty and is more and more evident both to others and to himself.[70]

It is during puberty that the retarded person begins to be rejected by social institutions, adults, and peers.

Society deals with mentally retarded children in two basic categories: educable mental retardation (EMR) and trainable mental retardation (TMR). Even though states tend to vary in their definitions of these terms, the division is usually derived from the individual's score on a standardized intelligence test. Most systems regard mental retardation as an IQ score of below 75; a score of 50 to 75 is regarded as EMR, a score of 25 to 50 as TMR status.

Acknowledging definitional problems, the 1970 White House Conference on Children estimated that there are 2.5 million mentally retarded children under the age of twenty in the United States. Seventy-five percent were estimated to be mildly retarded (EMR), 15 percent moderately retarded (TMR), 8 percent severely retarded (some TMR), and 2 percent profoundly retarded.[71] R.W. Conley is the only researcher of mental retardation we have seen referred to who considers data at all by age: 679,000 aged zero to four and 1,916,000 aged five to nineteen.[72] The Maternal and Child Health Service provides a breakdown by age of patients served in mental retardation clinics (see Table 3-2). The data are not particularly helpful, since tables using generic categories of causation report the largest number of patients under "Uncertain Cause." Forty-nine and one-tenth percent of the 79.6 percent who were medically classified had unknown causes and on most charts the category "other" is well represented. As R-1220 says, although many youth are being served under the Mental Retardation Clinic program, we really don't know who they are, what they are suffering from, and what they need.[73]

For a good many EMR individuals, the labeling of the mental impairment may persist only during the school years. In fact, it has been said that two-thirds of the adolescents and adults in this subcategory lose this label when they leave school.[74]

Very little information is available about adolescents who are classified as TMR. The interest, at least in reports, appears to be solely in the EMR individual.

Very little information is available about an area of great concern to practitioners: the sexual vulnerability of the mentally retarded adolescent. Lack of self-knowledge and self-control, compounded by others' insensitivity, makes the retardate a target for sexual abuse. This is a subject widely discussed among professionals as meriting further attention.

Finally, not much is known about the impact one's previous history of

Table 3-2
Number and Percent of Patients Served in Mental Retardation Clinics by Their Status and Age

	All Patients		New Patients		Other Patients	
Age Group	Total	Percent	Total	Percent	Total	Percent
All ages	60,859	100.0	27,988	100.0	32,871	100.0
Under 6 months	772	1.3	598	2.1	174	0.5
6-11 months	1,193	2.0	832	3.0	361	1.1
1-2 years	5,903	9.7	3,400	12.1	2,503	7.6
3-4 years	10,353	17.0	5,325	19.0	5,028	15.3
5-9 years	27,422	45.1	12,058	43.1	15,364	46.7
10-14 years	12,031	19.9	4,705	16.8	7,376	22.4
15-17 years	2,146	3.5	743	2.7	1,403	4.3
18-20 years	989	1.6	327	1.2	662	2.0
Median age	7.2	–	6.6	–	7.7	–

Source: U.S. Department of Health, Education and Welfare, *Mental Retardation Clinic Services, 1971*, Maternal and Child Health Service, 1972. Reported from: James S. Kakalik et al., *Services for Handicapped Youth: A Program Overview*, R-1220 (Santa Monica, Cal.: Rand Corporation, 1973), p. 244

failure has as one approaches adolescence. The role that such a steady accretion of failures plays during the identity-seeking years is not a research area we see being explored.

Learning Disabled

Presentations at the 1974 International Conference of the Association for Children with Learning Disabilities in Houston gave indication of the lack of attention being paid to the learning disabled young adolescent. From more than one hundred papers presented at the conference, only ten pertained to adolescents, and the majority of those dealt with the role of learning disabilities in juvenile delinquency.

There are many different definitions of learning disabilities. According to federal guidelines, specific learning disabilities are disorders in one or more of the basic psychological processes involved in understanding or using language, spoken or written. These disorders may manifest themselves in imperfect ability to listen, think, speak, read, write, spell, or do mathematic calculations. These include perceptual handicaps, brain injury, minimal brain dysfunction, dyslexia, and developmental aphasia. The term "learning disabilities" does not refer to children who have learning problems caused primarily by visual, hearing, or motor handicaps, mental retardation, emotional disturbance, or environmental disadvantage.[75]

The young adolescent with a learning disability may have suffered from a long history of failure, even though his intelligence is usually average or above average.

On the other hand, some disabilities may not surface until junior high school. A bright child can compensate for deficiencies in the early school years. When school achievement begins to depend more and more heavily on reading proficiency, after elementary school, the influence of brain dysfunction combined with more difficult school work may begin to take a serious toll.

The opposite may also occur. By adolescence, many of the characteristic features of neurologic deficits may be masked by impulsiveness and irritability. Minimal brain damage thus masquerades as a personality disorder, or may be seen as being "normal adolescence," varying with the intensity of the behavior aberration and the biases of the observer.

Or the increased emotional and social control gained developmentally may benefit the learning disabled adolescent. Thus, parents will often be advised to wait and see if the child "grows out of it" during adolescence.

Weiner cautions that although adolescent development may mitigate behavior manifestations of minimal brain dysfunction, there are adolescent behavior patterns frequently associated with organic impairment that should flag our attention: rigid, stereotyped behavior patterns; limited ambiguity tolerance and a high level of anxiety in unstructured situations; difficulty in grasping complex aspects of interpersonal relationships; inability to distinguish in social situations between the important and trivial; and unmangeability.[76]

Rigidity, anxiety, poor judgment, and impulsiveness are not unique to organic brain syndromes, but must not be ignored as indications of brain dysfunction in the underachieving adolescent.

Treatment of the learning disabled adolescent should usually combine remedial education, family counseling, perhaps psychotherapy and drugs. Remedial education needs to begin in the early grades. The learning disabled adolescent whose problems were not identified earlier is usually not considered a promising candidate for special school services. If the disability is not identified before age ten, the chance of rehabilitation may be only one in four, worse than that for the seriously mentally ill.

Nevertheless, as Weiner says, remedial classes or individual tutoring in subject areas where cognitive disabilities cause deficiencies can be of benefit, as can a curriculum tailored to take maximum advantage of the adolescent's strengths and to minimize the impact of deficiencies.[77]

Programs have begun on a limited basis only recently at the elementary school level; junior high schools often do not provide a continuing program. Of the twenty-four demonstration projects in twenty-one states funded by the Learning Disabilities Act of 1969 through the U.S. Office of Education, only three dealt exclusively with secondary school children.[78] Thus, age-specific programs for the young adolescent are sorely lacking. A growing number of exemplary projects are being funded for young children with learning disabilities. When programs are continued into secondary schools, the overwhelming sense of hopelessness on the part of these adolescents, compounded by the lack of training on the part of their teachers, leads often to an unsuccessful experience. What has been accomplished, then, is labeling without effective intervention.

Special Education

Rand Report R-1220 estimates that in our country about 9 percent of our school-age youth need special education of some kind, and that only 59 percent of these handicapped students receive it.[79] Funding priorities among age groups tend to be established by each state. About 63 percent of the federal funds go to preschools and elementary schools, with only 30 percent devoted to secondary schools (junior and senior highs), and about 7 percent to postsecondary or higher education. These are estimates, since budget or population breakdowns are not available by age groups for one-third of the total expenditures. The federal government encourages schools to educate the very young by paying 90 percent of the cost of experimental preschool programs for handicapped youth.[80]

R-1220 reports that the retarded stand a better chance of receiving educational services than do any other handicapped children. Forty-three percent of all federal dollars for handicapped youth are spent on the mentally retarded. (Speech impaired, emotionally disturbed, and learning disabled receive 10 to 11 percent each.)

R-1220 reports, as do almost all other sources, that the number of youth receiving special education services is woefully inadequate, and varies markedly across the various states and the various types of handicaps. Since the federal government supplies only 12 percent of funds targeted for handicapped youth, it does not have the leverage needed to induce state and local governments to increase the quantity or improve the quality of special education services. To compound the problems, data for planning are lacking. Estimates of the population in need, numbers served, cost of services, and impact of services on handicapped are based on inadequate information.[81]

Even data according to category of handicaps have been sorely lacking. As Dr. Alan Abeson at the Information Clearinghouse for Exceptional Children (CEC) says, this data collection is important because most of the existing statistics are either incorrect or misleading. He attributes this largely to the difficulty in collecting information from all states, each of which uses different methods of classification and different nomenclature. Abeson expects that there will be vast improvement by 1977 in the data collection with the implementation of The Education of All Handicapped Children Act of 1975 (Public Law 94-142), which requires reporting as to category.

Despite the considerable barriers, because of recent research and educational innovations the handicapped child in public school in America has a significantly better chance of being in an educational situation suitable to personal needs than a decade ago. It has been estimated that in 1966 only 35 percent of the handicapped children were receiving special education, as compared to 59 percent in 1972. More children are being served better, particularly in the lower grades. Special teachers for children with reading problems, visual and perceptual problems, and communication problems, as well as physical education and media specialists, offer supportive services to elementary classroom teachers in many areas of America today. Although there is often a team of teachers and specialists tailoring programs to meet individual needs, the learning situation usually takes place within a confined classroom that has the possibility of being comfortable and familiar. There is usually one teacher responsible for the overall development of the child. It is a more child-centered classroom than later grades provide.

What happens to these children when they leave this environment and move into the junior high school at about age twelve? The first problems they encounter may be physical ones: if they have orthopedic or visual problems, they may have trouble getting from one class to another on time, or indeed in handling stairs at all; if they have hearing problems, they may be unaware of the many bells and signals that mark the schedule progression. Will they be able to carry their books from class to class? Will they be able to see the blackboard clearly or hear the teacher in a large classroom? They may also have difficulty moving to the more abstract thinking required by subject-oriented material. They will be dealing with the emotional effects of prior failures. And inevitably they will be undergoing the complex emotional changes related to the onset of puberty. They will face these problems usually without the presence of the single teacher who, in elementary school, was aware of their needs and could potentially construct a reasonably comfortable situation for them. They will have, instead, a series of teachers, each of whom probably sees at least 150 students a day.

It seems unexplainably difficult to find out just what does become of these young handicapped adolescents. Many, of course, drop out of school. Others move into residential schools more geared to their particular needs. Of those that remain, how many are able to get the kind of instruction they need? The junior high can be a nightmare for handicapped youth. Nearly all junior high programs are seriously deficient in adequately trained counselors to arrange educational and counseling programs suited to the needs of the handicapped.

One important study on mental retardation, encompassing a six- to twenty-year age span, bears watching. This is the longitudinal project at Temple University under the direction of Beth Stevens.[82] The study by Stevens and her colleagues compares retarded and nonretarded youngsters through three different age groupings—six to ten, ten to fourteen, and fourteen to eighteen. The project covers an eight-year span. In an analysis of moral conduct, Stevens and her colleagues have found that there is an arrestation in development in retarded subjects during the ages of twelve through sixteen. However, the retarded subjects sixteen through twenty continue to make gains, although not at the same rate as the normal subjects. This is an extremely provocative finding, since most observers would tend to conclude, on the basis of a four-year plateau in development, that the retardate had reached maximum potential and should leave school. Stevens's findings suggest that such a decision, made during early adolescence, may deprive the older adolescent of the benefits of schooling when developmental gains can be expected to resume.

Dr. Henry Cobb of the President's Committee on Mental Retardation acknowledges that research and educational efforts have generally tended to center on young children, with a fair amount of interest in vocational training for adolescents above age fifteen. The difficulty in discovering trends, highlights, or exemplary programs in special education for young adolescents stems simply from what Dr. Cobb describes as a gap in service.[83]

There is, in addition, considerable disillusionment with special education in general. Dr. William A. Daniel has written that special education has been a failure. Adolescents are not given really "special" education, there are not enough teachers, enough dollars, or enough vocational programs.[84]

Before a suitable curriculum can be implemented, there has to be valid research to establish what youths of various handicaps can and should learn during adolescence and how this can be taught. There also have to be trained teachers to handle the multiple problems of these students. As the pressure for mainstreaming handicapped children into the regular classroom grows, higher education falls more and more behind, failing to train teachers for the changes in elementary and secondary education. Until this gap is remedied, localities will be dependent upon in-service work with classroom teachers, and will be looking for specialists who, at this point, are still groping with the problems posed by handicapping conditions and adolescent education. And in the end, there has to be a social commitment to providing meaningful work for these adolescents when their schooling is completed.

Staff and Staff Training

Although educators agree that there is generally less special instruction in the junior high than at any other level, the difference is extremely difficult to measure quantitatively and qualitatively. The Division of Personnel Preparation of the Bureau of Education for the Handicapped (BEH) has collected data on the numbers of special education teachers working at the preschool, elementary, and secondary levels; the data have not been collated, for want of funds.[85] The division of special education in one state admitted it kept no records on the percentage of teachers working at each grade level, and suggested that the only means of discovering the actual count would be to contact each individual superintendent of schools in each district. The "unofficial guess" of the office was that between two-thirds and four-fifths of the special education teachers were working in the elementary schools.

Although we do not have these concrete statistics, we do have access to two reports based on the School Staffing Survey conducted in the spring of 1970 by the National Center for Educational Statistics. These surveys, Metz and Cramer's *Professional Staff for the Handicapped in Local Public Schools*,[86] and Borinsky's *Provision of Instruction to Handicapped Pupils in Local Public Schools*,[87] offer projected statistics based on a representative sample of 1,996 public elementary and secondary schools.

Table 3-3, from the study by Metz and Cramer, shows the number of professional personnel and the type of instructional situation by handicapping condition and by level of school. In every category except instruction for the blind, the table shows a significant concentration of professional staff at the elementary school level. (Rand report R-1220 notes that more per capita is spent on the blind than on any other handicap.) Once we know the numbers of professionals working at each level, we can assess comparative coverage by examining the numbers of handicapped children to be taught at each level.

Table 3-4, from the study by Borinsky, reveals that there are, indeed, considerably more handicapped children in the elementary schools than in the secondary schools. Perhaps the elementary schools did an outstanding job in correcting these handicaps. Or perhaps the problems are not being identified in older children. Or perhaps secondary schools demand too much and offer too little, forcing students to drop out or to change to a residential school.

The important figures on Table 3-4 for this report, however, are the ones that reveal that although there are fewer identified handicapped secondary students, there also is less chance of their receiving any special instruction at all. In every type of handicapping condition except mental retardation, the percentage of secondary students needing special instruction and not receiving it is greater than for younger children. One should also note that these statistics do not distinguish between the junior and senior high schools, so there is no way to determine whether the young adolescents are receiving more, the same, or less special attention than the older adolescents.

Some insight into the priorities of special education as it exists in most states, and on the adequacy of teacher preparation for it, can be gleaned from examining certification requirements for teachers of the handicapped in the various states. A few require no special training at all, but the general qualification is a certificate in elementary or secondary education, plus twelve to thirty hours of special education in the handicap area. There are few requirements that the special education courses be centered on the age level at which the teacher will be working, and little indication that methods courses dealing with the particular handicapping areas take into consideration the developmental stage of the student at all. For instance, in almost all states the certification is called Special Education, not Special Elementary Education or Special Secondary Education.

Even more revealing are the courses either required or suggested for certification. While twenty-four states specify child psychology as a requisite, and seventeen specify child growth and development, only four states *suggest* adolescent psychology as a requirement for secondary teachers and no states require training in adolescent growth and development.[88]

Therefore, there are not only fewer teachers of special education in the secondary schools; there is every indication that the ones who are there have had less preparation for coping with the particular needs of their students than have the teachers working with younger children.

An argument can be made on the basis of market mechanisms that, given the surfeit of teachers projected through the 1980s, the demand for adolescent special education services will be met at the very least by self-interested individuals concerned for their jobs. This change has not taken place, nor do we see any trend towards its occurrence. The demand is hypothetical. There will be no movement in this direction until pressures from unmet demands are felt at the priority-setting level. At this point, there are unmet needs unaccompanied by mobilized demand, so we anticipate no remedy.

An Emerging Trend: Mainstreaming

Although special education for handicapped elementary school students may generally be said to be more satisfactory than the offerings in the junior high, there is growing national discontent with the entire concept of separate special education classes. In many cases, separation from the mainstream has been shown to be a stigmatizing process and detrimental to the child's progress. Incorrect diagnosis has frequently placed children in totally unsuitable and limiting educational environments. Many children in separate classes who undeniably need special instruction nevertheless suffer from lack of exposure to the many-faceted social institutions they could encounter in the regular classroom.

It has not been the educators who have led the movement toward mainstreaming. Sol Blatt, a psychologist active in the field of mental retardation, has stated, "More and more I comprehend the powerful positive influence that lawyers, if not laws, now exert within my field of work. . . . [Lawyers are] heroes, even now, to some of us today."[89] Though Dr. Blatt may have overstated the case, it is clear that since 1954, when the U.S. Supreme Court handed down its famous school desegregation decision, the courts have been among the major forces for change in the institutions in this country that relate

Table 3-3

Number of Professional Personnel and Type of Instructional System by Handicapping Condition and by Level of School

Type of Handicapped Pupils Taught	All Professional Staff for the Handicapped		Teachers of Separate (Special) Classes		Regular Teachers Who Provided Special Instruction in Regular Classes		Specialized Professional Personnel Who Provided Individualized Instruction	
	Number	Percent	Number	Percent	Number	Percent	Number	Percent
All schools[a]								
Speech impaired	96,700	100	35,100	37	31,400	32	30,200	31
Learning disabled	123,000	100	27,900	23	81,400	66	13,700	11
Mentally retarded	102,500	100	54,300	53	41,900	41	6,200	6
Emotionally disturbed	74,100	100	11,300	15	48,800	66	14,000	19
Hard of hearing	21,200	100	2,000	10	12,500	58	6,700	32
Deaf	6,200	100	2,300	38	3,000	48	800	14
Crippled	13,400	100	1,800	14	8,200	61	3,400	25
Partially sighted	20,200	100	800	4	16,100	80	3,300	16
Blind	6,900	100	500	8	4,600	66	1,800	26
Elementary schools								
Speech impaired	75,900	100	30,600	40	22,600	30	22,800	30
Learning disabled	97,000	100	19,700	20	66,400	69	10,800	11
Mentally retarded	64,700	100	31,700	49	28,500	44	4,500	7
Emotionally disturbed	53,700	100	8,200	15	36,000	67	9,500	18
Hard of hearing	13,600	100	1,500	11	6,900	51	5,200	38
Deaf	4,400	100	1,900	43	1,800	42	700	15
Crippled	7,800	100	900	11	4,500	58	2,400	31
Partially sighted	11,600	100	500	4	9,000	78	2,000	18
Blind	2,100	100	200	10	900	44	1,000	46

Secondary schools								
Speech impaired	14,500	100	3,000	21	5,000	34	6,600	45
Learning disabled	24,100	100	8,000	33	13,500	56	2,600	11
Mentally retarded	30,900	100	18,500	60	10,900	35	1,400	5
Emotionally disturbed	18,700	100	2,800	15	11,500	61	4,500	24
Hard of hearing	7,500	100	500	7	5,500	73	1,500	20
Deaf	1,700	100	200	15	1,200	74	200	11
Crippled	4,800	100	800	17	3,100	65	900	18
Partially sighted	8,000	100	300	4	6,500	82	1,100	14
Blind	4,800	100	300	7	3,700	75	900	18

[a]Professional staff in combined schools, with both elementary and secondary grades, are included in the "all schools" category but not in the detail by school level.

Note: Percentages are computed on unrounded numbers.

Source: A. Stafford Metz and H. Leslie Cramer, *Professional Staff for the Handicapped in Local Public Schools* (Washington, D.C.: U.S. Government Printing Office, 1970).

Table 3-4

Number of Handicapped Pupils in Local Public Schools, and Number and Percent That Received Any or No Designated Type of Special Instruction or Assistance–By Type of Handicap and Level of School (50 States and D.C., Spring 1970)

Type of Handicap	Total Handicapped Pupils		Handicapped Pupils Receiving Designated Types of Special Instruction or Assistance										Designated Types of Instruction or Assistance Not Received	
			Separate (Special) Classes				Individualized Special Instruction or Assistance							
			All of Instruction		Part of Instruction		In Regular Classroom by Regular Teacher		By Specialized Professional Personnel: In Own School		By Specialized Professional Personnel: In Another School and/or Agency			
	Number	Percent	Number	Percent	Number	Percent	Number	Percent	Number	Percent	Number	Percent	Number	Percent
All Schools[a]														
Speech impaired	1,793,300	100	1,600	–[c]	850,900	47	92,200	5	462,100	26	14,600	1	569,400	32
Learning disabled	1,160,400	100	80,700	7	337,500	29	245,000	21	95,500	8	8,600	1	512,000	44
Mentally retarded	935,900	100	498,600	53	104,700	11	99,400	11	32,700	4	46,100	5	208,100	22
Emotionally disturbed	555,600	100	54,500	10	30,200	5	82,200	15	95,200	17	26,300	5	303,000	55
Hard of hearing	131,100	100	3,400	3	6,800	5	9,800	7	12,600	10	13,300	10	89,600	68
Deaf	23,200	100	14,700	63	1,900	8	1,900	8	2,100	9	2,000	9	2,200	10
Crippled	81,700	100	5,300	7	10,200	12	7,400	9	9,400	12	4,300	5	51,800	63
Partially sighted	64,300	100	1,500	2	3,400	5	8,600	13	5,900	9	1,600	2	47,200	73
Blind	6,200	100	600	9	1,800	29	1,900	31	2,900	47	400	6	400	6
Elementary Schools														
Speech impaired	1,519,600	100	200	–[c]	778,400	51	71,000	5	384,400	25	10,500	1	447,200	29
Learning disabled	778,700	100	68,000	9	215,500	28	197,200	25	69,100	9	6,600	1	313,400	40
Mentally retarded	605,900	100	323,500	53	27,800	5	74,500	12	15,400	3	30,700	5	152,700	25

Emotionally disturbed	370,700	100	36,500	10	21,300	6	61,200	16	63,600	17	14,000	4	198,100	53
Hard of hearing	70,800	100	2,900	4	3,900	6	5,700	8	9,200	13	2,000	3	50,400	71
Deaf	18,300	100	12,700	70	1,100	6	1,500	8	1,800	10	1,900	10	500	2
Crippled	40,400	100	3,200	8	4,700	12	4,100	10	5,600	14	3,200	8	23,600	58
Partially sighted	30,300	100	1,200	4	1,900	6	5,900	20	3,700	12	800	3	19,200	63
Blind	3,200	100	500	16	800	26	1,100	33	1,500	48	100	3	–[b]	1
Secondary Schools														
Speech impaired	197,600	100	–[b]	1	45,000	23	12,800	6	60,000	30	2,800	1	93,800	47
Learning disabled	314,400	100	11,700	4	122,000	39	44,800	14	19,100	6	1,100	–[c]	142,100	45
Mentally retarded	257,300	100	129,600	50	71,800	23	19,300	8	15,200	6	13,100	5	39,400	15
Emotionally disturbed	159,600	100	15,700	10	8,700	5	14,700	9	30,900	19	12,000	8	89,300	56
Hard of hearing	50,400	100	500	1	2,900	6	4,000	8	3,500	7	11,200	22	29,600	59
Deaf	3,100	100	580	18	800	26	400	12	300	11	100	3	1,400	45
Crippled	36,000	100	1,000	3	5,500	15	3,000	8	3,800	11	700	2	24,800	69
Partially sighted	23,000	100	–[b]	–[c]	1,500	6	2,300	10	2,200	9	500	2	18,800	79
Blind	2,000	100	100	2	1,000	34	800	30	1,400	50	200	8	200	7

[a]Pupils in combined schools, with both elementary and secondary grades, are included in the totals but not in the detail by school level.

[b]Quantity more than 0 but less than 50.

[c]Percent more than 0 but less than 0.5.

Note: Percentages were computed on unrounded numbers. Percentages add to more than 100 percent because some pupils participated in more than one designated type of instruction.

Source: Mark E. Borinsky, *Provision of Instruction to Handicapped Pupils in Local Public Schools* (Washington, D.C.: U.S. Government Printing Office, 1974).

to the young. Nowhere is this seen more clearly at present, besides the issue of desegregation, than in another issue of integration—the integration as against exclusion of "different" children into the regular classroom.

The area of exclusion where litigation has been most widespread and has had the greatest impact is special education. In 1972 it was estimated that over one million children across the country were totally excluded from public schools because of various handicaps. This exclusion was justified on the basis that such handicapped children could not benefit from a public education, a position that has been generally discredited.[90]

The first major challenge to such exclusion came in the case of *Pennsylvania Association for Retarded Childen v. Commonwealth of Pennsylvania,*[91] an action seeking to require the state of Pennsylvania to provide an appropriate education for all those children who had previously been excluded from school because of some handicap. The court in *PARC* asserted that Pennsylvania's failure to offer any education to severely retarded children represented a denial of equal protection and that assignment of youngsters to programs for the retarded, unless preceded by notice and the opportunity for a hearing, denied them due process of law. In addition to requiring that the state locate all children previously excluded and develop an educational program that could meet these children's needs, the court also ordered a procedural system that would insure that the classification procedure itself was fundamentally fair.

In addition to the *PARC* case, there have been legal cases in Washington, D.C., (*Mills*) and California (*Diana vs. Board of Education*), which involve the element of racial stereotyping.[92]

Several states, including Massachusetts and California, to name only two, have enacted legislation bearing on the classification and education of handicapped children that seeks to abolish many of the injustices prevalent in public schools. The widespread judicial and legislative trend can be described as an effort to extend "due process" to children with special needs: whether a child is physically, mentally, or emotionally handicapped, or a juvenile delinquent or an abused and neglected child, he has rights. These rights involve access to treatment suited to these needs, and freedom from stereotyping classifications that identify a need without providing appropriate treatment. In short, if a child is to be singled out as "different," then proof of his deviancy must be substantiated and a suitable educational or correctional situation provided for him. Using special classification as a means of exclusion has long been a practice of our society, and these legal measures are aimed at correcting this practice.

In their evaluation of the effect of these recent movements Kirp, Kuriloff, and Buss point out that in general the outcomes have fallen far short of the intent. Local educational units have been quick to spot loopholes in new laws and in many cases have successfully ignored them altogether. This action, or inaction, is not necessarily a result of disagreement with the ideal, but may be a result of the realities of the situation. Legislatures frequently mandate change for which they do not provide adequate resources. "A Court order or a legislative mandate can do little to improve a situation if there is little or no raw material out of which that improvement can be wrought."[93] Understaffed, underfinanced institutions cannot provide the high calibre of individualized programs required for the handicapped.

The Children's Defense Fund (CDF) of the Washington Research Project has selected as an area for special impact "Right to Education, Classification, and Labelling." According to CDF, the more than one million children between the ages of seven and fifteen reported by the census as not enrolled in schools is merely the tip of the iceberg. In addition, children who are in groups that are disproportionately out of school share a common characteristic of differentness—race, income, language, handicap. CDF states that "most children who are out of school are out not because of choice but because they have been excluded by a range of overt or covert policies and practices." CDF conducts studies of educational services (for instance, in Mississippi) for children requiring special attention for mental, physical, emotional, and other health impairments as precursors to pushes for legislation and court action.[94]

Afterword

The issues involving physically, emotionally, and mentally handicapped young adolescents are complex and painful. Society turns to those institutions that provide services to those young people—the schools and the agencies for the handicapped—for clarification and leadership.

It seems unlikely, for unexplainable reasons, that it will be educators or agencies for the handicapped who will speak out most forcefully. There seems proportionally less concern for the young adolescent age group among those responsible for their educational development than among any of the other professionals who provide services for them. More concern comes from the legal profession. The major concern comes from a small number of professionals in the fields of medicine and psychology who are intimately aware of the delicate relationship of physical and emotional forces at this age; professionals who indeed realize that early adolescence is a recognizable, crucial developmental stage that differs from all others in the problems it creates and potentials it offers.

There is very little literature on handicapped adolescents, let alone on the impact of handicaps of *early* adolescence. *Issues in the Classification of Children*, for instance, two volumes representing the best work we have seen on the many facets of serving the handicapped, discusses adolescents mainly in terms of social deviance—that is, antisocial delinquent behavior. There is only one article not about delinquency that concerns adolescents, a review of issues in mental health that takes a developmental perspective. It is this perspective that is missing in almost all work on handicapping conditions.

Early identification and intervention are so critical, and corrective or compensatory education is seen as so difficult as children grow older, that specialists zero in on the young child. Also, the added psychological dimensions in adolescence may magnify problems within older children and in their relationships with special teachers.

Nevertheless, children grow. There are developmental epochs in childhood, and they include early adolescence. The handicapped will not stop growing because we stop serving them.

4 The Family and the Young Adolescent

Introduction

The educational and occupational attainment of parents, the physical resources of the home, the personal relationships between parents and children—these factors and many more are what we mean by family background. The impact of this background is visible early in the life of a child; his intelligence and ability to perform in school are in part predictable from knowledge of his background. Later, in adolescence, his educational and occupations aspirations are predictable in part from the attainments of his parents. Still later, his own attainments reflect quite clearly the stamp of his family background. Not only are his attainments influenced by family background; his values, attitudes and mental health are all subject to the pervasive and continuing effects of the family.[1]

The family is not a biological or instinctual imperative, but a social invention designed to care for and instruct the young. Families may change in composition and differ among cultures, but basically they exist for the rearing of children.[2]

The family is the most enduring and universal of human institutions. It appears early in human prehistory and occurs more ubiquitously than church, state, or any other social institution.[3] Family structure and function are the elementary basis of social organization, and therefore the keystone of both the status quo and radical revolution. We all come from, and live in relation to, families.

The family is potentially the most effective influence on the development of a person. Professionals in child-serving agencies will at least give lip service to the notion that "no child should be approached, assessed, treated, nursed, taught, or corrected without the parental influence being taken into account. . . . Without knowledge of the parents' influence neither the child's developmental successes and failures nor his social adjustments and maladjustments can be seen in their true light."[4] The 1970 White House Conference on Children and Youth, asserting that programs for children could not circumvent the family, urged increasing participation of and concern for the family.[5]

If the family has been the most enduring of our human institutions, it has also been one of the most protean.[6] Richard Farson has listed eight areas of significant change in the American family:

1. The shift from the extended kinship system to the nuclear family. [Fifty years ago half of the households in the nation had at least one other adult besides the parents: today, fewer than five percent do.]

2. The disappearance of the family functioning as a unit in the economic, religious, and social spheres.
3. The trend from lifetime monogamy to "chronological polygamy and polyandry" [the divorce and remarriage cycle].
4. A loss of influence, so that the family today is considered a secondary, rather than primary, group of orientation.
5. Major family life-cycle changes due to changing social conventions and longer life expectancies. [In 1890, the average wife was a widow when the last child left home; today she and her husband have another fifteen years of life together.]
6. The upheaval connected with the changing roles of women—roles which become less and less family-oriented.
7. The corresponding increase in egalitarian relationships between husband and wife.
8. The generally acknowledged fact that the family is surrendering some of its socialization influence to various other social institutions and informal groups.[7]

Theorists and researchers predict problems for the family and adolescents. Chief among these seems to be vanishing social support for parents. Our society no longer views child-bearing and child-rearing as automatic. The so-called support system for parents holds few rewards. Parents of troubled adolescents find they usually receive blame from counselors, teachers, and other youth workers, regardless of the circumstances. Feeling they have little control of their own family situation, parents often throw in the towel and begin to deny any obligation to or responsibility for their adolescents.[8]

Adolescence is more difficult for the family and the child today. Before, there were more helping hands available in the home and in the community. As the American family developed, it shed in-laws, grandparents, cousins, aunts, boarders, and retainers. It handed production over to offices and factories, religion to the churches, the administration of justice to the courts, formal education to the schools, medical attention to the hospitals. It has been stripped down to the bare frame of being marriage-centered and child-fulfilled. Today, the nuclear family, with "occupants" living next door instead of neighbors, is on its own.

At the same time, researchers report that social institutions serving children (and, we would assume, adolescents, although no research has been conducted to prove or refute this) achieve greater success when the family is intimately involved programmatically. Even though historically socialization has been taking place more and more in society at large and less in the family, Earl Schaefer's research, for instance, shows that parent-centered child development programs, when compared with "child-centered" programs, have equal immediate effectiveness, greater long-term effectiveness, greater cost effectiveness, and greater "spin-off" impact on the family and community.[9]

Bronfenbrenner, in discussing the interrelatedness of such issues as nutrition, housing, family life, parents' employment and schooling, says that the involvements of parents is of critical importance for sustaining the child's learning in school. This necessary participation implies, then, "a major reorientation in the design of intervention programs and in the training of personnel to work in this area."[10]

On the one hand we are told that the family is "on its own," with few supports, and on the other that its participation must be broadened. What, in fact, is known about the family and young adolescents? How far are we from having the information that would undergird the implementation of policy recommendations such as Bronfenbrenner's?

The family is often one of the most important influences on a person; adolescence is often a "last chance" stage in the development of a person. The widening gulf between family and society and concurrent calls for its increased participation should be important. It would be reasonable to assume that the effects of changing society and family functions are under heavy study. It would be reasonable, but not correct.

Research on the Family and the Early Adolescent

Of the major research studies reviewed for this report, not a single one deals specifically with the early adolescent. The Social Research Group has estimated that close to 10 percent of all federally funded adolescence research in fiscal years 1973 and 1974 involved the family. The primary focus may not have been on the family, however. Comparable figures are not available for fiscal year 1975. The Interagency Panel's Third Annual Report cites a 3.3 percent funding level of both adolescence *and* early childhood projects whose primary focus was on the family as representing a +36.1 percentage change in dollars between FY '74 and FY '75. It is not known what proportion of any of this funding deals specifically with the family and the early adolescent, but indications are that it is minimal. Further, the Group reports that there were "no new starts" on federally funded research projects dealing with the family in fiscal year 1973—all were continuations of projects begun earlier. Similarly, the Smithsonian Institution's Science Information Exchange, covering state and privately funded research, lists no significant studies of the family and the early adolescent.

Since the early adolescent is beginning the process of separating himself and his identity from the family, it is logical to assume that considerable research on family-adolescent relations would focus on the early adolescent. It may be logical, but once again it is not the case. The only major research on the family and the adolescent focuses on the late adolescent.

Reviewing this research, and attempting to glean factors that tell us something about the early adolescent, we must bear in mind that it is the late adolescent that actually is under study, and that we must assume that the factors significant for the late adolescent are of some significance for the early adolescent.

The Social Research Group has suggested some research questions that relate to family and early adolescence.[11] The research that directly addresses these questions has not been done, and except in rare instances is not under way. Instead, there is a random hodge-podge of *ad hoc* research on family size, sibling relationships, single-parent and typical family groupings, working mothers, family background, family and peer orientations, and parenting styles. None of these, as indicated earlier, focuses specifically on the early adolescent.

Following is a question-by-question review of research using the Social Research Group's six major questions.

1. *Can the family continue to perform the major socializing function for the young that it has in the past?*

There is no research that addresses this question as it regards the early adolescent and the family. There are studies on peer-group and family orientation, sibling relationships, family composition, and family background, and they are summarized selectively below:

Peer-Group and Family Orientation. The early adolescent's shift from family- to peer-orientation is a topic well-researched and documented. Of particular relevance is David P. Ausubel's satellization theory, whereby the young child first identifies and derives status from his family. During adolescence, the process of "desatellizing" usually takes place, as children begin to look beyond their parents for sources of attitudes and values.[12] The most comprehensive study in this field was conducted by Charles E. Bowerman and John W. Kinch, who recognized in their research the potential conflict of a transitional period during which the child strives to achieve status in the two conflicting or competing primary groups, parents and peers. For adequate socialization and personal adjustment, the transition must occur.[13] These researchers surveyed 686 students from fourth through tenth grade, asking them to respond to questions that would measure three separate types of orientation: "identification" (whom does the child single out for admiration, for a model for him/her self, for advice?), "association" (whom does the child prefer as a companion?), and "norm" (with whose values and decisions does the child agree?).

On the basis of their responses, the students were divided into three categories: family-oriented, peer-oriented, or neutral. Eighty-seven percent of the fourth graders were family-oriented, but only 50 percent of the eighth graders and only 31 percent of the tenth graders fell into this category.

The greatest shift from family to peer orientation was with respect to "association," and the least change was in the area of "identification." Females seemed to make the orientation switch a year earlier than boys, and early adolescents from large families with four or more children made a more rapid and complete transfer from family to peer orientation.

The Family. Peer group orientation, however, is not an all-or-nothing relationship. Denise Kandel and Gerald Lesser, in *Youth in Two Worlds*, a cross-cultural study of Danish and American adolescents, found that adolescents usually differentiated between family and peers in terms of specific need fulfillment. Results indicated the family was sought out often for advice (similar to Bowerman and Kinch's "identification") and peers were often sought out for companionship (similar to Bowerman and Kinch's "association").[14]

Gisela Konopka, in her study of adolescent girls, disputes assumptions that the family is becoming malfunctional for adolescents. The family, as reported by the subjects of the study, is the most powerful influence on a girl's life, whether for "joy and hope" or "fear and shame." Girls not only list parents as important, but list them highest in their regard for adults.

Especially esteemed are mothers, named by the large majority of the girls as the person they feel closest to. (Konopka sees this as a change from the 1950s, because there is now less emphasis on pleasing the male in the family and therefore less competition between mother and daughter.)

The girls' relationships with their fathers differ from that with their mothers. About 25 percent report positive relationships, and these are mostly girls who relate positively to both parents. The fathers are often remote, if not invisible, seen as someone who does not want the girl to grow up. A more formal relationship grows between father and daughter, which she accepts with resignation.

One-quarter of Konopka's respondents said that they are not very close to their mothers or that they actively dislike them. This was said with regret and hurt.

The second most important adult listed by the girls was the grandmother, again reaffirming the strength of adolescents family ties.[15]

John Condry and Michael Siman classified 766 sixth graders as primarily adult- or peer-oriented, then examined the two groups for differences in behavior, attitude, and family situation.

Adult-oriented children had parents who were described as more active in parental responsibilities, more nurturant, more consistent and demanding in discipline, and more available for companionship.

The most common parental characteristics of peer-oriented children were mothers who nagged or otherwise "expressively rejected" the children, who lacked disciplinary control over the children, or who exhibited a pattern of passive neglect.[16]

Bachman found an upward shift in parent-child relations between grades ten and twelve, implying that parent-child relations are at a low point during early adolescence.[17] Changes in the child may cause existing parenting styles to fail, and force parents to adopt extreme styles.

Offer also notes a similar phenomenon. In his subjects, rebellion manifested itself most clearly at ages twelve and thirteen. These young adolescents described themselves as getting into fights with their parents over seemingly insignificant issues. Rule-breaking was constant: refusal to take the garbage out, coming home late, not making beds, skipping church. Rebellious behavior carried over to interaction with schoolteachers, church workers, and especially significant males. By the time the teenager entered high school, most of these overt behavioral forms of rebellion had ceased. Nearly all the parents in Offer's sample stated that the early adolescent years (12-13) were the most difficult of their parenting years.[18]

As Hill has noted:

> Adolescence for most is a relatively pacific period not characterized by stormy intrafamilial relationships. And, when the latter do characterize adolescence, available information suggests that it is more often a function of extreme parenting styles than a solely intrapsychic matter.[19]

These "intrapsychic" phenomena are anything but negligible, of course. The move toward independence from parents is critical, allowing adolescents to revise defensive and adaptive patterns that are ill-suited for adult functioning.[20] The adolescent must maintain a balance between loyalties to family and peers that is personally functional. Tensions caused by changing patterns of intrafamilial relating are inevitable. Turmoil, the generation gap, the tyranny of the peer group, and other commonly assumed characteristics of adolescent-family distress, are not.

One conclusion that can be drawn, in keeping with the studies cited, is that negligent or extreme parenting styles force the adolescent into precocious and extreme "desatellization," seeking a position within a peer group that the family may find unacceptable. It is the family, in other words, that in such cases often pushes the adolescent out; the peer group alone cannot pull him or her out.

Sibling Relationships. Charles Bowerman and Rebecca Dobash studied relationships among adolescent brothers and sisters, and found that 65 percent of the seventh through twelfth graders studied felt a closeness to their siblings, with siblings of the same sex usually preferred. Early adolescents tended to feel closer to family-oriented brothers and sisters, older adolescents selected older siblings more rooted in peer society and therefore a reminder of their more mature status. Also, the researchers found that increased family size, and the resultant complexity of family relationships, heightened the potential for conflict in the family.[21]

Family Composition. The ability of the family to function as a socializer for adolescents is affected, Dr. Thomas Langner has found, by its composition. Rating different family structures for their potential to cause mental impairment of children, Langner found the natural child-intact family to be the least potentially damaging.

Langner's ten-year study, "Psychiatric Impairment in Urban Children Over

Time," is reported in *Children Under Stress*. More than 2,000 families with children six to eighteen years of age were interviewed. In single-parent families where the father was absent, Langner and his associates found the absence of a parent is by no means as important to the child's psychological development as the parenting style of the available parent. The single most damaging factor was found to be maternal coldness.

A significant relationship was found in the more than 1,000 control families between the father's absence or the child's isolation from peers, and increases in fighting and delinquency.[22]

Family Background. Volume II of Gerald Bachman's *Youth in Transition* summarizes the extensive and wide-ranging effects that family background has on all aspects of the adolescent's life.

Bachman found that male adolescents from small families with one or two children are advantaged. They score higher in the Quick Test (a test of general intelligence) and they rate higher in academic achievement, academic self-concept, political knowledge, and academic and occupational aspirations.

These effects, while due in part to the higher socioeconomic level associated with small family size, held true when researchers controlled for socioeconomic level. The study also found that boys in small families report strong family relations, and that as family size increased the quality of family relations decreased.[23]

2. *In what ways has this function changed?*

There is no research on how the family function has changed as it specifically affects the young adolescent.

3. *How can traditional roles be made more effective?*

Again, there is no research on how the traditional family roles toward the early adolescent can be made more effective. There is research on parenting styles, summarized below:

Parenting Styles. Before discussing how parents cope, a description of what they must cope with should be helpful. Cohen and Frank describe the preadolescent child:

> As his confidence and reasoning improves, he feels less need to rely on his parents' explicit injunctions. He may seem to deliberately devalue his parents—to disobey, underestimate and criticize with great gusto. He appears very sensitive to the exercise of adult power and prerogatives, embarrassed to submit to adult

good manners or to accept adult help openly, revolted by praise or punishment perceived as infantilizing. In spite of his continuing need and desire for support and guidance, he may hesitate or altogether cease to play with or to communicate feelings to adults.[24]

As the child enters early adolescence, these behavior patterns may continue in a more intense form. New cognitive skills make it possible for the young adolescent to compare behavior against ideals, a process that may undermine his respect for parental behavior and reasoning. Criticism of parents, defiant rejection of parents' rules and standards, and (more noted with girls) a withdrawal and concern for privacy may occur.[25]

While the young adolescent needs peer support and companionship to help him develop new beliefs and values, he needs his parents to provide models for comparison and possible imitation; he needs a set of values, to adopt or modify. More importantly, he needs the family to value and esteem him, to credit him with the ability to make wise decisions.[26] But most of all he needs parents who do not see his life as entirely parent-regulated or entirely self-regulated.

There was a flurry of work in the 1950s in patterns and consequences of child-rearing practices, like Sears, Maccoby, and Levin's *Patterns of Child Rearing* (1955) and Bandura and Walter's *Adolescent Aggression: A Study of the Influences of Child-Training Practices and Family Interrelationships* (1959). Work on parenting styles continues, although more quietly, into the 1970s.

The best known work on parenting styles is being conducted by Diana Baumrind of the University of California at Berkeley.

Baumrind's longitudinal study concerns the effect of different types of parental authority on a number of child behaviors, including the development of competence, the child's conception of the legitimacy of parental authority, change in definition of sex roles as a function of the child's age and pattern of parental authority, and creativity of the child.

Baumrind has delineated four major types of parental control: "authoritative" (combination of strong and clear parental control with warmth); "authoritarian" (consisting of strong parental control, punitiveness, coldness, suspiciousness); "permissive" (weak control, moderate warmth, overindulgence of child); and "harmonious" (control exercised through information, consideration without overindulgence, warmth and encouragement of autonomy).[27]

In her article, "Early Socialization and Adolescent Competence," Baumrind discusses in detail various hypotheses about parenting and patterns of authority. Certain points are particularly relevant to this review.

First, it is Baumrind's hypothesis that because of developmental and secular factors (adolescence reached at earlier ages) it may be increasingly important for parents to be sensitive to their children's changing needs for control. Many parents may tend to exert control too firmly and too long, thus adversely affecting young adolescents.

Second, the effects of various authority patterns are sex-related. Independence in girls, as against overconformity, is associated with high parental demands and a lack of overprotectiveness. Resistance to adult authority in girls is not related to low achievement, as it may be for boys. And dominance and stridency in girls may signify that they are resisting sex-role pressures to underachieve. According to Baumrind, it is possible that parents should stimulate reactive aggression in girls to assure independence and achievement. Too much warmth and support seem to be debilitating.[28]

Third, "harsh, exploitive, arbitrary treatment by parents is strongly associated with antisocial rather than prosocial aggression in children and adolescents." This proposition together with the proposition that traditionalist parents most effectively circumvent the alienating effects of society, has received the most extensive support in the research literature.[29]

To avoid an entirely one-sided perspective, it should be noted that antisocial behaviors caused by parental punitiveness serve to reinforce in the parents' minds the need for further, and perhaps more extreme, measures. Thus, a vicious cycle begins, with the parents' behavior being both reactive and contributive to the adolescent's behavior. Bachman found this a very important factor in his study of high school attrition.[30]

Also to avoid one-sidedness, it is noteworthy that in his study of "modal" adolescents, Offer reports that parents' capacity to change with their children was impressive. "They went through their sons' adolescence together with them and seemed to show a relatively high degree of tolerance and understanding. . . . The only exception . . . is the early adolescent years, when . . . there was openly rebellious behavior by the teen-agers." Offer hypothesizes that once the "hurdle" of early adolescence is negotiated by both parents and children, there starts the "psycho-social moratorium," with parents beginning to "consider seriously that their children were no longer to be treated as children."[31]

Kandel and Lesser found a democratic parenting pattern to be consistently associated with most positive interactions and attitudes towards parents (communication, closeness, reliance for advice, desire to model after parents) and that the most distance between parent and adolescent was found when the parent was perceived as being permissive.[32]

Young adolescents can be very provocative, requiring changes in parenting styles. While the reciprocal relationship of the infant and its caregiver is being studied, thus acknowledging the complexities of interactional situations, parallel studies concerning young adolescents have not appeared.

John P. Hill is concerned with parenting, although he is not actively involved in research in this area. What are the changing roles of son and daughter during the growth spurt, he asks, noting that "unfortunately, the longitudinal study that would need to be done to describe and isolate the effects of the biological change on parental demands and expectations has not yet been done." Hill agrees that overcontrol and overpermissiveness in early adolescence have negative effects, "but the relation of such parental practices and *change* in parental practices to the onset of puberty awaits longitudinal investigation."

Hill makes a beautiful comment about the considerable subset of parents who, common observation suggests, do not modify their expectations of the son or daughter role around puberty. He wonders whether what is commonly seen as adolescent negativism may be the adolescent's reaction to the parents' failure to modify expectations. "It is striking," he points out, "that the period around two—the earlier time when the organism changes dramatically by the addition of speech and self-locomotion—also attracts the same high-frequency parental cries of negativism."[33]

Even though the terminology for parenting styles varies from researcher to researcher, the basic findings are similar:

1. Extreme parenting styles (authoritarian or permissive, for example) are not beneficial and are highly inappropriate.
2. Democratic styles that allow the adolescent input into family and personal decisions are the most advantageous for the adolescent's development.
3. Parents need to alter their attitudes toward the adolescent in keeping with developing cognitive, social, and physical maturity.

These studies are in the main conducted on white, middle-class families, and do not specifically address low-income or minority group families.

4. *What is the effect on young people of changes in family functions and the consequent reduced amount of time spent in the company of parents, siblings, and other family members?*

There is no research that addresses this question as it regards the early adolescent. The working mother, perhaps one of the most important phenomena of the decade, has been researched. But most of the research focuses on the infant or preschool child and the working mother, and says very little about the effect on the early adolescent, the father, or the family as a whole. What does seem relevant is summarized below.

The rapid rise in the proportion of mothers working outside the home has been viewed by some critics as a major cause of family disintegration and dysfunction. Studies, however, show that the mother's employment outside the home has few detrimental effects on adolescents. Alice Propper studied about 500 adolescents, and was unable to find any statistically significant effects of maternal employment. She did find a slightly higher incidence of arguments between adolescents and working mothers, and noted that sons of working mothers awarded their fathers slightly lower status than some of nonworking mothers.

Propper concluded, however, that the adolescents' perception of parental interest, parental help with school and personal problems, and feelings of closeness to parents were unrelated to the employment status of the mother.[34]

Glen Elder cites Elizabeth Douvan's work in *Employment and the Adolescent*, where female adolescents with working mothers expressed higher degrees of admiration for their mothers, were more independent in judgment, and were generally more self-reliant.[35] It is important to note, however, that the girls involved in this study felt that their mother's work held some degree of status and demanded competency.

Coopersmith, in his study of sons of "intact" nuclear families, *The Antecedents of Self-Esteem*, found that both parents of children with high self-esteem lead active lives outside the family. They do not rely on the family as their sole or even major source of gratification. Referring specifically to working mothers who enjoy working, Coopersmith says:

> This study reveals that such mothers are likely to have children who are high rather than low in their self-esteem and who are less likely to manifest anxiety and psychosomatic symptoms. The significance of the mother's absence from home apparently depends upon how she, her child, and the other members of the family view such absence; that is, it is not the treatment but how the treatment is perceived in the family context that determines its effects upon the child.[36]

5. *To what extent can and should other institutions pass on the information, skills, and values that were once received from long association with the nuclear and extended family?*

There is no research that addresses this question as it affects the early adolescent. Researchers may either assert that the family (for children of all ages) is no longer inculcating values, skills, or information, or else they may incorporate the assumption into their research. Nowhere, it appears, have they documented and proven the validity of the assertion or assumption.

Even when the assertion or assumption is made, little mention is made of other institutions that could take over this function. There appears to be a thoroughgoing dread of even addressing such a potent question. The major thrust of the recommendations coming from researchers is to suggest ways to strengthen the family so that it can (assuming it is not) perform this function.

6. *How do various agents interact to effect the socialization of youth?*

Again, and for the last time—since this is the last question—there is no research that attempts to show how the family and other social institutions work together to help the young adolescent become a fuller member of society. There is some doubt that child-serving agencies work successfully with parents to any significant degree. Further, there is some question as to whether they even interact among themselves.

In addition to the six unaddressed questions cited from the Social Research Group, there are specific research areas on the family developed by the Interagency Panel on Early Childhood Research and Development, all of which could be applied with benefit to the family and the early adolescent:

Investigations to determine the various family structures that exist in the United States; frequency; effects on parents (adults) and children;

Study of decision-making processes in families;

Experimental studies which indicate how parents learn to act as parents;

Studies of values in families concerning sex education;

Results of the impact of increased geographical mobility of families;

Effect of the family/home on the child's learning, life-style, and future educational achievement;

Effects of varying degrees of involvement of children in family activities upon the value structure of adolescents;

Research on the adjustment potential of the family; the kinds of changes . . . the family is capable of making and how these skills can be acquired;

Investigations of the environmental and sociocultural factors impinging upon families (e.g., schools, hospitals, type of housing, geographical region, cultural group norms, etc.) and their relationship to child-rearing practices, family roles and functioning, etc.;

Determination of the influence of the role of the school in the community in which the family is a part; i.e., how do school programs (e.g., adult education) affect the family?

Exploration of areas in which family may be legally supplanted, e.g., mechanisms for supplying children with homes away from home; mechanisms for maintaining as many primary ties as possible, especially those that might keep children in their old neighborhoods;

Research on the impact of media and dissemination of various types of information upon families;

Determination of how parent behaviors are learned; how parents structure and amend their environment when they rear children; how to build in intervention that will help them learn what we think is important to child development;[37]

and, as suggested by Baumrind,

The coinciding of the parental middle years, with their ensuing perspective and status changes, and the adolescent period, with its similar patterns of change.[38]

Another crucial task is that of impressing upon parents the importance of parenting. As the research has clearly shown, indifferent and suppressive parenting often causes antisocial or illegal behaviors which make the intimacy of the parent-child relationship of public concern. As Hill and others (Blos, Bronfenbrenner) point out, parenting education is by and large left to the mass media, and in particular is shaped by the stereotypes and distortions presented on television. Classes and teaching materials are abundant for the care of infants and young children. The most popular and widely read child-rearing experts heavily concentrate on this early period. The majority of adult education offerings in parenting and family counseling services are offered in the most popular area: early childhood. It is perhaps a fatalistic sense of inevitable failure that makes active and concerned parenting more infrequent during adolescence. Parents often take their adolescent's growing independence and value change as a personal affront, and act in a retaliatory fashion. Also, it must be noted, parents are under heavy pressures in their careers and personal and marital lives during the time their children reach early adolescence.

Afterword

An uncertain trumpet heralds the new status of the young adolescent in the family. He has been told by his family who he is, who he may become, what is right, what is wrong, what is true, what is false. He has accepted these messages from the family because they came from his family.

His drive to establish his identity, aided by his developing logical competence, encourages him to test the previously untested values the family taught him. He perceives gaps between what he has been told is the truth and what is true, between what is and what should be. He has been told that the truth will set him free and he wants to be free. He seeks out his peers and other adults to test reality, and more or less puts the family on "hold." The songs he learned at mother's knee, though with him still, no longer enchant.

To the family, already under stress because of the life-cycle changes of its adult leaders, the young adolescent is yet another challenge to be faced unprepared and unaided. Parents in particular may react to the adolescent's changing behaviors with increasingly authoritarian responses, thus creating a stormy cycle of overreaction.

Whatever the quality of the relationship between the family and the young adolescent, wherever he goes, the family will go also, and be a part of him. We can never go home again. It is also true that we can never leave home.

5 Voluntary Youth-Serving Agencies

Introduction

All of the largest national youth-serving agencies came into existence as a reaction to the changing character of American life between the middle of the nineteenth century and 1916.[1] The YMCA, the YWCA, the Boys' Clubs and the settlement and community house movements developed largely in reaction to industrial and urban growth.

The Boy Scouts of America, the Girl Scouts of America, the YWCA, the YMCA, the Boys' and Girls' Clubs of America, and the 4-H Clubs formed an integral part of white, middle-class American life. These institutions were considered important allies of the home, the church, and the school. They set out explicitly to inculcate their set of ethical and moral values and to practice the Judeo-Christian concepts of brotherhood and tolerance. They had wide appeal and spread to smaller cities and towns. The objectives of the agencies—cleanliness of mind and body, health and character development, leadership training, development of a sense of responsibility and good citizenship, fun and adventure—were close to the hearts of most middle-class parents. Participation in the organizations was encouraged and considered a desirable and even an essential part of growing up.

Today these national, adult-supervised, leisure-time youth groups are appealing to a relatively small portion of the youth population.[2] Although in our rhetoric, society still seems to believe that organized youth groups are "avenues to character development" and useful in keeping adolescents out of mischief, the decline in membership in some of the organizations indicates two things. First, the value systems of these agencies, with a few exceptions, are largely outmoded. Second, because of their overwhelmingly hierarchical structure, these agencies have been unsuccessful in adjusting to the social dilemmas of our urban and ethnic postindustrial society.

Youth-Serving Agencies

Just as autonomy and aggression have their roots in the American tradition, so have neighborliness, civic concern, and devotion to the young. It is to these that we must look if we are to rediscover our moral identity as a society and as a nation.[3]

Following are descriptions of a few youth-serving agencies with long-standing traditional foundations. They are faced with the problems of remaining relevant to youth in the 1970s.

Boy Scouts of America and Girl Scouts of America

The Boy Scouts of America (BSA) and the Girl Scouts of America (GSA) have hierarchical organizational structures staffed by paid professionals who are primarily administrative and who seldom work directly with their members. Volunteers recruited from the community provide the direct leadership necessary for the institutions' existence. The recruiting and training of these volunteer leaders is directed by a fixed national program; the scouts participate in a standardized promotional system, using a national handbook. The basic purposes of scouting have remained the same for sixty-four years. The traditional values and rhetoric of scouting are still held in high esteem by well-meaning administrators, who seek to provide scouts with sound bodies and a code of ethics that will enable them to lead productive, meaningful lives in a white, middle-class, urban, market-oriented society.

The Girl Scouts and the Boy Scouts are designed to transmit noncognitive skills and moral qualities by finding valuable roles for youngsters to play. For example, the Girl Scout Constitution states that the motivating force in scouting is a spiritual one but the purpose is that of "inspiring girls with the highest ideals of character, conduct, patriotism, and service that they may become happy and resourceful citizens."[4] The Boy Scouts of America share a similar purpose: "To build desirable qualities of character, to train in the responsibilities of participating citizenship, and to develop in them personal fitness. . . ."[5] Scouting is still camping, doing a Good Turn daily, and living up to the Scout Oath and Law.

The problem is that these older institutions fail to fulfill an important need of youth, to feel that they have a function in the initiation, development, and execution of activities. The ritual ceremony and paramilitary structure are no longer enough to attract new membership, and in fact both agencies have experienced a decline in membership, particularly in urban areas. In 1970, membership in the BSA was 6,183,086, and the GSA 3,920,000. In 1973, the Boy Scouts reported having 4,753,634 members and the Girl Scouts 3,726,000.[6]

Young Men's Christian Association and Young Women's Christian Association

The YMCA, the oldest youth-serving organization in existence today, began in England during the nineteenth century as a place where young working men could improve themselves and where they could develop and maintain their Christian attitudes. The YMCA has come to place less emphasis on evangelical Christianity and more on character education. Membership is nondiscriminatory–people of any religion may join.

The Young Women's Christian Association was founded in Boston in 1866 with the specific goal of providing the influence and protection of a Christian home for women and girls who had left their homes to come to the city. The YW did not restrict its interest to females, but worked in the community with a "missionary zeal for all who suffered or were unfortunate."[7]

Both the YMCA and YWCA have special programs for junior high school students which are social, educational, and recreational in nature. Older adolescents have not remained members–many join to buy a service (such as the use of a swimming pool or a first-aid course) rather than to belong to an organization. As a result, membership has been unstable.

The organization of the Ys is handled by a paid administrative staff, but these people are working directly with members, unlike the BSA and GSA. National and regional programs are available, but local programs develop out of group and community needs.

Church-Related Organizations

Churches have found that in order to attract and keep young people as members in their youth organizations they have had to develop programs in tune with their changing interests and values. Where they have been fortunate enough to have enlightened pastoral leadership, programs have been developed that allow adolescents freedom to have discussions on drugs, dating, family life, death, race, and personal problems. Innovations in the presentation of church services and in programs that bring adolescents together with their parents and the older members of the congregation have begun to open up important avenues of communication.

The B'nai B'rith Youth Organization and the three main branches of Judaism stress Jewish culture and religious heritage with their members as well as the practice and development of a sense of community responsibility. The Young Men's Hebrew Association, the Young Women's Hebrew Association, and the Jewish Community Centers have programs and clubs for all ages. In the latter organization, the family is emphasized. Membership is not restricted to Jews.

The Catholic Youth Organization (CYO) has one of the largest youth programs in the country. As no strong national program exists, local traditions and interests govern the needs. Sports and recreational programs are offered to both boys and girls. The CYO is strongest in large, industrial cities, where each chapter retains a great deal of autonomy.

4-H

4-H is a national organization administered by the Cooperative Extension Services of the U.S. Department of Agriculture. Traditionally, 4-H programs operated in rural communities to provide young people with an opportunity to learn technical skills in agriculture. 4-H is unusual in that its monetary and administrative support is federal, state, and local. The State Extension Service and local county agents provide the administrative leadership, but volunteers are needed on the community level to form the clubs and provide the basic leadership. Meetings are held in members' homes, schools, or community centers. Today its programs have wider appeal, but its membership continues to be greatest among rural youth. In 1973, close to 70 percent of the members lived on farms, in small towns with less than 10,000 population, or in open country. Forty-nine percent of the members were pre-teens (9-11), 36 percent were twelve through fourteen years old and 16 percent were fifteen through nineteen years old. Total enrollment in 1973 was 3,340,000.[8]

The 4-H Clubs are occupation-oriented and seek to prepare youth for future economic roles. The programs focus on club activities or special interest courses. Profit provides the initial incentive for 4-H Club members, although profit has nothing to do with the organization's objectives. Emphasis is placed on constructive citizenship, leadership, and the ability to cooperate for the improvement of services in the home, on the farm, and in the local community. Although the program has been enlarged to attract urban youth, the goals of the earlier period remain: "Head to clearer thinking; Heart to greater loyalty; Hands to service; Health to better living for club, community and country."[9]

National Federation of Settlements and Neighborhood Centers

The National Federation of Settlements and Neighborhood Centers began in urban centers as religiously motivated, advantaged people tried to help the disadvantaged in deprived neighborhoods to seek a better life, improve living conditions, and achieve a just society. It is a federation with 180 corporate entities bound to the national organization by dues and policies. These policies are not binding and allow for a great deal of autonomy. Settlements vary significantly in their programs and there is a wide disparity between the resources of the older settlements in the East and Northeast, which are well-endowed, and the ones in the Southwest and Midwest, which are not. Settlements have always concentrated on working with the smaller units of society—the family, the neighborhood, and the community. They are centers of neighborhood initiative, experimentation, and coordination.

Save the Children Federation

Another agency serving the disadvantaged is Save the Children Federation. Unlike the National Federation of Settlements, its emphasis is on community service in rural regions. It uses a community development approach of working with parents, who define the needs for their children and the community at large. The parents, and not the children, make the decisions. They are supported by private foundations and federal grants, and are staffed by a small number of professionals who administer programs and do the field work. Save the Children Federation and the National Federation of Settlements and Neighborhood Centers concentrate on integrating the family unit into its community context. Save the Children Federation, particularly, focuses on moving the youth and his family out of their familiar context to achieve a level of cooperation in the community. Both organizations try to instill the idea of community responsibility in the youths they serve.

Coordinating Agencies

There are two relatively new agencies, consultative in nature, that are providing adolescents with opportunities to feel needed by helping them make contributions to their communities. One is the National Commission on Resources for Youth, a nonprofit organization begun early in 1967 by a group of educators, social scientists, and businessmen. The Commission has no set of moral values to inculcate. It exists to research, develop, and promote models of programs in which youth can assume responsible roles. The Commission maintains a central office run by a small staff of four or five professionals who function as a switchboard, plugging into youth projects, validating their originality, and transmitting these innovations to practitioners across the country.[10]

The second new organization is the National Youth Alternatives Project, a nonprofit agency founded in 1973 as a spin-off from a Washington-based group. It acts as a national clearinghouse for alternative youth programs. It runs, among other programs, crisis intervention centers and runaway centers to serve youngsters from eleven to seventeen years of age, and also provides services to older adolescents who have not yet assumed the responsibilities of adulthood. This organization is funded by private foundations, church groups, welfare services, and United Ways. It depends on paraprofessionals to staff its agencies around the country.

Changes to Serve Today's Youth

The attitude of the community determines what happens to youth groups because the community itself supplies the three basic ingredients: leadership, membership, and financial support. (4-H is the exception because financial support is also provided by federal and state funds.) At the same time, the major youth-serving organizations have established national headquarters that develop programs, print materials, and house an ever-increasing administrative staff. With continued growth the direct input adolescents have had into programming has waned. The administrative staff has become divorced from the membership.

One questions whether these adult-supervised youth agencies can continue to provide meaning and purpose in the lives of adolescents when they have lost their proximity to their clients. Vast and rapid social changes, like the growth of mass media and a more pervasive peer group culture, and the early introduction of drugs and alcohol offer new interests and create new problems for maturing adolescents to solve.[11]

Gisela Konopka's recent study of adolescent girls reveals some causes for the trend away from membership in youth-serving organizations. One-third of the sample included in her study belonged at one time or belongs at present to a voluntary agency. Eighty-three percent of the girls who had once belonged to a youth organization were no longer affiliated, the most common ages for "dropping out" being twelve and thirteen. In seeking to determine what forces were at work, she investigated both their reasons for joining originally and their reasons for leaving. The most frequently mentioned reasons for joining were interest in the program, pressure from parents, desire for friends, and personal conviction. The prime cause of disengagement were childish and boring activities, domineering adult leaders, and a group size too large for close personal relationships. The girls frequently complained of having no opportunity to share in decision making or engage in meaningful activities.[12]

With the exception of the consultative organizations mentioned (the National Commission on Resources for Youth and the National Youth Alternatives Project) and religious groups, the purposes of the national youth agencies remain decidedly educational, holding a limited, individualistic view of citizenship. Their attention has focused on developing in their members the attributes of self-reliance, integrity and patriotism, values favored by the middle-class adults which have historically guided the groups.

Many organizations serving the disadvantaged in urban areas are as "educational" in their goals. Boys' and Girls' Clubs of America offer boys and girls "a place to go and a way to grow." The Girls' Clubs' core programs hope to build responsible mothers, homemakers, and citizens of the community.

A different approach to the problem of coping with today's adolescent and his needs is made by Resources for Youth through its programming. Many of the programs under their guidance do in fact give young people an opportunity for experiential learning while they perform valuable services for their communities. In their files are more than 800 examples of such innovative programs. They have initiated two programs to serve as models for adaptation elsewhere—Youth Tutoring Youth and the Day Care Youth Helper Program. In the first program underachieving teenagers across the country are learning by tutoring younger underachievers on a one-to-one basis. In the other program high school students help out in day-care centers. The agency's aim is to develop programs for school children, particularly adolescents. The importance of doing this is best summarized by a ninth grade teacher in the Community Participation Project, Kirkwood, Missouri. When asked what she thought was the most valuable aspect of the program, she replied:

> You know what everybody thinks about junior highs—that they're neither here nor there. These students are regarded as being too old to be supervised constantly, yet too young to assume responsibility. In this course many of them discover that what they can do can make a difference. There is a feeling of self worth. I cannot think of anything more imporant. . . .[13]

By allowing youngsters to exercise initiative, industry, independence, and to assume some responsibilities, Resources for Youth helps provide both relevant and practical experiences necessary for adolescents.

The Boy Scouts and other traditional, adult-supervised groups have utilized the files of the National Resources for Youth to look for meaningful projects that their own organizations can adopt.[14] In order to survive, youth agencies are trying to modify existing programs to update them, to give members more responsibility, and to offer expanded services to the disadvantaged whites, blacks, and other ethnic groups in both urban and rural areas.

To reach urban youth Ys have had to change their mode of operation. Instead of waiting for youngsters to come through their doors, they now find it more effective to send workers into the street to recruit and provide programs for adolescents. Children in rural areas are physically isolated and find it very difficult to get back to a church or school or someone's house for meetings. In these rural areas the Boy Scouts of America has begun to offer scouting during activity periods at school.

Even 4-H Clubs, which in the past exemplified a wholesome farm life, have begun to design programs to attract urban members. A 1964 study of Emory Brown and Patrick Boyle, *4-H in Urban Areas*, reported that many fourth, fifth, and sixth graders, a majority female, were attracted to the 4-H programs. Few of the members were from the lower socioeconomic levels.[15] 4-H now offers adult-sponsored groups that provide havens against such urban problems as heavy drug use or early sexual activity. To correlate and not compete, The National Federation of Settlements and Neighborhood Centers has linked some of its programs to 4-H operations in cities.

Youth organizations are placing more emphasis on counseling and working with small, closely-knit groups similar in backgrounds (age, interests, and education). The Ys also employ vocational counselors to assist interested members.

Because so much of the child's future is determined in the home, some of the youth-serving agencies are winning federal support in sponsoring programs that emphasize parent education and parent involvement. In 1973, Save the Children Federation received a grant from the Office of Child Development for a project entitled "Teenagers as Child Advocates." This demonstration program is a cooperative endeavor between private and public agencies and the parents of a rural Appalachian community to recruit members and provide learning experiences in which teenagers obtain the skills and knowledge to become effective future parents. In this program, teenagers learn about child development in out-of-school classes and work in day-care centers or children's homes. These teenagers are then expected to use their new skills and knowledge as child advocates throughout the community. The program goals have been to reinforce learning through experience, to provide needed services to parents and children of the community as well as to train adolescents to become effective future parents, and to introduce teenagers to a possible career in working with younger children. The program has attracted some criticism from persons who are concerned that it may be imposing a constricted definition of "family" on adolescents. These critics also feel that the goals of the program may be conflictual: teaching adolescents the importance of having a mother at home to care properly for the children while preparing them for jobs outside the home as child-care workers.

A similar program is being offered in urban areas by The National Federation of Settlements and Neighborhoods in conjunction with the Office of Child Development (OCD), involving adolescents in practical work settings.

OCD, as part of its Education for Parenthood Program, is supporting projects like these in national voluntary organizations. What is significant here is that OCD, in addition to funding school curriculum development contracts, has gone outside the schools to the voluntary agencies. The investment of millions of dollars in voluntary agencies reflects OCD's belief that these agencies are not outmoded, but actually reach millions of adolescents.

Conclusion

If voluntary national youth-serving agencies came into existence as a reaction to the changing character of American life in the second half of the nineteenth century, then they must learn how to satisfy the needs of adolescents living in the urban, ethnic, postindustrial society of the last quarter of the twentieth century. Although some alterations are apparent, most adult-sponsored youth organizations are suffering from a confusion of purpose and have not yet set themselves a new set of goals for the 1970s.

Gisela Konopka believes that there is "hidden gold" in agencies, which can be a "rich source" of opportunities for adolescents to explore themselves and the world around them, to develop meaningful relationships with peers and adults, and to find commitment and self-direction. Among her recommendations for youth agencies outlined in *Young Girls: A Portrait of Adolescence*, are: (1) allowing adolescents to participate actively in planning and executing youth projects; (2) furnishing opportunities for adolescents to discuss their problems; (3) establishing co-ed activities; (4) reducing organizational structure to leave groups small, informal, and fairly autonomous; (5) active recruiting of "youth in trouble"; and particularly, (6) encouraging significant participation in the public life of the community.

Today most agencies continue to attempt to build character by aiming their special services at particular, separate age groups. However they choose to change their programs, they must offer the adolescent the sense of personal worth that comes from feeling that one can make a difference in the world.

The Young Adolescent in the Juvenile Justice System

Introduction

It is the central argument of this study that young adolescents receive relatively little of our nation's attention in terms of research and programs; there is, however, one group which at present is of grave concern to government agencies and the lay citizen alike: the juvenile offender.

Large sums of public and private funds are spent each year on delinquency prevention and rehabilitation, as well as on the system that arrests, adjudicates, and maintains in custody our society's youthful criminals. In this section, we will discuss the effectiveness of our system's efforts in dealing with this group of adolescents and will point out certain current issues in juvenile corrections.

Most programs and publications dealing with juvenile delinquency include all children under age sixteen. A few studies offer age-specific information, and where possible we include this. In general, however, the information included in this section does not relate exclusively to early adolescents.

Who Are the Juvenile Delinquents?

> . . . this nation has reached a turning point in the way we handle children in trouble. It is imperative that this nation devote its resources and talents to resolving the legal and social issues involved in the prevention and control of delinquency. We can continue upon the same paths, locking children up in institutions, often for acts which are not crimes, where the only "rehabilitation" is brutalization or, at best, alienation. Alternatively, we can seize upon a unique opportunity—the chance to develop new methods of redirecting behavior that endangers society, unhampered by the forms and restrictions of our traditional juvenile correctional system.[1]

The number of young people who are adjudicated "delinquents"—that is, who have been processed through the juvenile court system and who have been found guilty—represents only 2.9 percent of youths ten to seventeen.[2] Yet alarming statistics can be cited concerning the scope of juvenile delinquency in regard to the rising national crime rate. Reports from the Children's Bureau of the Department of Health, Education, and Welfare (DHEW) indicate that "one in nine youths and one in six male youths will be referred to juvenile court before their eighteenth birthday."[3]

Between 1960 and 1970, the arrests of juveniles for all infractions doubled, but the arrests of juveniles for violent crimes increased 216 percent. Perhaps even more significant is the fact that youths under the age of eighteen were arrested for slightly more than half of the serious crimes in the United States in 1970.[4]

A conservative estimate of the total number of juvenile arrests in 1970 is about two million. . . . About half of the individuals arrested were sent to court and about half of those—some 500,000 youngsters—were formally removed to the juvenile correctional system.[5]

In an article in the *New York Times*, Diane Ravitch reports on the incidence of school crime in New York:

. . . for the 1973-74 school year, the New York City school system reported almost 5,000 "incidents." No matter how the figures are added up, the total is not reassuring. Juvenile crime is an increasingly serious problem. . . . The growing consensus is that the problem of crime in the schools is merely one dimension of the far greater problem of juvenile crime. In 1973 over 20,000 children under the age of 16 were arrested in New York City. Almost 15,000 of those arrests were for felony offenses, an increase of 16 percent in the last year alone.[6]

It is significant that the statistics quoted refer precisely to the early adolescent.

Large numbers of youths appear to be committing delinquent acts. Self-report studies indicate that up to 90 percent of all young people have committed acts that could bring them into the web of the juvenile justice system. Since a much smaller percent are caught, it would be impossible to create a representative profile of the delinquent youth. We can, however, look at the characteristics of the much smaller group that is officially defined as delinquent. (See Table 6-1 for arrests by offense, ages 11-15.)

The President's Commission on Law Enforcement and Administration of Justice issued a report in 1967: "the most comprehensive study of crime and juvenile delinquency undertaken in the nation's history . . . based upon eighteen months' work with 175 consultants and hundreds of advisors representing a broad range of opinions and professions; countless visits to courts, prison and police stations; three national conferences, five national surveys; hundreds of meetings; and interviews with tens of thousands of people."[7] This description is a result of findings by the Commission:

1. Official delinquents are predominately male. In 1965 boys under 18 were arrested five times as often as girls. Four times as many boys as girls were referred to juvenile court. [This figure is changing in light of current skirmishes with sexual role reversals—female crime is surging in volume.]
2. Boys and girls commit different kinds of offenses. Children's Bureau

statistics based on large-city court reports reveal that more than half of the girls referred to juvenile court in 1965 were referred for conduct that would not be criminal if committed by adults; only one-fifth of the boys were referred for such conduct. . . .

3. Delinquents are concentrated disproportionately in the cities, and particularly in the larger cities. Arrest rates are next highest in the suburbs, and lowest in rural areas.
4. Delinquency rates are high among children from broken homes. They are similarly high among children who have numerous siblings.
5. Delinquents tend to do badly in school. Their grades are below average. Large numbers have dropped one or more classes behind their classmates or dropped out of school entirely.
6. Delinquents tend to come from backgrounds of social and economic deprivation. Their families tend to have lower than average incomes and social status.
7. More important than the individual's situation is the area in which a youth lives. One study shows that a lower class youth has little chance of being classified as delinquent if he lives in an upper class neighborhood. Numerous studies have revealed the relationship between certain deprived areas . . . and delinquency.[8]

Gerald Bachman makes an extremely forceful statement about the role of the family: "The relationships between our background measures and the summary index of delinquency can be reported very quickly. Only the family relations measure shows a meaningful association with delinquency; the better a boy gets along with his family, the less delinquency he reports."[9]

This thumbnail sketch of the officially defined delinquent is further amplified by the results of a more recent study, published in 1972, *Delinquency in a Birth Cohort,*[10] which confirms the high incidence of arrests of nonwhites and furnishes significant age statistics. This study, conducted by Wolfgang, Figlio, and Sellin, is frequently cited by workers in the field as one of the best analyses of youthful crime available. In a study of all male age cohorts born in 1945 and living in Philadelphia between their tenth and eighteenth birthdays, the investigators were able to follow the progress of 9,945 youths through their adolescent years in their contacts with societal institutions such as schools and courts.

A major pattern became evident in the data collected on the contact of these youths with the police and the courts. Beginning at age ten, there is a steady rise in arrests, peaking at age sixteen and dropping rather markedly at age seventeen. "We may take the years fourteen to seventeen as being those in which adolescent delinquency blooms."[11]

Of particular relevance to our concern for young adolescents are the statistics in the study concerning age of onset of delinquency. Although the mean age of onset for all white offenders was 14.2 and for nonwhite offenders 13.3, the mean age of onset for *chronic* offenders was approximately two years lower (12.0 for white and 11.6 for nonwhite).[12] The authors report that "the

Table 6-1
Arrests, by Offense

Offense Charged	Ages 11-12	13-14	15
Total	146,080	433,202	356,309
Percent distribution	2.1	6.2	5.1
Criminal homicide:			
Murder and nonnegligent manslaughter	20	165	268
Manslaughter by negligence	12	23	26
Forcible rape	92	549	651
Robbery	2,376	7,456	6,279
Aggravated assault	1,806	5,501	4,647
Burglary—breaking or entering	16,423	42,783	31,488
Larceny—theft	44,771	98,477	63,663
Auto theft	2,077	15,484	18,084
Violent crime[a]	4,294	13,671	11,845
Percent distribution	1.6	5.0	4.3
Property crime[b]	63,271	156,744	113,235
Percent distribution	5.6	14.0	10.1
Subtotal for above offenses	67,577	170,438	125,106
Percent distribution	4.8	12.2	9.0
Other assaults	5,857	14,615	10,438
Arson	1,038	1,723	857
Forgery and counterfeiting	122	534	624
Fraud	258	629	611
Embezzlement	33	68	56
Stolen Property; buying, receiving, possessing	1,548	4,831	4,221
Vandalism	15,841	26,356	13,518
Weapons; carrying, possessing, etc.	960	3,500	3,359
Prostitution and commercialized vice	9	119	173
Sex offenses (except forcible rape and prostitution)	844	2,726	2,118
Narcotic drug laws	1,098	10,622	15,706
Gambling	29	300	394
Offenses against family and children	25	113	126
Driving under the influence	15	81	209
Liquor laws	574	7,021	12,423
Drunkenness	550	5,276	7,244
Disorderly conduct	10,992	30,290	24,931
Vagrancy	299	1,567	1,786

Table 6-1 (cont.)

Offense Charged	Ages 11-12	13-14	15
All other offenses (except traffic)	20,329	63,779	52,204
Suspicion	1,276	3,750	3,558
Curfew and loitering law violations	4,167	20,644	22,983
Runaways	12,639	64,220	53,664

[a]Violent crime is offenses of murder, forcible rape, robbery, and aggravated assault.

[b]5,649 agencies: 1971 estimate. Based on: Pop. 155,446,000. Property crime is offenses of burglary, larceny, and auto theft.

Extracted from: *Sourcebook of Criminal Justice Statistics*, 1973, U.S. Dept. of Justice, LEAA, U.S. Government Printing Office, Aug. 1973.

earlier the offender commits his first offense, the greater the number of offenses he will have commited by the end of his seventeenth year,"[13] and even more specifically, "boys who began their delinquency at age thirteen (mean and mode) committed more offenses from the onset years through age seventeen than boys who began at any other year."[14]

These reports tell us how many youthful offenders there are and who they are likely to be. Of equal importance is a consideration of what they have done, or how our society defines delinquency functionally.

According to the 1971 *Annual Report of the Youth Development and Delinquency Prevention Administration*, one-third of juvenile arrests are for serious crimes such as murder, rape, aggravated assault, and robbery; however, "at the other end of the scale another one-third (approximately) of the arrests were for offenses that are not crimes in the adult sense—running away from home, violation of curfew laws, incorrigibility, truancy. . . ."[15]

Although youths account for a disproportionate number of criminal violations, they are frequently referred to the courts for what are commonly named "status offenses." The definition of a status offense is that conduct which, though illegal for a minor, if engaged in by an adult would not result in legal action. Examples from juvenile court laws are:

Violates any law or ordinance
Immoral conduct around school
Immoral or indecent conduct
Associates with vicious or immoral persons
Enters, visits house of ill repute
Patronizes gaming place
Patronizes public poolroom
Patronizes saloon
Wanders about railroad yards or tracks
Absents self from home without consent

Smokes cigarettes in public
Begging or receiving alms
Uses vile or obscene language[16]

Anthony Platt, University of California criminologist, contends that our society's definition of juvenile delinquency and its system of juvenile corrections historically grew from the child-saving movement at the end of the nineteenth century.[17] Although a major concern of the reformers was to protect youth from "the horrors and excesses of the adult courts," its primary preoccupation was the definition and control of youthful deviance. As Dr. Saleem A. Shah, Chief of the Center for Studies of Crime and Delinquency at the National Institute of Mental Health, points out, "not only did the child-savers voice strong humanitarian concerns and ideologies, but they brought attention to, and in fact, invented, new categories of youthful misbehavior which had not previously been viewed as requiring formal societal efforts at prevention and control."[18]

Although this movement was able to bring about some actual improvement in the handling of young offenders, it also permitted the inclusion of previous noncriminal behavior into the justice system, thereby equalizing the handling of the various offenses of the young. As a result, the runaway or the truant has been subjected to the same legal processes or lack thereof that govern our society's treatment of the youthful murderer or robber.

There is evidence, in fact, that in the actual workings of the juvenile justice system status offenders receive more punitive treatment, and little or no evidence that they receive more therapeutic attention. Studies comparing the fates of delinquents committing offenses in nineteen major cities revealed the following facts: (1) status offenders are more likely to be detained in detention facilities than serious delinquents (54% vs. 31%); (2) once detained, status offenders are twice as likely to be detained for more than thirty days longer than serious delinquents (51% vs. 25%); (3) status offenders are more likely to receive harsher dispositions in juvenile court and to be sent to confinement placement than serious delinquents (26% vs. 23%), with the average stay being much longer for the status offender.[19]

Once status offenders are sentenced, they are frequently placed in institutions or training schools that also house serious offenders, and are given little or no differential treatment. Under varying conditions, large numbers are placed in jails that house adult criminals.

Although there is widespread support for removing the "delinquent" label from status offenders, the Honorable Justine Wise Polier, who has served as a judge since 1935 and has wide experience with the juvenile corrections system, contends that appropriate custodial attention for status offenders is justified, since one finds a high proportion of emotionally disturbed children and youths who require residential treatment among status offenders.[20] The point nevertheless remains that although the status offenders may be seriously in need of treatment, they have not yet committed a criminal act that justifies their being placed in punitive detention, in an atmosphere more likely to aggravate their problems than to correct them.

The previously quoted statistics bear witness to the fact that juvenile delinquency is a serious problem in our society, and that our corrections system is fraught with inequities and contradictions. The statistics also point to an unprecedented increase in all kinds of juvenile offenses which cannot be explained by population expansion alone. These are problems of great concern to our public institutions and to the population at large.

The reports indicate not only that more juveniles now commit offenses, but also that they begin at a younger age.[21] The great public concern centers, of course, on the rise of violent crimes perpetrated by the young. The 216 percent increase cited earlier is a startling figure. Reaction from the public is growing; there are demands for stronger controls of juvenile crime, and for laws and legal processes that protect the victim rather than the criminal.

Given the growing national concern over the criminal acts of the young, changes, perhaps extensive ones, are inevitable in our juvenile justice system. At issue here is whether or not our institutions, in moving to meet these concerns, will continue to treat status offenders and criminals in the same manner. If legal processes become stricter for the young violent criminals, will they also become stricter for all the categories listed under the umbrella of juvenile deviancy, or will serious efforts be made to differentiate, both in penalty and treatment? There is evidence, to be presented later, that both federal and state efforts are toward such a differentiation.

Prediction and Prevention

Based on what information researchers have furnished regarding individual and societal sources of deviancy, widespread efforts have been made by public and private agencies to identify high risk youths and to forestall their delinquent activity; in other words, to predict and prevent. In actual fact, the development of prevention programs has been so rapid and extensive that many critics feel that they have developed without proper direction by thorough research and continue to function without any real evidence that they are effective. As Shah points out, only a small fraction of 1 percent of the criminal justice system's budget is spent on research.[22]

One of the most important findings of *Juvenile Delinquency Prevention Programs*, based on a review of over 6,600 pertinent abstracts and contact with more than 200 agencies and institutes, supports earlier reports: there is very little quality evaluation of the prevention programs being funded. In 1970 "the federal government alone spent 11.5 billion dollars . . . for juvenile delinquency and related youth development programs. Fifty-seven percent of these programs had no evaluation at all. Of those programs with evaluation, only 18 percent included descriptive or statistical assessments. . . . Of those reports containing empirical data (or approximately 8 percent of the total), few were considered to be methodologically sound."[23]

The staff for the study reviewed evaluations of programs in nine categories: Juvenile Court Programs, Volunteer and Indigenous Nonprofessionals, Individual and Group Counseling, Social Casework, Street-Corner Workers, Area Projects and Youth Service Bureaus, Educational and Vocational Programs, Community Treatment Programs, and Miscellaneous Programs.

Their conclusions are not optimistic and echo what other evaluators before them have said:

> In summary . . . an extremely small percentage of delinquency and youth development efforts are ever evaluated, even minimally. Furthermore, even when adequate evaluation is performed, few studies show significant results. Finally, information which policy makers are most interested in is virtually nonexistent.[24]

On the basis of the few adequate evaluations available, the group makes the following recommendations: (1) Recreation programs, guided group interaction, social casework, and detached worker-gang worker projects have shown no evidence of having been effective in preventing juvenile crime and should be discarded. (2) Community treatment, the use of volunteers, diversion programs in general (including the Youth Service Bureaus), and special school projects are beginning to show some success, and should be further explored and evaluated.[25]

The report gives further specific recommendations for encouraging diversion, differential treatment, community treatment, decriminalization of status offenses, expanded use of volunteers, prevention-treatment programs aimed at females, special school programs, and the creation in each state of a Central Children and Youth Agency.

While admitting that delinquent behavior like all human behavior is extremely difficult to change, and that "there is little in the way of effective programs" in delinquency prevention, the authors of the report take some hope in the newer programs they recommend for further evaluation.[26]

Some students of crime, however, take a more pessimistic view of delinquency prevention. Edwin M. Lemert, a sociologist at the University of California at Davis, contends in *Instead of Court* that neither the prevention techniques aimed at individuals nor the broad-scale social amelioration programs have made any significant contribution to delinquency prevention. A major problem is that of predicting who the target group or individual should be in prevention activities. Though researchers have shown that there are high risk groups and some psychiatrists have postulated that there are certain predelinquent types or pathological personalities, Lemert contends that there is ultimately no way accurately to predict who will or will not become delinquent.[27]

Saleem Shah states that although most predictive techniques do identify the majority of actual predelinquents, they overidentify or falsely identify a significant number as well. It is not only inefficient and expensive to treat more youths than necessary, Shah points out, but the whole idea of delinquency prevention raises the "serious social policy and Constitutional issues of intervening in the lives of persons especially when they have not yet displayed any behavior which makes them subject to the community's social defense efforts."[28]

Lemert asserts that preventive programs fail not only because of the difficulty of identifying accurately a target group, but also because of their diffuse impact, inability to be validated, and their failure to crystallize into stable institutional structures.[29] He concludes, "The conception of delinquency prevention, being ill-conceived and devoid of demonstrable results, should be abandoned."[30]

Another student of crime, James Q. Wilson, professor of Government at Harvard University, agrees with this conclusion. In *Thinking About Crime*, Wilson urges our institutions to abandon the ineffectual effort to prevent crime by searching for its causes. His argument, in short, contends that although researchers have presented a fairly convincing picture of the impact of family situations on forming delinquent behavior, such knowledge is actually of little use in informing public policy.[31]

Wilson states:

> There are, we now know, certain things we can change in accordance with our intentions and certain ones we cannot. We cannot alter the number of juveniles who first experiment with minor crimes. We cannot lower the recidivism rate, though within reason we should keep trying. . . .[32]
>
> I believe that our society has not done as well as it could have in controlling crime because of erroneous but persistent views about the nature of man and the capacities of his institutions. . . . The gravity of the offense must be appropriately impressed on the first offender, but the effort to devise ways of reeducating or uplifting him in order to insure that he does not steal again is likely to be wasted—both because we do not know how to reeducate or uplift and because most young delinquents seem to reeducate themselves no matter what society does.[33]

Although the views of Professors Lemert and Wilson vary widely on many points, they are apparently in accord in urging the institutions of our society to turn from fruitless efforts to prevent crime toward effective methods of control.

The primary issues raised by the scholars and practitioners in the area of juvenile prevention are serious ones. Evidence seems convincing that so far preventive programs have failed to make any significant impact. In our society, social defiance has usually been regarded like other handicaps, in which early intervention is essential to save money, disability, and heartbreak. How will America's institutions react to the mounting research evidence that delinquency cannot be predicted with accuracy or prevented with any adequate degree of success?

Control and Treatment: The Juvenile Justice System

Present Problems and Abuses

The vast number of persons concerned with juvenile crime, the social workers, the criminologists, the scholars, the authorities of the courts, the politicians, the victims, and even lay citizens, though representing widely divergent points of view, agree on one point: the juvenile justice system is a failure as it now functions.

Nicholas Hobbs, writing a consensus report of the evidence presented by the authorities on juvenile justice for the Project on the Classification of Exceptional Children, asserts that the "correctional system as it currently functions has no discernible rational basis."[34] This is only one of many reports indicating the almost total failure of our judicial system's efforts to control and treat juvenile crime.

The burden placed on the juvenile justice system is unwieldy. In short, the role of the court permits interference in the lives of young people, whether or not they have committed a crime, promises to "cure" them, and is not required to allow them the opportunity to refuse treatment. Theoretically it is responsible for the rehabilitation of over one million adolescents annually. It is failing to do so for many reasons, but primarily because:

(1) the courts do not have the resources in manpower or knowledge even effectively to screen and decide on the proper disposition of cases. Usually only large metropolitan areas have specialized courts for children. In other areas judges usually have no particular training for juvenile cases and in some areas no legal training at all. Almost all courts have inadequate probation and clinical services;
(2) often the courts are working with the wrong youth to start with, the frightened runaway who needs a changed family situation rather than therapy or punishment, or the abandoned or neglected child needing foster home placement; and most importantly,
(3) the institutions to which the courts send the youths for therapy are overcrowded, understaffed, and seriously deficient in the kind of differential treatment that might possibly benefit the offender. In general, they do

not know *how* to rehabilitate, and therefore the whole system becomes one of punishment rather than treatment.

Although a majority of the youths who are brought before the juvenile courts are released to the responsibility of their parent(s) or put on a relatively informal probation, a considerable number, 500,000,[35] are detained by the juvenile corrections system, and approximately 150,000 are formally placed in juvenile or adult correctional facilities each year.

There is a current trend to place these youths in small group homes and community centers. However, the vast majority of predelinquent and delinquent children are still housed in large congregate juvenile training schools.[36]

That these traditional training schools cannot meet the widely varying needs of the youth referred there is evident. Courts, however, are seriously limited by the alternatives available to them. There are not enough relaxed family-type homes for the youths who would benefit from this type of approach, nor are there enough facilities equipped to cope with the seriously disturbed and violent adolescent. In his study of the New York State corrections system, Ted Morgan reports: "There does not exist a single city or state facility equipped to handle this type of [disturbed and violent] youth."[37]

It is not unusual, then, for the child-murderer and the rapist to be placed in close institutional quarters with the runaway and the truant. It is not unusual for the runaway and the truant to be exposed to the same harsh treatment meted out to the violent. And in the boring and hostile atmosphere that pervades most large institutions, many of the status offenders are "reeducated" into criminals.

Reports of the abuses of training schools are legion, and the rate of recidivism of their inmates testifies to their failure. More serious than the fact of their failure to rehabilitate is the growing evidence that they actually increase delinquency and other deviant behavior.

There is growing awareness as well that not only the youths actually incarcerated by the corrections system suffer ill results, but that mere contact with the juvenile justice system at any point may serve to push the adolescent into deviant conduct.[38]

Wolfgang, Figlio, and Sellin conclude: "the juvenile justice system, at its best, has no effect on the subsequent behavior of adolescent boys, and, at its worse, has a deleterious effect on future behavior."[39]

It is not totally on the basis of ineffectiveness that our juvenile justice system is attacked. Mention has already been made of the courts' violation of due process; critics also eschew the inequities and prejudices that prevent equal protection under the law. Previously cited statistical studies show the high incidence of detention of blacks and low-income youth. Law enforcement and court officials across the country are far more likely to release a middle-class youthful offender to the responsibility of his parents than they are to return, without incarceration, a low-income youth to an inner-city environment. Courts assume that a middle-class family will secure from the community or provide itself with the therapeutic and custodial services needed. The recent movement toward community based treatment comes, in part, from efforts to provide for all youths the less punitive, less stigmatizing, and frequently more effective treatment that has more commonly been available to middle-class youth.

More recently, critics have pointed out that girls are in a disadvantaged position in the current system. Not only are there fewer youth development programs designed for girls, there is evidence that girls are discriminated against judicially: they are more likely to be incarcerated for promiscuity and given longer sentences for status offenses than males receive for criminal violations.

In addition to its failure to provide equal protection and due process, the juvenile corrections system is also under attack for violating youths' right to privacy. Although a major initial promise of the juvenile justice system was to preserve the privacy of youthful offenders, information concerning case histories circulates rather freely in many areas and is frequently shared with police departments, armed services, and private employers.[40]

Despite the pessimism of many critics, there are many professionals concerned with juvenile delinquency who feel that changes in the correctional system can effect better control and rehabilitation, while protecting certain basic rights. In the next section we will review current trends that are working toward equity and effectiveness in the judicial system.

Emerging Trends in Juvenile Justice

We have discussed some of the factors involved in defining and determining delinquency, and have attempted to portray the broad scope of the problem of juvenile delinquency among adolescents. Also, we have investigated some of the issues raised by efforts to predict, prevent, and treat youthful crime, and have pointed to some of the ways in which the correctional system is failing to perform its professed purpose.

The whole concept of delinquency, its treatment and prevention, is undergoing vigorous change. It is obvious that the juvenile justice system has failed in achieving its dual objectives: "serving the best interests of individual youth while contributing to public safety by controlling and reducing youthful crime."[41] The findings of some of the theorists and practitioners quoted here and various commissions, including the President's Commission on Law Enforcement and Administration of Justice, have played an influential role in shaping the current new trends in juvenile justice.

The National Assessment of Juvenile Corrections (NAJC), a study conducted at the University of Michigan under the direction of Rosemary C. Sarri and Robert D. Vinter, is surveying the situation on a nationwide basis. This five-year study, 1971-1976, is supported by a grant from the National Institute of Law Enforcement and Criminal Justice of the Law Enforcement Assistance Administration, LEAA. We will be relying heavily on the findings of this study in the following sections.

Statutory Change

One of the most basic sources of inequity in the juvenile system is the juvenile code itself. Recent court cases, most notably the Supreme Court decision *in re Gault*, 1967, have considerably redefined the role of the juvenile court. The *Gault* decision did not quarrel with the laudable purposes of the courts.

But in view of the failure of the system to deliver treatment and rehabilitation, the court altered the primary role of the juvenile court from informally identifying wayward youth to emphasizing due process in the classification scheme of the court. The court-based social work is now subservient to legal due process, and the court is charged with the responsibility of forcing the state to prove its right to intervene in the life of the child.[42]

The NAJC survey discovered that general dissatisfaction with the juvenile justice system coupled with the precedent set by *Gault* have led to substantial revision of almost all but a handful of state codes.[43]

The most significant of these changes have occurred in statutes dealing with jurisdiction, detention, adjudication, and disposition.

Jurisdiction. There is a definite trend toward establishing separate categories to differentiate status offenders from perpetrators of criminal acts. Approximately half of the states still do not differentiate; half do. These states, in altering their statutes, have introduced somewhat ambiguous labels such as "children in need of supervision," "unruly children," or "incorrigible children."

There is a less definite trend in changes in age limitations for juvenile court jurisdictions. The ages range from seventeen to fifteen. In most states, the maximum age is seventeen. What these figures do not reflect is that, while there have been many recent statutory changes, they have both lowered and raised the age limitations.

Detention. The provisions covering the processes for handling juveniles once they have come in contact with the judicial system are changing in some states. Restrictions on fingerprinting juveniles, for instance, occur in many state codes, as does provision for detention hearings. The NAJC study points out, however, that ambiguity as to what factors are to be considered at detention hearings still leaves considerable freedom to the local judicial authorities.

The provisions for length of detention before adjudication varies widely among the states. Few states have altered their codes to place definite limits, varying from three days to sixty days.[44]

While an increasing number of state codes advise against placing youths in jail, very few absolutely prohibit it. As a result of ambiguous statutes and unclear provisions, almost 100,000 youths are held annually in jails that house adult criminals.[45]

Adjudication. The *Gault* decision has made its greatest impact on the adjudication process of the juvenile corrections systems, causing it to resemble more closely adult trials in several states.

There has been movement to limit the type of evidence presented at the hearing to facts bearing only on the charge at hand, rather than permitting wider background information on the accused youth's history and past offenses.

A major impact of the *Gault* decision was the requirement that the juvenile be assisted by legal counsel.

Disposition. Although "unlimited discretion without guidelines dominates the disposition phase of the juvenile justice process," a few states have moved to stipulate the procedures that should be followed in decision making, including requiring that probation have a definite time limit, that a periodic review of probation cases be required, that a maximum limit be placed on institutionalization, and that the agencies of commitment be permitted to terminate a juvenile's commitment.[46]

Despite the efforts in several states to control decision making, "nineteen states permit the agency of commitment to transfer a juvenile to an adult correctional institution without approval of the juvenile court."[47]

In the summary of their findings, the NAJC group point out that some of the recent statutory changes "suggest greater punitiveness toward youth by imposition of more stringent sanctions; other changes provide clarification and extension of civil liberties and due process guarantees."[48]

It is as yet too early to assess what impact on state statutes the Juvenile Justice and Delinquency Prevention Act of 1974 will have. States may receive grants if they devise programs in line with the recommendations of the Act: juvenile status offenders should be channeled to other agencies, leaving the courts freer to handle serious youth crime; states should develop advanced techniques to prevent juvenile crime, to divert juveniles from the juvenile justice system, and to provide community based alternatives to juvenile detention and correction facilities; juveniles are not to be confined with incarcerated adults. The Act further clarifies the Federal Juvenile Delinquency Act by setting due process for court cases: it stipulates conditions of custody, duties of magistrates, proceedings in district courts, detention prior to disposition, speedy trial, safeguards in disclosure of juvenile records, commitment in appropriate juvenile rather than adult facilities, and regularization of parole processes.

Institutionalization

In speeches and in publications, the majority of persons working in the area of juvenile corrections espouse a commitment to the reduction in the incarceration of youthful offenders. Evidence of the ineffectiveness of such incarceration (the increasingly high recidivism rate of incarcerated offenders) coupled with the mounting costs (as high as $36,000 per year per youth in some states) have led to recommendations for alternate methods of handling problem youth.

Because of the dominance of this point of view in the literature and because of the publicity given to Massachusetts' dramatic closing of training schools between 1969 and 1972, this trend would seem to have gone beyond the conceptual stage into policy making.

The NAJC study found, however, that "the national picture is one of decreasing institutionalization, but the change is neither radical, uniform, nor precipitous."[49] Most states, while altering the outlines of their judicial systems, have made few substantial changes in the actual workings of the institutions in which the youths are confined.

One exception is Massachusetts, which is a pioneer in the area of institutional reform. In working toward more humane and effective treatment of young offenders in the state, the Department of Youth Services' plan has passed through three phases: first, relaxation of repressive and punitive regulations in the large training schools; second, decentralization of large training schools into small cottage-type living facilities which accent group therapy sessions; and third, closing of training schools and establishment of a network of community-based facilities and services.[50]

Evaluations of the second phase of the program, therapeutic cottages, "demonstrate consistently that decentralized cottage treatment and group therapy could lead to remarkably better reactions and experience even for youth within the same institutions" and that the "data revealed reactions from youth and staff that justifies such efforts elsewhere."[51]

Despite the success of many group therapy cottages within the institution, the Commissioner of the Department, Dr. Jerome Miller, concluded that therapeutic communities might be more successful outside the institution.[52] This decision led to the final closing of most large state institutions in 1971-72, and the establishment of seven regional units to coordinate and implement treatment services for youth in the community. The regional units, being administrative offices only, do not house youths, but refer them to appropriate community residential or nonresidential programs.

Although the Massachusetts Department of Youth Services opted finally for abolishing large institutions altogether (except secure facilities for seriously disturbed or violent youths), as have several other states, the results of their experimentation with institutional reform can furnish valuable guidelines for other states who are interested in making changes in their existing institutions.

Diversion

With the growing awareness that incarceration, at least in its present form, is an ineffectual and inappropriate method of handling the social and emotional problems of deviant youth, new methods are being devised to prevent and treat delinquency. Programs to divert adolescents from the juvenile justice system have been increasing in all regions of the country.

Diversion programs are offered prior to adjudication and after official police contact in order to deal with illegal behavior through noncriminal means. There are also growing numbers of programs that divert people after adjudication in order to "minimize penetration."[53]

Edwin M. Lemert, mentioned earlier as a proponent of control rather than prevention, views diversion as a method of control and treatment. Deploring the present practice of the courts in "causing" delinquency "by processing cases of children and youth whose problems might be ignored, normalized in their original setting, or dealt with as family, educational, or welfare problems,"[54] he urges that statutes be changed to allow juvenile court action only for serious felonies or dangerous disturbances. The other cases should be absorbed into the community or "funneled into some type of diversion institutions, staffed and organized to cope with problems on their own terms rather than as antecedents to delinquency."[55]

Lemert offers several practical suggestions for ways in which diversion agencies might work, but urges that the organizational form of the agency, as long as it is operationally oriented toward problem solving, is less important than the idea which infuses it. "Diversion of children from the official court system is a state of mind; once it is established as a predominant social value, the questions of adaptation of means to end should be more easily answered."[56]

The principle of diversion is somewhat ambiguous and can be identified both in certain informal dispositions of juvenile offenses as well as in carefully formulated programs. The policeman who warns rather than arrests, and the court authorities who refer a youth to a mental health facility rather than to a correctional institution, are equally engaged in diversion activities.

There are, however, large and institutionalized diversion programs, the best known of which is the Youth Service Bureau. The President's Commission on Law Enforcement, which recommended the establishment of the program, stated: "The Youth Service Bureau–an agency to handle many troubled, troublesome young people outside the criminal justice system–is needed in part because society has failed to give the juvenile court the resources that would allow it to function as its founders hoped it would."[57]

The general findings of a National Study, conducted by the State of California Youth Authority, were that in 1971-72 approximately 50,000 youths were serviced by 140 of these bureaus away from the juvenile justice system, and that in addition over 150,000 more participated in the programs.

What is the typical Bureau like? From analyses of 195 written responses, the California authorities come up with the following composite:

Individual counseling and referral were the most important services for at least 75%. . . . Included were referral and general follow-up; family counseling; group counseling; drug treatment; job referral; tutoring and remedial education; recreation programs; medical aid; and legal aid.

At least 2/3 of the programs were located in an urban core city or model city neighborhoods, socio-economic conditions for the areas were usually considered lower income with a high crime rate, unemployment, and limited facilities. . . . The target group was adolescents 14-17 years old.

The "typical" program provided intensive services for 350 cases per year; about 60% were male and 40% female. The average age was 15.5 years. Primary sources of referral were school, law enforcement and self. Primary reasons for referral were unacceptable behavior, personal difficulties, or some professional services needs. Drugs and delinquency were the primary reasons for police referral.[58]

On the basis of information already presented, it would seem that the further a young status offender penetrates the juvenile justice system, the more likely he is to become actually delinquent. Why, then, is diversion not automatically employed in this type of case? The failure to do so is partially due to the attitude of mainstream America that punitive measures are preferable to lax and unproven rehabilitative measures in controlling the spread of juvenile crime. There is also evidence that possibly the diverted youth may not be getting a better deal.[59] Since the diversion program can often entail more time on an "informal" basis than actual jail sentences, it must be questioned whether it is justifiable to commit a youth to longer detention in a diversionary program than he would receive from adjudication.

Another factor hampering effective diversion is the lack of information based on evaluation of various diversion programs. Some evaluations have been conducted, but results are contradictory and confusing. Nevertheless, a very thorough recent study of New York City's multimillion-dollar prison reform program has brought to light some disconcerting facts. The major features of the program for adults and juveniles alike are diversion or rehabilitative alternatives to prison. The study, directed by Robert Fishman and financed by LEAA, revealed that 41 percent of adults and juveniles enrolled in the diversion programs had at least one arrest within one year of entering the programs.[60] Even more sobering are the statistics concerning young adolescents:

The worst record of recidivism—a rearrest rate of 51 per cent—was found in youngsters aged 13 to 15. One of every three of these juveniles was apprehended on charges of having committed a violent crime.[61]

The Fishman report, branding the diversion programs a failure, calls for their abolition. The study reveals that lavishly funded diversion programs offering a wide variety of quality services are no more successful in preventing further criminal activity than are the modest programs.

The report urges that the "city consider 'preventive detention' for persons accused of violent crimes and swifter trials as more practical alternatives to halting the steady crime rise" in New York City,[62] and recommends in general a tougher system which provides "adequate, immediate, certain, and consistent" punishment.

The Fishman study has come under attack by some criminologists and correction workers for using faulty research procedures and has been defended by others as sound and admirable. The results are obviously disappointing to the large body of judicial workers who have looked to diversion as a humane and effective solution for many of the nation's criminal offenders.

The question of how much that is learned about programs in large urban areas can be transferred to other smaller communities remains unanswered. Further evaluation and experimentation must be made with different systems in different areas to assess other possibly conducive conditions for therapeutic community treatment.

Community Based Intervention

As a result of the trend away from institutionalizing adolescents, the term "community based treatment" has become the catch phrase for alternatives to incarceration. Like "diversion" this concept is ambiguous and is interpreted in various ways. Diversion is aimed primarily at protecting the noncriminal offender, while community based treatment is aimed at "retaining in the community those offenders who are eligible for institutional placement because they cannot be placed safely and effectively under probation supervision."[63] Most community alternatives fall into one of three classifications: (1) specialized units of probation and parole agencies; (2) nonresidential intensive treatment (attendance centers, guided group interaction programs); or (3) residential programs and out-of-home placement alternatives.[64]

Specialized units of probation and parole agencies are a result of caseload research in the sixties. It was found that reducing the caseloads of parole officers was not as significant in improving parole performance as was the classification of offenders and the development of appropriate treatment models. The California Youth Authority's Community Treatment Project (CTP) was established "to test the feasibility of substituting intensive supervision of juveniles in the community for the regular program of institutionalization plus parole and to develop optimum treatment/control plans for defined types of offenders."[65] Another form of community based treatment in this category is the Positive

Action for Youth (PAY) Program operating in schools in Flint, Michigan, since September 1966. Provided here are intensive treatment and counseling to male juvenile probationers including work experience, family counseling, and individual counseling with the school and social agency concerned. Various programs such as these have allowed greater flexibility to courts in disposition of offenders for whom neither probation nor institutionalization is suitable.[66]

The nonresidential intensive treatment classification includes such alternatives as the attendance or day care center for those requiring more intensive care than probation but not incarceration. Offenders live at home and concentrate solely on a school and counseling program. Attendance centers provide a structured correctional "in-house" program. Placement in such a program is an alternative to commitment, not to probation. It is the result of a court order and is a condition of probation.[67]

Another type of nonresidential treatment is guided group interaction. The GGI programs are:

> . . . primarily concerned with peer group dynamics and the operation of the peer group in restructuring the youth "subculture" around more socially acceptable norms and values. These programs also depend sometimes to a considerable extent on the involvement of youth in their own treatment.[68]

These programs differ from traditional group therapy in that authority given the group itself in decision making is greatly increased, on the theory that group support is as important for social as for antisocial behavior.

The last category in community based treatment is the out-of-home placement and residential treatment. The judge chooses this alternative when he deems that the youth must be removed from his home because conditions there are obstacles to his rehabilitation.

Foster-home placement is the most traditionally used alternative to institutionalization for juvenile probationers. The National Survey of Corrections reported that 42 percent of the 233 probation departments utilized it.[69]

The group home is another form of residential treatment. Mostly group homes are operated by organizations like churches or civic groups and often referred to as "halfway houses." This facility normally accommodates eight to thirty youths. "It was initially conceived as a stepping-stone between the institution and the community, but a recent trend has evolved of utilizing it as a diversion program for individuals who otherwise would be committed to a traditional state training school program."[70]

Community based treatment programs of these types are emerging as a definite alternative to the institution, but NAJC finds them only in a limited number of states and in no case sufficient in number to handle all those youths requiring referral to them.

The residential models are guided by various philosophies, but two major ones stand out: guided group interaction and behavior modification.

The behavior modification programs being implemented in this country, especially Achievement Place in Lawrence, Kansas, and the programs that have grown out of it, have attracted a great deal of attention.[71] Despite glowing descriptions of such programs by their proponents, no clear evaluation has been conducted—that is, no rigorous follow-up studies have proven their effectiveness. Whether community programs utilize guided group interaction or behavior modification, the point to be made is that the evaluative procedures need to be sharpened to ascertain how effective any of these programs is in dealing with youthful offenders.

Radical Nonintervention

NAJC has not identified radical nonintervention as an emerging trend, but it has been discussed heatedly by various people disenchanted with the program-oriented approaches being taken by juvenile corrections organizations. A very interesting and rigorous examination of selected programs by Stevens H. Clarke at the Institute of Government, University of North Carolina at Chapel Hill, shows that the studies reviewed "presented little evidence that the juvenile offender treatment programs succeeded in reducing delinquency, and much evidence that they failed."[72] Clarke's point is that "it is morally right to treat 'captive' juvenile offenders as long as their 'captivity' is not *prolonged* by the treatments."[73]

The ethical question involved in funding programs for youthful offenders is a serious one, especially when studies by Martin Gold indicate that being apprehended does not reduce subsequent delinquency,[74] and Wolfgang, Figlio, and Sellin found that the severity of juvenile court dispositions does not discourage and may encourage further delinquency.[75] Clarke gives some thoughtful suggestions or guidelines for further treatment programs for offenders:

1. Announce future programs as experiments and evaluate them rigorously.
2. Restrictions on an offender's liberty should be justified only in terms of protecting public safety and *never* in terms of a perceived need for treatments.
3. Rehabilitative treatment programs should be based on facts.
4. Concentrate resources on serious offenders and first index offenders. These are the people whom society can justify incarcerating on the basis of the threat they pose to society.
5. For status offenses avoid involvement with the juvenile court and experiment with strictly voluntary community service programs.
6. In evaluating new programs, use randomly selected treatment and control groups whenever possible, and include a "no treatment" group when conditions permit.[76]

The radical noninterventionist policy would be to adopt a standard that seeks to find the alternative least detrimental to the deviant young person while still considering the overall needs of the society. Such a standard would opt in many cases to do nothing with respect to deviant young people unless they were a clear threat to themselves or others (except where a program could be identified that clearly had a positive rehabilitative effect). The standard would also emphasize keeping young people in their community and out of institutions on the grounds that such an approach is less detrimental to the young people involved.

As compelling as such an argument may seem to be, the impact of deviants on the peer group involves the question of the epidemiology of violence and juvenile crime, a subject about which we know little. Bronfenbrenner's warning, made in a different context, is relevant to this question.

> . . . the effect of a peer group on the child depends on the attitudes and activities which prevail in that peer group. Where group norms emphasize academic achievement, the members perform accordingly; where the prevailing expectations call for violation of adult norms, these are as readily translated into action. In short, social contagion is a two-way street. . . .[77]

Delayed Intervention

There is little doubt that the research carried out by Wolfgang, Figlio, and Sellin in Philadelphia is beginning to be felt in trends in delinquency control. The implications of the study on recidivism have had the greatest impact. Scholars as widely different in general points of view as Saleem Shah and James Q. Wilson have espoused the idea of delayed intervention.

What the study revealed, among other things, was that of the 9,945 age cohorts of the study, 3,475 of the boys committed at least one offense which brought them to the attention of the court. Forty-six percent of these juveniles did not commit a second offense; 18 percent of them (or 6 percent of the entire cohort, 667 youths) were chronic offenders who were responsible for over one-half of all offenses.[78]

A major question that concerned the group is at what point in a youth's delinquent career society should intervene both for the benefit of the youth and the society. "One answer would be that the best time is that point beyond which the natural loss rate, or probability of desistance, begins to level off. Because 46% of the delinquents stop after the first offense, a major and expensive treatment program at this point would appear to be wasteful."[79] Delaying intervention would reduce the number of youths substantially through the third offense, after which the desistance probabilities level off.

A public policy of delayed intervention could possibly find favor with the juvenile workers who feel youths should have as little contact as possible with the judicial system; it also could relieve some of the problems of an overburdened, understaffed, underfinanced judicial system, and would concentrate society's efforts on the small percentage of identified chronic offenders.

Should delayed intervention become public policy, however, other questions will need answering. Will the courts have any responsibility for securing aid and direction for the first and second offenders whom they identify and release? Once the chronic offender is identified, what resources exist to treat him or her?

The basic trends that have been identified as emerging and ongoing represent the major ones being discussed and/or implemented in this country. They are broad issues and balk at close definition or categorical description. Sarri and Isenstadt state that these trends are "lines of movement appearing in enough states to suggest that they may eventually characterize much of the nation."[80]

Conclusion

In an effort to present an overview of our nation's juvenile justice system, we have reported facts and statistics on the nature of criminally deviant behavior among adolescents; we have examined the prevalent theories and opinions of professionals in regard to causes, cures, and control of delinquency. In addition, we have discussed some of the myriad problems and abuses of the current corrections system, and have pointed to major recent efforts to make the system both more effective and more equitable.

We cannot help concluding that the sum total of the facts, opinions, and theories we have examined offers a very slender basis on which to develop firm public policy for controlling juvenile crime. There is no clear directive; there is little evidence that our society can in any consistent way, on the basis of present knowledge, prevent or treat or control juvenile delinquency. There is a great deal of evidence that what we try to do is frequently more harmful, both for the individual and society, than simply doing nothing at all.

We are brought once more to the statement, quoted on the first page of this section, made by the Senate Judiciary Committee in its presentation of the bill that became the Juvenile Justice and Delinquency Prevention Act of 1974: "This nation has reached a turning point in the way we handle children in trouble." That our present system is a failure is evident. What will replace it is at present uncertain.

There seem to be two clearly different alternatives, each with its vociferous band of supporters. One approach advocates strong repressive measures: certain and consistent punishment, at least for serious offenders. The professionals who hold this view feel that certainty of incarceration would act as a real deterrent to crime, as well as reduce the crime rate by removing the chronic offender from the streets.

The alternative to this approach seems to be a vigorous, coordinated, massively funded research effort to uncover new possibilities in prevention, treatment, and control. Many feel that our society's failure to discover more effective answers to the problems of deviant behavior lies in our inadequate funding of research and evaluation. This point of view is reflected in the Juvenile Justice Act of 1974, the major thrust of which is to encourage research into delinquency prevention and to evaluate programs already in existence. The Act also seeks to coordinate the nation's attack on delinquency, by centering all programs under one office. (In April 1974, there existed 116 separate federal juvenile delinquency and youth development programs.[81]) Indications are that without vigorous implementation of this Act, and other measures, our corrections system will continue its present ineffective practices and the crime rate will continue to rise. Our citizens' reaction to increased juvenile delinquency may well be a call for far more repressive measures.

We have not yet, as a society, fully committed ourselves to the earnest, expensive task of reclaiming our troubled youth. Perhaps such an expensive and often wasted effort would not be necessary if we, as a society, had a real commitment to all youth. Perhaps the general lack of concerted research efforts aimed at a better understanding of adolescence as a developmental stage contributes as much as anything else to our failure to understand and help troubled juveniles. We do not thoroughly comprehend how they grow, we have inadequate knowledge of how they learn, we rarely understand what alters the delicate emotional structure of their inner world. We know that for many of them our society is an unhealthy place, and we do not know how to cure either them or ourselves.

7 Conclusion

The years twelve to fifteen do not form a coherent unit of life. It has been an irony of this study that we have often concentrated on these years as if they do not represent the extreme variability among individuals that we have documented. We have done this in order to call attention to the tendency of American society to formalize the age period erroneously. These years are socially defined as a "stage" and then neglected.

The variability among young adolescents and their vulnerability to external events can be both positive and negative attributes for social institutions. Young adolescents are vulnerable not only to negative social forces. Choices involving education, health, careers, personal relationships, societal interactions, and many others, are being made or remade. They can be redirected or at least strongly influenced at this strategic time.

Society's present grasp of early adolescence is inadequate. We have underscored over and over again the paucity of meaningful research on early adolescence, the inadequacies of effective educational and voluntary programs, the perplexing and often intractable inequities of the juvenile justice system, the apparent unwillingness to meet the special needs of the handicapped, and the pervasive myths that undermine familial as well as other relational functioning.

We have looked at early adolescence from two vantage points: what research tells us about young adolescents, and some of those societal forces that may be affecting the lives of these young people. We have done this in the hopes of promoting greater understanding of what is known, of what is not known, and of the ways in which various social domains impinge simultaneously upon a little studied and little served population. The next step must be to promote an integrative dialogue about early adolescence.

Several themes have surfaced time and time again during the preparation of this study. We were not looking for them.

That this group is hardly studied and is underserved has been constantly repeated. What does exist appears and disappears seemingly at random, determined by no priorities, proliferated by no policy decisions.

Also startling has been the almost total lack of communication among people who are concerned with young adolescents. Researchers in one discipline are isolated from researchers in adjoining disciplines. Practitioners in one institution are unaware of the work of practitioners in other institutions, at times even when they are serving overlapping constituencies. Researchers and practitioners are light years apart. There is no central clearinghouse for adolescence research and programs. We were struck by the wastefulness of a society that does not utilize the information it has in order to enlighten its institutions.

The lack of options for young adolescents became a recurrent theme. It has its counterpoint in the lack of alternatives in training for youth workers, including teachers.

What is needed is a reconceptualization of our entire mode of thinking about and serving youth. There is no set of national centers of excellence in the study of adolescence to spur such thoughtfulness. There are no federal priorities to fund it. There is less than a handful of universities with youth development centers capable of identifying youth problems, of collecting and of promoting youth research–and here we are talking about all adolescents, not the twelve-to-fifteen-year range that is the most severely neglected among adolescents.

In Part I, we cite John Money's sensitive observation that "it is very difficult for some youngsters to be caught in that no-man's land between their chronological age and their physique age, trying to keep up their social age, their academic age, their personality age, in conformity with their chronological age." We do not know very much about this no-man's land. Researchers and practitioners have not dedicated themselves in great numbers to easing these difficulties.

This does not mean, however, that nothing is known. If research reports gathering dust on shelves were available to practitioners, and if the everyday wisdom of practitioners were communicated to researchers, we might save ourselves years of work. And if doctors knew what teachers do, and vice versa, and teachers knew what parents knew, and vice versa, we might save adolescents many hours of grief.

We see as a major task the creation of mechanisms for establishing correlates among what is already known about early adolescence. This is not to underestimate the need for paying attention to the extraordinary gaps in research and programs, but to underscore the necessity for attempting what we see as the harder effort of integrating what already exists.

The *New York Times* of July 21, 1974, published an article by Diane Ravitch about crime in the city's schools. Ms. Ravitch's article concluded, "Now some educators are coming to see that . . . the schools are only a part of an entire child development network which many feel needs urgently to be rethought and redirected." This was good news. We were unaware of who the "some" and the "many" were, but were encouraged that the rethinking process had begun. We asked Ms. Ravitch how the child development network was being conceptualized, and by whom. She answered, in a letter dated August 3, 1974:

> In my original draft of the article, I stated in conclusion that no one institution had full responsibility for the problem of juvenile justice, and that the entire child development network . . . needed to be rethought and redirected. My

editor told me that it sounded like editorializing, and it was rewritten to state that "some educators" had come to that conclusion. So I cannot refer you to particular people who are rethinking the problem, because at this stage there is very little consciousness that it exists.

We agree that the entire child development network needs urgently to be rethought and redirected. We also agree that there is very little conceptualization of this network, because there is little awareness of the problem. Ravitch's views have been deeply affected by Lawrence Cremin, President of Columbia Teachers College, who has written about the significance of educational configurations. Cremin argues that you cannot look at any one educational institution by itself. Educational institutions include schools, the family, the media, churches, community organizations, youth groups, labor unions, libraries, etc.—formal and informal agencies that influence values and behavior. What one agency accomplishes in educating or miseducating children is affected by what the others are doing. A similar holistic or network approach is found in the works we have cited by Urie Bronfenbrenner and John Hill.

These people are telling us deep truths about the way we feel about and rear our young. It is the conclusion of this report that the chaotic fragmentation of research and services is a surface manifestation of a dangerous underlying social confusion about how we want to grow up in America. The dialogue had better begin.

Appendix

Table A-1
The Early Adolescent Population

Ages[a]	Total	White	Negro	Other Races
12	4,183,341	3,512,236	554,764	59,685
13	4,101,977	3,495,074	548,936	57,967
14	4,095,359	3,485,620	552,177	57,562
15	4,029,034	3,440,465	531,985	56,584

Ages[b]	Chinese	Japanese	Filipino
12	7,853	10,447	6,011
13	8,116	10,576	5,695
14	8,034	11,249	5,755
15	7,751	10,508	5,458

Ages[c]	Puerto Ricans	Puerto Rican Birth and/or Parentage		
		Northeast	North Central	South*
12	33,595	27,104	3,881	1,425
13	33,181	26,838	3,566	1,469
14	32,420	26,070	3,673	1,522
15	30,300	24,244	3,232	1,731

Ages[c]	Spanish Mother Tongue	English Mother Tongue
10-13	61,373	6,587
14-15	28,021	2,772

	American Indian Population				
Ages[d]	Total	Northeast	North Central	South	West
12	19,526	829	3,860	4,684	10,153
13	19,408	814	3,607	4,783	10,204
14	19,213	839	3,790	4,828	9,756
15	18,966	856	3,444	4,960	9,706

[a]U.S. Bureau of the Census, *1970 Census of Population*, vol. 1, *Characteristics of the Population, United States Summary*, p. 265.

[b]U.S. Bureau of the Census, *Japanese, Chinese, and Filipinos in the United States*, July 1973.

[c]U.S. Bureau of the Census, *Puerto Ricans in the United States*, June 1973.

[d]U.S. Bureau of the Census, *American Indians*, 1973.

*West about the same as South.

Table A-2
Adolescents in Institutions and Other Group Quarters

All Institutions	
Ages	Number
11	12,659
12	16,664
13	20,801
14	27,213
15	33,822
16	35,296

Mental Hospitals and Residential Treatment Centers				
Ages	All Races	White	Negro	Spanish
All Ages	433,890			
0-5	401	268	112	0
5-9	3,198	2,518	655	97
10-13	7,581	5,950	1,597	316
14	2,942	2,312	593	40
15-17	12,670	10,375	2,144	371

Homes and Schools for the Mentally Handicapped (Public and Private)				
Ages	All Races	White	Negro	Spanish
All Ages	201,992			
0-5	3,593	3,136	407	118
5	1,879	1,593	254	133
6	2,198	1,908	261	44
7-9	10,537	8,930	1,374	321
10-13	23,121	19,205	3,646	532
14	6,813	5,798	923	178
15-17	21,611	17,989	3,214	627
18-19	12,672	11,046	1,462	205
20-24	25,377	22,374	2,714	521
25-29	17,667	16,086	1,400	362
30-over	Numbers Become Progressively Smaller			Numbers Vary Up and Down

Homes and Schools for Physically Handicapped				
Ages	All Races	White	Negro	Spanish
All Ages	22,739	19,284	3,102	859
0-5	518	435	78	22
5	836	721	115	22

Ages	All Races	White	Negro	Spanish
6	741	607	114	0
7-9	2,935	2,485	413	207
10-13	5,821	4,877	823	114
14	1,365	1,162	189	0
15-17	4,273	3,687	527	155
18-19	1,779	1,545	211	47
20-24	986	836	131	28
25-over	3,485	2,929	501	264

Persons in Homes for Dependent and Neglected Children

Ages	All Races
All Ages	47,594
0-1	463
1-4	1,639
5	902
6	1,273
7-9	6,937
10-13	17,288
14	4,836
15-17	10,529
18-19	1,392
20-24	260
25-29	85
30-over	1,990

Persons Confined for Juvenile Delinquency

	Training Schools		Detention Homes	
Ages	All Races	Black	All Races	Black
All ages	66,457	24,099	10,272	3,329
0-5	162	12	207	75
5	75	0	36	15
6	100	4	23	4
7-9	669	113	215	76
10-13	7,291	3,078	1,986	700
14	8,272	3,160	1,656	556
15	13,001	4,998	2,260	758
16	12,761	4,230	2,144	685
17	9,601	3,145	1,182	304
18	4,452	1,612	298	97

Table A-2 (cont.)

Ages	All Races	Black	All Races	Black
19	2,952	1,260	53	20
20-24	4,271	1,822	47	6
25-over	2,850	665	165	33

Source: U.S. Bureau of the Census, *Persons in Institutions and Other Group Quarters*, July 1973.

Notes

Chapter 1
Research Review

1. Gisela Konopka, "Requirements for Healthy Development of Adolescent Youth," *Adolescence* 8, no. 31 (Fall 1973): 314. Reprinted by permission.

2. Edgar Z. Friedenberg, *The Vanishing Adolescent* (New York: Dell Publishing Co., 1959), p. 19.

3. Donald Cohen and Richard Frank, "Preadolescence: A Critical Phase of Biological and Psychological Development," in *Mental Health in Children*, vol. 1, ed. D.V. Siva (Westbury, New York: PJD Publications, Ltd., 1975), p. 140.

4. Erik Erikson, *Identity, Youth and Crisis* (New York: W.W. Norton, 1968), p. 91.

5. Ibid., p. 208.

6. Glennard H. Elder, Jr., "Adolescence in the Life Cycle: An Introduction," in *Adolescence in the Life Cycle: Psychological Change and Social Context*, ed. Sigmund E. Dragastin and Glen Elder, Jr. (Washington, D.C.: Hemisphere Publishing Corp., 1975), pp. 1-22.

7. David Bakan, "Adolescence in America: From Ideal to Social Fact," *Daedalus* 100, no. 4 (Fall 1971): 981.

8. Ibid., p. 989.

9. John P. Hill, "Some Perspectives on Adolescence in American Society" (Position paper prepared for the Office of Child Development, United States Department of Health, Education, and Welfare, mimeographed, Washington, D.C., May 1973), p. 21.

10. Joint Commission on Mental Health of Children, *Mental Health: From Infancy Through Adolescence* (New York: Harper and Row Publishers, 1973), pp. 209-10.

11. Friedenberg, p. 17.

12. Ibid., p. 18.

13. Elder, p. 13.

14. Gisela Konopka, "Adolescence in the 1970s," *Child Welfare* 50, no. 10 (1971): 553.

15. Konopka, "Requirements for Healthy Development," pp. 301-2.

16. Hill, p. 2.

17. Ibid., p. 7.

18. Elder, p. 20.

19. Judith E. Gallatin, *Adolescence and Individuality: A Conceptual*

Approach to Adolescent Psychology (New York: Harper and Row Publishers, 1975).

20. Hill, pp. 11-12.

21. Ibid., p. 88.

22. Ibid., p. 87.

23. Deborah Waber, Department of Psychiatry, Children's Hospital Medical Center, Boston, Mass., letter of July 9, 1974.

24. Hill, p. 88.

25. National Institute of Child Health and Human Development, "Expanded Programs in Adolescent Development," mimeographed, Washington, D.C. (August 1973), p. 2.

26. The Boys Town Center for the Study of Youth Development, "The Boys Town Research and Training Complex," mimeographed, n.d.

27. Social Research Group, *Toward Interagency Coordination: An Overview of Federal Research and Development Activities Relating to Adolescence.* First Annual Report (Washington, D.C.: The George Washington University, 1973), p. 11.

28. Hill, p. 9.

29. "Boys Town Research and Training Complex," p. 3.

30. *Toward Interagency Coordination* (1973), pp. 50-51.

31. Elder, p. 14.

32. Hill, pp. 10-11.

33. Cohen and Frank, p. 150.

34. Social Research Group, *Toward Interagency Coordination: An Overview of FY '74 Federal Research and Development Activities Relating to Early Childhood*, Fourth Annual Report (Washington, D.C.: The George Washington University, 1974), p. 19.

35. Donald Cohen, letter to Terry Saario, Ford Foundation, 8 January 1974, p. 2.

36. Gilman D. Grave, "Introduction," *The Control of the Onset of Puberty*, ed. Melvin M. Grumbach, Gilman D. Grave, Florence E. Mayer (New York: John Wiley and Sons, 1974), p. xxiii. © 1974 by John Wiley and Sons. Reprinted by permission of John Wiley and Sons, Inc.

37. James M. Tanner, "Sequence and Tempo in the Somatic Changes in Puberty," in *The Control of the Onset of Puberty*, p. 455.

38. Rose E. Frisch, "Critical Weight at Menarche, Initiation of the Growth Spurt, and Control of Puberty," in *The Control of the Onset of Puberty*, p. 409.

39. Hill, p. 17.

40. Rolf E. Muuss, "Adolescent Development and the Secular Trend," in

Adolescent Behavior and Society: A Book of Readings, ed. Rolf E. Muuss (New York: Random House, 1971), pp. 56-57.

41. *The Maternal and Child Health Service Reports on Promoting the Health of Mothers and Children, FY 1973.* DHEW Publication No. (HSA) 74-5000.

42. Cited in United States Senate's Select Committee on Nutrition and Human Needs, *To Save the Children: Nutritional Intervention Through Supplemental Feeding* (Washington, D.C.: U.S. Government Printing Office, 1974).

43. National Academy of Sciences, *Maternal Nutrition and the Course of Pregnancy*, Summary Report of the Committee on Maternal Nutrition, Food and Nutrition Board (reprinted, Washington, D.C.: U.S. Government Printing Office, 1974), p. 10.

44. National Academy of Sciences, *Extent and Meanings of Iron Deficiency in the United States*, Summary Proceedings of a Workshop of the Committee on Iron Nutritional Deficiencies, March 8-9, 1971 (Washington, D.C.: Food and Nutrition Board, National Academy of Sciences, 1971). The Food and Nutrition Board's Committee on Maternal Nutrition is working on a report on iron nutriture and adolescence which is not available for this review.

45. Herbert G. Birch and Joan Dye Gussow, *Disadvantaged Children: Health, Nutrition and School Failure* (New York: Harcourt, Brace and Jovanovich, 1970).

46. John McKigney, NICHD, telephone conversation, June 1974. See, for instance, Felix P. Heald, Patricia S. Remmell, Jean Mayer, "Caloric Protein and Fat Intakes in Children and Adolescents," in *Adolescent Nutrition and Growth*, ed. Felix P. Heald (New York: Appleton-Century Crofts, 1969), now out of print; also see the 1930 White House Conference's Committee on Nutrition, where the call went out for "renewed interest in food consumption of our young population" (p. 17).

47. National Institute of Child Health and Human Development, "Nutritient Requirements in Adolescence," mimeographed (Work group recommendations, meeting held at Airlie House, Va., 3-6 June 1973).

48. Smithsonian Science Information Exchange, "Notices of Research Projects," (Washington, D.C.).

49. Sol Klotz, "Appendix," George van Hilsheimer, *How to Live With Your Special Child* (Washington: Acropolis, 1970).

50. Roger J. Williams, *Nutrition Against Disease: Environmental Prevention* (New York: Bantam Books, 1973), p. 43.

51. Ray C. Wunderlich, *Allergies, Brains, and Children Coping* (St. Petersburg, Fla.: Johnny Reads, 1973).

52. Ben F. Feingold, "Hyperkinesis and Learning Disabilities (H-LD) Linked to the Ingestion of Artificial Food Colors and Flavors," mimeographed

(Presentation before the Committee on Education, Legislative Hearings, California State Legislature, Sacramento, 31 July 1974).

53. Frisch, in *The Control of the Onset of Puberty*, pp. 404-6.

54. Rose E. Frisch, "Demographic Implications of the Biological Determinants of Female Fecundity" (Paper presented at the Population Association of America annual meeting, New York, April 1974), p. 8.

55. Tanner, in *The Control of the Onset of Puberty*, p. 467.

56. Ibid., p. 448.

57. Grave, in *The Control of the Onset of Puberty*, p. xxiv.

58. Julian M. Davidson, Department of Physiology, Stanford University, Palo Alto, Cal., letter of 8 August 1974.

59. J.M. Davidson, "Hypothalamic-Pituitary Regulation of Puberty: Evidence from Animal Experimentation," in *The Control of the Onset of Puberty*, p. 80.

60. R.A. Gorski, "Extrahypothalamic Influences on Gonadotropin Regulation," in *The Control of the Onset of Puberty*, pp. 182-183.

61. Judson Van Wyk, Division of Endocrinology, University of North Carolina, telephone conversation of 17 July 1974.

62. Judson Van Wyk et al., "The Somatomedins: A New Class of Growth-Regulating Hormones," *American Journal of Diseases of Children* 26 (November 1973): 705-10.

63. H.E. Kulin and E.O. Reiter, "Delayed Sexual Maturation, With Special Emphasis on the Occurrence of the Syndrome in the Male," in *The Control of the Onset of Puberty*, p. 239.

64. Ibid., p. 253.

65. Tanner, in *The Control of the Onset of Puberty*, discussion, pp. 261-63.

66. John Money, in *The Control of the Onset of Puberty*, pp. 264-65.

67. Van Wyk, telephone conversation of 17 July 1974.

68. Hill, p. 27.

69. John Money, Johns Hopkins University, telephone conversation of 26 July 1974.

70. Robert E. Grinder, ed., *Studies in Adolescence: A Book of Readings in Adolescent Development*, 2nd ed. (London: Macmillan and Co., 1969), p. 431.

71. Donald Cohen letter of 8 January 1974, p. 1.

72. George Christakis, Department of Epidemiology and Public Health, University of Miami, letter to Sol Chafkin, Ford Foundation, 13 February 1975.

73. Judson J. Van Wyk, Professor of Pediatrics, University of North Carolina at Chapel Hill, letter of 17 March 1975.

74. Hill, p. 27.

75. Elder *Adolescence in the Life Cycle.*

76. Robert E. Grinder, Arizona State University, letter of 2 August 1974.

77. Jerald G. Bachman, *Young Men in High School and Beyond: A Summary of Findings from the Youth in Transition Project* (Final Report, U.S. Department of Health, Education, and Welfare, Washington, D.C., May 1972), p. 7.

78. Ibid., p. 8.

79. Jerald G. Bachman, Swayzer Green, Ilona D. Wirtanen, *Youth in Transition, Vol. 3: Dropping Out–Problem or Symptom?* (Ann Arbor, Mich.: Survey Research Center, Institute for Social Research, 1971), p. 179.

80. Bachman, *Young Men in High School and Beyond*, p. 39.

81. Ibid., p. 21.

82. Ibid., pp. 21-22.

83. Cohen and Frank, pp. 132-133.

84. Muuss, *Adolescent Behavior*, pp. 252-53.

85. Hill, p. 93.

86. Daniel Offer, *The Psychological World of the Teen-ager* (New York: Basic Books, 1969), p. 179.

87. Hill, p. 32.

88. Ibid., p. 36.

89. Ibid., p. 37.

90. Ibid.

91. Center for Youth Development and Research, *Youth Encounters a Changing World*, Seminar Series No. 3 (Minneapolis: University of Minnesota Center for Youth Development and Research, August 1972), p. 13.

92. Offer, pp. 180-81.

93. Ibid., p. 222.

94. Elizabeth Douvan and Joseph Adelson, *The Adolescent Experience* (New York: John Wiley and Sons, 1966).

95. Gallatin, pp. 205-7.

96. *Center for Youth Development and Research*, p. 40.

97. Elder, p. 2.

98. Hill, pp. 53-54.

99. Gisela Konopka, *Young Girls: A Portrait of Adolescence* (Englewood Cliffs: Prentice-Hall, in press), mss. p. 55.

100. Hill, p. 64.

101. Judith Gallatin, Department of Psychology, Eastern Michigan University, Ypsilanti, Mich., letter of 10 November 1974.

102. John A. Clausen, "The Social Meaning of Differential Physical and Sexual Maturation," in *Adolescence in the Life Cycle*, pp. 25-47.

103. John A. Clausen, Institute of Human Development, University of California, Berkeley, letter of 18 July 1974.

104. Clausen, "The Social Meaning."

105. Ibid., pp. 33-34.

106. Hill, pp. 59-60.

107. Clausen, p. 35.

108. Ibid., p. 46.

109. National Institute of Child Health and Human Development, "Expanded Program," p. 15.

110. Social Research Group, *Toward Interagency Coordination: Early Childhood*, p. 23.

111. Benjamin Bloom, *Stability and Change in Human Characteristics* (New York: John Wiley and Sons, 1964).

112. David Elkind, "Recent Research on Cognitive Development in Adolescence," in *Adolescence in the Life Cycle*, p. 49.

113. National Institute of Child Health and Human Development, "Expanded Program," p. 9.

114. Elkind, pp. 49-50.

115. Lawrence Kohlberg and Carol Gilligan, "The Adolescent as Philosopher: The Discovery of Self in a Postconventional World," *Daedalus* 100, no. 4, (Fall 1971): 1061.

116. Muuss, *Adolescent Behavior and Society*, p. 286.

117. Elkind, p. 53.

118. Ibid., p. 55.

119. David Elkind, "Egocentrism in Adolescence," *Child Development*, 1967, 38, 1025-1034; and in *Adolescent Behavior*, pp. 43-45.

120. Ibid. © 1967. The Society for Research in Child Development, Inc.

121. Ibid., p. 46. © 1967. The Society for Research in Child Development, Inc.

122. John P. Hill and Wendy J. Palmquist, "Social Cognition and Social Relations in Adolescence: A Precursory View" (Paper presented at the meeting of the Eastern Psychological Association, Philadelphia, April 1974), n.p.

123. Kohlberg and Gilligan, p. 1065.

124. Elkind, "Recent Research," p. 52.

125. Hill and Palmquist, p. 4, citing E. Dulit, "Adolescent Thinking à la Piaget: The Formal Stage," *Journal of Youth and Adolescence* 1 (1972): 281-301.

126. Elkind, "Recent Research," p. 56.

127. William D. Rohwer, Jr., "Elaboration and Learning in Childhood and

Adolescence," in *Advances in Child Development and Behavior*, ed. H.W. Reese (New York: Academic Press, 1973), p. 67.

128. Hill, p. 20.

129. Hill and Palmquist, p. 14.

130. Ibid., p. 15.

131. Ibid.

132. Hill, p. 30.

133. Elkind, "Recent Research," p. 59.

134. Deborah Waber, "Developmental Trends and Biological Bases of Gender Differences in Mental Abilities," mimeographed dissertation abstract, Yale University, New Haven, Conn., n.d.

135. Deborah Waber, letter of 9 July 1974.

136. Lawrence Kohlberg, "The Development of Children's Orientation Toward a Moral Order," *Vita Humana* 6 (1963): 30.

137. Ibid., p. 11.

138. Carol Gilligan, "Fostering Moral Development in Children," *EDC News*, issue 4 (Spring 1974): 8.

139. Ibid., p. 9.

140. Gilligan will not be asking them in relation to early adolescence any more. She is shifting the focus of her research to college age students because it is among these students that she feels she will be able most effectively to study the development of formal operations. There are so few thoughtful researchers in the area of early adolescent cognition that one can only comment upon this with a certain ruefulness.

141. Joseph Adelson, "The Political Imagination of the Young Adolescent," *Daedalus* 100, no. 4 (Fall 1971): 1029.

142. Ibid., p. 1013.

143. Ibid., p. 1015.

144. Ibid., p. 1019.

145. Joseph Adelson and Robert P. O'Neil, "Growth of Political Ideas in Adolescence: The Sense of Community," in *Adolescent Behavior*, p. 192.

146. Adelson, p. 1028.

147. Adelson has influenced many students of the development of political thinking in adolescents. He has said that his most recent work in this area is his "valedictory statement" in this area of research. Once again, one can only regret the departure of such an erudite and articulate investigator from the field of adolescence.

148. Judith Gallatin, with Joseph Adelson, Robert O'Neil, and Lamar Miller, "The Development of Political Thinking in Urban Adolescents," mimeographed (Final report, Project No. 0-0554, National Center for Educational Research and Development, DHEW, Washington, D.C., December 1, 1972), p. 8.

149. Ibid., p. 126.

150. Ibid., p. 127.

151. Ibid., p. 136.

152. Robert Hogan and Ellen Dickstein, "Moral Judgment and Perceptions of Injustice," *Journal of Personality and Social Psychology* 23, no. 3 (1972): 412.

153. Esther Blank Greif and Robert Hogan, "The Theory and Measurement of Empathy," *Journal of Counseling Psychology* 20, no. 30 (1973): 281.

154. Robert Hogan, "Moral Conduct and Moral Character: A Psychological Perspective," *Psychological Bulletin* 79, no. 4 (1973): 219.

155. Robert Hogan, letter of September 14, 1976.

156. Elizabeth Leonie Simpson, "Moral Development Research: A Case Study of Scientific Cultural Bias," *Human Development* 17 (1974): 219.

157. James Gallagher, Frank Porter Graham Child Development Center, University of North Carolina, Chapel Hill, conversation of 20 June 1974.

158. Jacob W. Getzels and Philip W. Jackson, "The Highly Intelligent and the Highly Creative Adolescent: A Summary of Some Research Findings," in *Adolescent Behavior*, pp. 121-33.

159. Ibid., p. 132.

160. Diana Baumrind, "Coleman II: Utopian Fantasy and Sound Social Innovation," *School Review* 83, no. 1 (November 1974): 69-84.

161. National Institute of Child Health and Human Development, "Expanded Program," pp. 10-12.

162. Social Research Group, *Toward Interagency Coordination: Adolescence '73*, p. 80.

163. Participating Member Agencies of the Interagency Panel for Research and Development on Adolescents: ACTION; Department of Agriculture; Department of Commerce—Bureau of the Census; Department of Health, Education, and Welfare (DHEW)—Assistant Secretary for Planning and Evaluation (ASPE), Bureau of Community Health Services (BCHS), National Institute on Alcohol Abuse and Alcoholism (NIAAA), National Institute of Child Health and Human Development (NICHD), National Institute of Education (NIE), National Institute of Mental Health (NIMH), National Institute of Neurological and Communicative Disorders and Stroke (NINCDS), Office of Child Development (OCD), Office of Civil Rights (OCR), Office of Education (OE), Office of Human Development (OHD), Office of Youth Development (OYD), Social and Rehabilitation Services (SRS); Department of Justice—Law Enforcement Assistance Administration (LEAA); Department of Labor; Office of Management and Budget (OMB).

164. Social Research Group, *Toward Interagency Coordination: FY '75 Federal Research and Development Activities Pertaining to Adolescence*, Third

Annual Report (Washington, D.C.: The George Washington University, 1975), p. 3.

165. Social Research Group, *Toward Interagency Coordination: Adolescence '73*, pp. 80-82.

166. Social Research Group, *Toward Interagency Coordination: Adolescence '75*, pp. 54-55.

167. Ibid., p. 56.

168. Social Research Group, *Toward Interagency Coordination: Early Childhood '74*, p. 26.

169. Social Research Group, *Toward Interagency Coordination: Adolescence '75*, p. 21.

170. Robert E. Grinder, Associate Dean, College of Education, Arizona State University, Tempe, letter of 2 August 1974.

171. Hill, pp. 182-87.

172. Konopka, "Requirements for Healthy Development," pp. 312-13.

173. Social Research Group, *Toward Interagency Coordination: Adolescence '73*, p. 56.

Chapter 2
Schools and the Young Adolescent

1. Donald Wells, Headmaster, Carolina Friends School, Durham, N.C., unpublished manuscript.

2. See Michael B. Katz, *Class Bureaucracy and Schools: The Illusion of Educational Change in America* (New York: Frederick A. Praeger, 1971); and William Greenbaum's overview of this viewpoint in "America in Search of a New Ideal: An Essay on the Rise of Pluralism," *Harvard Educational Review* 44, no. 3 (August 1974): 411-40.

3. Greenbaum, p. 431.

4. Cited in The Ford Foundation, *A Foundation Goes to School: The Ford Foundation Comprehensive School Improvement Program, 1960-1970* (New York: Office of Reports, The Ford Foundation, November 1972), p. 8.

5. Carl Bereiter, *Must We Educate?* (Englewood Cliffs, N.J.: Prentice-Hall, 1973), pp. 64-65.

6. Ibid., p. 93.

7. Ibid., p. 23.

8. Charles E. Silberman, Foreword to *Young Lives at Stake* by Charity James (New York: Agathon Press, 1972), pp. vii-ix.

9. Urie Bronfenbrenner, *Two Worlds of Childhood: U.S. and U.S.S.R.*

(New York: Russell Sage Foundation, 1970. Cited Edition in Pocket Book, 1973), pp. xxiv-ix.

10. Ibid., p. 162.

11. G. Vernon Bennett, *The Junior High School* (Baltimore: Warwick and York, 1919), pp. 2-3.

12. Ibid., p. 4.

13. Ibid., p. 79.

14. Ibid., pp. 4-5.

15. Ibid., pp. 6-7

16. Thomas H. Briggs, *The Junior High School* (Boston: Houghton Mifflin Co., 1920), p. 24.

17. Ibid., p. 37.

18. Ibid., pp. 25-26.

19. Ibid., pp. 83-84.

20. Ibid., p. 34.

21. Ralph W. Pringle, *The Junior High School: A Psychological Approach* (New York: McGraw-Hill Book Co., 1937), p. 25.

22. Ibid., p. 13.

23. Anita A. Summers and Barbara L. Wolfe, "Which School Resources Help Learning? Efficiency and Equity in Philadelphia Public Schools," Federal Reserve Bank of Philadelphia *Business Review*, February 1975, p. 7.

24. See, for instance, Thomas Gatewood, "What Research Says About the Middle School," *Educational Leadership* (December 1973); and the work of the Middle School Resource and Research Center, a Title III project in the Indianapolis public school system.

25. Maurice McGlasson, *The Middle School: Whence? What? Whither?* Phi Delta Kappa Fastback No. 22 (Bloomington, Ind.: Phi Delta Kappa Educational Foundation, 1973), p. 14.

26. Thomas Gatewood, Central Michigan University, Mount Pleasant, telephone conversation, 16 October 1974.

27. McGlasson, p. 27.

28. John Henry Martin et al., *Report of the National Panel on High Schools and Adolescent Education*, Washington, D.C.: U.S. Office of Education, March 1974.

29. McGlasson, p. 22.

30. Ibid., p. 23.

31. J. Lloyd Trump, "Dynamic Junior High-Middle-Intermediate Schools," *National Association of Secondary School Principals Bulletin* 58 (April 1974): 4.

32. Martin, p. 8.

33. Ibid., p. 11.

34. Keith Goldhammer et al., *Elementary Principals and Their Schools: Beacons of Brilliance and Potholes of Pestilence*, Center for the Advanced Study of Education, University of Oregon (Washington, D.C.: Capitol Publications, 1971).

35. Sal DiFranco, Principal, MacDonald Middle School, East Lansing, Mich., telephone conversation, 16 October 1974.

36. Rose Frisch, Harvard University, Cambridge, Mass., letter of 17 September 1974.

37. Roberta G. Simmons, Florence Rosenberg, and Morris Rosenberg, "Disturbance in the Self-Image at Adolescence," *American Sociological Review* 38 (October 1973): 564.

38. Ibid., p. 562.

39. Mario D. Fantini, *Public Schools of Choice* (New York: Simon and Schuster, 1973).

40. James M. McPartland and Joyce L. Epstein, *Interim Report: School Organization and School Outcomes: A Study of the Effects of Open-Environment Schools* (Baltimore: Center for Social Organization of Schools, The Johns Hopkins University, December 1973), pp. 82-83.

41. Vito Perrone, Dean, Center for Teaching and Learning, University of North Dakota, Grand Forks, telephone conversation, 14 October 1974.

42. Gerald Weinstein and Mario D. Fantini, *Toward Humanistic Education: A Curriculum of Affect* (New York: Frederick A. Praeger, 1970), p. 10.

43. Tom Wilson, Center for New Schools, Chicago, telephone conversation, 16 October 1974.

44. Pauline M. Leet, "Socialization and the 'Middle' Child: A Twentieth Century Model of a Seventeenth Century Process" (Paper presented at the 1974 Annual Meeting, American Educational Research Association, Chicago, April 1974).

45. Ibid.

46. Gisela Konopka, "Requirements for Healthy Development of Adolescent Youth," *Adolescence* 8, no. 31 (Fall 1973): 312.

47. Social Research Group, *Toward Interagency Coordination: An Overview of Federal Research and Development Activities Relating to Adolescence*, First Annual Report (Washington, D.C.: The George Washington University, 1973), p. 86.

48. Ibid., p. 207.

49. Meredith A. Larson and Freya E. Dittmann, *Compensatory Education and Early Adolescence: Reviewing our National Strategy*, Educational Policy Research Center, Stanford University Research Institute, Research Report EPRC 2158-7 (May 1975).

50. Meredith A. Larson and Freya E. Dittmann, *Adolescence: Alternative Strategies For Compensatory Education*, Educational Policy Research Center, Stanford Research Institute (Prepared for the Office of the Assistant Secretary for Education, DHEW, Washington, D.C., July 1974), p. v.

51. Ibid., p. 24.

52. Ibid., p. 2.

53. Ibid., p. 25.

54. Ibid., p. 27.

55. Ibid., p. 32.

56. Ibid., p. 35.

57. Ibid., pp. 43-44.

58. Ibid., p. 59.

59. Ibid., p. 28.

60. Ibid., p. 39.

61. Ibid.

62. Ibid., p. 61.

63. Ibid., p. 46.

64. For a comprehensive analysis of the Coleman, Martin, and Brown reports, see Michael Timpane et al., *Youth Policy in Transition* (A working note prepared for the Department of Health, Education and Welfare, Rand Corporation, December 1975).

65. Martin, pp. 23-24.

66. Ibid., pp. 170-73.

67. Bronfenbrenner, p. 65.

68. James, p. 41.

69. Summers and Wolfe, Federal Reserve Bank *Business Review*, p. 10.

70. Ibid., p. 12.

71. Ibid., p. 16.

72. Ibid.

73. California Commission for Reform of Intermediate and Secondary Education, *RISE: Report of the California Commission for Reform of Intermediate and Secondary Education* (Sacramento: California State Department of Education, 1975), pp. 32-33.

74. Ibid., p. 33.

75. *RISE*, p. xii.

76. Social Research Group, *Toward Interagency Coordination: An Overview of FY '74 Federal Research and Development Relating to Adolescence*, Second Annual Report (Washington, D.C.: The George Washington University, 1974), p. 21.

77. Alaska, Office of Child Advocacy, "Needs Analysis of Children in America," mimeographed.

78. John M. Taborn, "Some Reflections on Meeting the Needs of Youth: Implications for Staff Awareness," *Center for Youth Development and Research Quarterly Focus* 1, no. 2: n.p.

79. David B. Tyack, *The One Best System: A History of American Urban Education* (Cambridge, Mass.: Harvard University Press, 1974), p. 85. Cited in Greenbaum.

80. Richard Rivera, "A Case for Puerto Rican Studies Program" in *Puerto Rican Perspectives*, ed. Edward Mapp (Metuchen, N.J.: Scarecrow Press, 1974), p. 38.

81. Magdalena Miranda, ed., *Puerto Rican Task Force Report* (New York: Council on Social Work Education, 1973), p. 8.

82. Jacquetta Hill Burnett, *Social Structure, Ideologies, and Culture Codes in Occupational Development of Puerto Rican Youths*, vol. 1 of Final Report (Urbana: Bureau of Educational Research, University of Illinois, Spring 1974).

83. Anthony Gary Dworkin, "A City Found, a People Lost," in *Introduction to Chicano Studies*, ed. Livie Isauro Duran and H. Russell Bernard (New York: Macmillan Co., 1973), p. 412.

84. Charles S. Knowlton, "Changing Spanish-American Villages of Northern New Mexico," in *Chicano Studies*, p. 304.

85. Kenneth R. Johnson, *Teaching the Culturally Disadvantaged: A Rational Approach* (Palo Alto, Cal.: Science Research Associates, 1970), p. 71.

86. Knowlton, in *Chicano Studies*, p. 326.

87. Paul M. Sheldon, "Mexican-Americans and the Public Schools," in *Report of the Conference on Understanding and Teaching Mexican-American Children and Youth*, California State Department of Education, Sacramento, Cal., 1964, p. 8.

88. John H. Haddox, "American Indian Values," in *Chicanos and Native Americans*, ed. O. de la Garza, Z. Anthony Kruszeruski, and Tomas A. Arciniega (Englewood Cliffs, N.J.: Prentice-Hall, 1973).

89. Burnett, p. 91.

90. Donald Smith, "The Black Revolution and Education," in *Black Self-Concept: Implications for Education and Social Science*, ed. James A. Banks and Jean D. Grambs (New York: McGraw-Hill Book Co.. 1972), p. 47.

91. Jean D. Grambs, *Black Self-Concept*, p. 199. For other discussions of inner-city black value systems see Richard W. Brozovich, "Characteristics Associated with Popularity Among Different Racial and Socioeconomic Groups of Children," *Journal of Educational Research* 63 (July-August 1970): 441-44; Monroe K. Rowland and Phillip Del Camp, "The Values of the Educationally Disadvantaged: How Different Are They?" *Journal of Negro Education* 37 (Winter 1968): 86-89.

92. In addition to the works cited, other writings that reflect this view are: John L. Johnson, "Special Education and the Inner City: A Challenge for the Future or Another Means for Cooling the Mark Out?" in *Black Psychology*, ed. Regional L. Jones (New York: Harper and Row Publishers, 1972), pp. 295-307; Gerald D. Bachman, *Young Men in High School and Beyond: A Summary of Findings from the Youth in Transition Project* (Washington, D.C.: Office of Education, DHEW, May 1972); and Jean D. Grambs, "Negro Self-Concept Reappraisal," in *Black Self-Concept*, pp. 175-205.

93. Daniel Levine, "Cultural Diffraction in the Social System of the Low Income School," *School and Society* 96 (20 March 1968): 206.

94. Donald Smith, in *Black Self-Concept*, p. 44.

95. Daniel Fader, *The Naked Children* (New York: Macmillan Co., 1971), p. 167.

96. Luis Fuentes, "Puerto Rican Children and the New York City Public School," in *Puerto Rican Perspectives*, p. 19.

97. Susan Navarro Uranga, "The Study of Mexican-American Education in the Southwest," in *Chicanos and Native Americans*, p. 19.

98. Rivera, in *Puerto Rican Perspectives*, p. 19.

99. Uranga, in *Chicanos and Native Americans*, p. 164.

100. Rivera, in *Puerto Rican Perspectives*, p. 38.

101. Alexander Vazquez, "Why Puerto Rican Students Drop Out of School," in *Puerto Rican Perspectives*, p. 23.

102. Uranga, in *Chicanos and Native Americans*, p. 167.

103. Burnett, p. 179.

104. John P. Hill, *Some Perspectives on Adolescence in American Society* (Paper prepared for the Office of Child Development, U.S. Department of Health, Education, and Welfare, Washington, D.C., May 1973), pp. 69-70.

105. Alan G. Green, "Planning for Declining Enrollments," *School Review* 82, no. 4 (August 1974): 597.

106. Konopka, p. 310.

107. Bronfenbrenner, p. 128.

108. Hill, pp. 66-67.

109. McGlasson, p. 24.

110. Bob Malinka, Middle School Resource and Research Center, Indianapolis Public Schools, telephone conversation, 16 October 1974.

111. Vito Perrone, telephone conversation, 14 October 1974.

112. Hill, pp. 26-27.

113. A. Otto and S.L. Healy, "Adolescents' Self-Perception of Personality Strengths," *Adolescent Behavior and Society: A Book of Readings*, ed. Rolf E. Muuss (New York: Random House, 1971), p. 297.

114. Larson and Dittmann, p. 67.

115. Joan S. Goldsmith, Co-Director, Institute of Open Education, Cambridge, Mass., letter, 21 October 1974.

116. Marian Wright Edelman, in a speech before the National Association of Young Children, reported in *Report on Pre-School Education* (November 1973), p. 2.

117. *Peter Doe v. San Francisco Unified School District*, No. 653 312 (Superior Court of California, San Francisco County, filed 20 November 1972).

118. See David Bazelon, "Implementing the Right to Treatment," University of Chicago *Law Review* 36 (1969): 742-45.

119. *Rodriguez v. San Antonio Independent School District*, 441 U.S. 1 (1973). The court held there was no constitutionally guaranteed right to an education. It did not rule on whether there exists a right to some minimum level of education.

120. J. Sugarman, "Accountability through the Courts," *School Review* 82, no. 2 (February 1974): 246.

121. Important documents for federally-funded research activity are: "Synopsis of Issues and Criteria for Definition of Functional Literacy," Essential Skills Program, National Institute of Education, 8 pp.; Joy Frechtling, Epp Miller, Ronald Leslie, Timothy Hodapp, and William Ashcraft, "Review of NIE Research and Development Projects Related to Reading: A Paper Prepared for the Essential Skills Planning Conference" (August 18-22, 1974); NIE, Conference Guidance Materials, *Conference on Studies in Reading* (August 18-22, 1974), 91 pp.; and position papers written as a result of that conference.

122. Education Commission of the States, *Legislative Review* 4, no. 17 (12 August 1974): 4.

123. National Council for Teachers of English, "Government Finds Illiteracy Among Teenagers to be Alarming," NCTE *Council-Grams* 35, no. 4 (September 1974): 21-22.

124. Essential Skills Program, NIE, pp. 5-6.

125. Gisela Konopka, *Young Girls: A Portrait of Adolescence* (Englewood Cliffs: Prentice-Hall, in press), mss. p. 148.

126. Ibid., mss. p. 196.

127. Ibid., mss. pp. 198-99.

128. Herbert G. Birch and Joan Dye Gussow, *Disadvantaged Children: Health, Nutrition and School Failure* (New York: Harcourt, Brace and Jovanovich, 1970), p. 259.

Chapter 3
Service Institutions and the Handicapped Young Adolescent

1. James S. Kakalik et al., eds., *Services for Handicapped Youth: A Program Overview* R-1220 (Santa Monica, Cal.: Rand Corporation, 1973), p. 273.

2. Samuel A. Kirk, *Educating Exceptional Children*, 2nd ed. (New York: Houghton Mifflin Co., 1972), p. 10.

3. Nicholas Hobbs, ed., *Issues in the Classification of Children*, 2 vols. (San Francisco: Jossey-Bass, 1975), 1:159.

4. Prudence M. Rains et al., "The Labeling Approach to Deviance," in *Issues in the Classification*, 1:99.

5. Kakalik et al., pp. 16-17.

6. Ibid., p. 21.

7. Ibid., p. 22.

8. Ibid.

9. Ibid., p. 16.

10. Dr. Harris Faigel, Director of Adolescent Medicine, Joseph P. Kennedy Jr. Memorial Hospital for Children, Brighton, Mass., letter of 19 September 1974.

11. Dr. Adele Hofmann, Department of Pediatrics, New York University Medical Center, New York, N.Y., letter of 1 August 1975.

12. Dr. William A. Daniel, Jr., Chief, Adolescent Unit, University of Alabama Medical Center, Birmingham, Ala., letter of 12 September 1974.

13. Harris Faigel, "Rehabilitating the Physically Handicapped Adolescent" (Paper delivered to the New England Pediatric Society, Boston, Mass., 12 December 1973), p. 7.

14. Ibid., p. 12.

15. Evelyn West Ayrault, *Helping the Handicapped Teenager Mature* (New York: Associated Press, 1971), p. 13.

16. Kakalik et al., pp. 13, 165.

17. Ibid., p. 16.

18. Ibid., p. 176.

19. Ibid., p. 178.

20. Ibid., pp. 203-4.

21. Ibid., p. 17.

22. Ibid., p. 224.

23. Daniel letter, 12 September 1974.

24. Ayrault, p. 27.

25. Ibid., p. 39.

26. Telephone conversation with adolescent psychologist, October 1974.

27. Ayrault, p. 59.

28. Randolph K. Byers, Preface to Ayrault, n.p.

29. Richard H. Israel, Alexander Graham Bell Association for the Deaf, Washington, D.C., telephone conversation, 8 October 1974.

30. Dr. Henry Cobb, President's Committee on Mental Retardation, Chapel Hill, N.C., personal interview, 19 June 1975.

31. Judith Gallatin, Department of Psychology, Eastern Michigan University, Ypsilanti, Mich., letter to Terry Saario, Ford Foundation, 7 April 1975.

32. Robert Deisher, "Youth Services in Europe," mimeographed (Seattle: University of Washington), pp. 18-19.

33. Irving B. Weiner, *Psychological Disturbance in Adolescence* (New York: John Wiley and Sons, 1970), p. 50.

34. J.R. Masterson et al., "The Symptomatic Adolescent: Comparing Patients in the Controls" (Paper presented to the American Orthopsychiatric Association, 1966), cited in *Psychological Disturbance*, p. 52.

35. J.R. Masterson, "The Symptomatic Adolescent Five Years Later: He Didn't Grow Out of It," *American Journal of Psychiatry* 123 (1967): 1343, cited in *Psychological Disturbance*, p. 52.

36. J. Roswell Gallagher and Herbert I. Harris, *Emotional Problems of Adolescents* (New York: Oxford University Press, 1964), p. 66.

37. Weiner, p. 4.

38. Donald J. Cohen et al., "Mental Health Services," in *Issues in Classification* 2:112-14.

39. Derek Miller, *Adolescence: Psychology, Psychopathology and Psychotherapy* (New York: Jason Aronson, 1974), p. 285.

40. Kakalik et al., pp. 232-33.

41. The Group for the Advancement of Psychiatry, *Normal Adolescence: Its Dynamics and Impact* (New York: Charles Scribners' Sons, 1968), pp. 77-78.

42. Gisela Konopka, *Young Girls: A Portrait of Adolescence* (Englewood Cliffs, N.J.: Prentice-Hall, in press), mss. p. 82.

43. Cited in Betty J. Hallstrom and Joachim M. Banda, *The Provision of Health Care Services to Adolescents in the 1970's* (Minneapolis: Minnesota Systems Research, 1972), pp. 70-71.

44. Miller, p. 300.

45. Sherwin A. Kaufman, "When Teenagers Ask for the Pill," *Family Planning* 2 (March 1970): 2.

46. Konopka, mss. p. 99.

47. Cohen et al., in *Issues in the Classification*, p. 114.

48. Ibid.

49. Weiner, p. 178.

50. Ibid., p. 189.

51. Ibid.

52. Konopka, mss. p. 189.

53. C.C. Rhors and J. Densen-Gerber, "Adolescent Drug Abuse: An

Evaluation of 800 Inpatients in the Odyssey House Program," (Paper presented at the American Psychiatric Association Annual Meeting, Washington, D.C., 3-7 May 1971), cited in *Issues in the Classification*, 1:397.

54. Hallstrom and Banda, p. 122.

55. For a discussion of free clinics, see Jerome L. Schwartz, "First National Survey of Free Clinics, 1967-69," *Health Services and Mental Health Administration* Health Reports (September 1971).

56. The Joint Commission on Mental Health of Children, *The Mental Health of Children: Services, Research, and Manpower* (New York: Harper and Row Publishers, 1973), p. 330.

57. Ibid., p. 426.

58. The Joint Commission on Mental Health of Children, *Social Change and the Mental Health of Children*, Report of Task Force II and Excerpts from the Report of the Committee on Children of Minority Groups (New York: Harper and Row Publishers, 1973).

59. Cohen et al., in *Issues in the Classification*, p. 113.

60. Ibid.

61. Jack Korlath, Michael Baizerman, and Shirley Williams, "Twin City Adolescent Health Attitudes, Knowledge and Behavior," *Center for Development and Research Quarterly Focus* (Winter 1976).

62. Cohen et al., in *Issues in the Classification*, p. 115.

63. Ibid.

64. Weiner, p. 352.

65. Cohen et al., in *Issues in the Classification*, p. 117.

66. Ibid., p. 112.

67. Ibid., p. 118.

68. See, for instance, Weiner, p. 4.

69. Weiner, p. 349.

70. Max Hutt and Robert G. Gibby, *The Mentally Retarded Child: Development, Education and Treatment* (Boston: Allyn and Bacon, 1965), pp. 220-21.

71. Kakalik et al., p. 234.

72. Cited in Kakalik et al., pp. 234-35.

73. Kakalik et al., p. 244.

74. Michael J. Begab, "The Major Dilemma of Mental Retardation: Shall We Prevent It?" *American Journal of Mental Deficiencies* 78, no. 5 (1974): 519-29.

75. Office of Education, *Federal Register* 38, no. 196 (11 October 1973): 28230-31.

76. Weiner, p. 251.

77. Ibid., p. 278.

78. Samuel Kirk and John Elkins, *Characteristics of Children Enrolled in Child Service Demonstration Centers*, Final Report to the Department of Health, Education and Welfare (Washington, D.C.: U.S. Government Printing Office, 1974), p. 2.

79. Kakalik et al., p. 17.

80. Ibid., p. 106.

81. Ibid., p. 94.

82. Beth Stevens, "Symposium: Developmental Gains in the Reasoning, Moral Judgment, and Moral Conduct of Retarded and Non-retarded Persons," *American Journal of Mental Deficiency* 79, no. 2 (1974): 113-15.

83. Cobb interview, 19 June 1975.

84. Daniel letter, 12 September 1974.

85. Dr. Herman Saettler, Division of Personnel Preparation, Bureau of Education for the Handicapped, telephone conversation, 25 May 1976.

86. A. Stafford Metz and H. Leslie Cramer, *Professional Staff for the Handicapped in Local Public Schools* (Washington, D.C.: U.S. Government Printing Office, 1970).

87. Mark E. Borinsky, *Provision of Instruction to Handicapped Pupils in Local Public Schools* (Washington, D.C.: U.S. Government Printing Office, 1974).

88. Alan Abeson and J.B. Fleury, eds., *State Certification Requirements for Education of the Handicapped* (Arlington, Va.: Council for Exceptional Children, 1972).

89. Sol Blatt, "The Legal Rights of the Mentally Retarded," *Syracuse Law Review* 23 (1972): 9.

90. Harvard University Center for Law and Education, *Classification Materials*, mimeographed (Cambridge, Mass., September 1973).

91. 343 F. Supp. 279 (E.D. Pa., 1972).

92. For a full and informative evaluation of the legal issues of special education see David L. Kirp, Peter J. Kuriloff, and William C. Buss, "Legal Mandates and Organizational Change," in *Issues in the Classification*, 2.

93. Nicholas Hobbs, *The Futures of Children: Labels and Their Consequences* (San Francisco: Jossey-Bass, 1975), pp. 178-79.

94. Children's Defense Fund, *Report of the Second Year Activities of the Children's Defense Fund of the Washington Research Project, Inc.* (Cambridge, Mass., 1974), pp. 11-14. A report about children out of school and special needs issues is available from CDF: *Children Out of School in America* (Cambridge, Mass., 1974).

Chapter 4
The Family and the Young Adolescent

1. Jerald G. Bachman, *Youth in Transition*, vol. 2, *The Impact of Family Background and Intelligence on Tenth-Grade Boys* (Ann Arbor, Mich.: Survey Research Center, Institute for Social Research, 1970), p. 194.

2. Max Lerner, *America As A Civilization* (New York: Simon and Schuster, 1957), p. 552.

3. Nelson Northrup Foote, "Family," *Encyclopaedia Britannica* 9 (Chicago: Encyclopaedia Britannica, 1963): 59.

4. Joseph Goldstein, Anna Freud, and Albert J. Solnit, *Beyond the Best Interests of the Child* (New York: Macmillan Co., 1973), p. 10.

5. Rochelle Beck, "The White House Conference on Children: An Historical Perspective," *Harvard Educational Review* 43, no. 4 (November 1973): 662.

6. James Walters and Nick Stinnett, "Parent-Child Relationships: A Decade Review of Research," in *A Decade of Family Research and Action*, ed. Carlfred B. Broderick (Minneapolis: National Council on Family Relations, 1971), p. 130.

7. Richard E. Farson et al., *The Future of the Family* (New York: Family Service Association of America, 1969), pp. 30-33.

8. Diana Baumrind, "Coleman II: Utopian Fantasy and Sound Social Innovation," *School Review* 83, no. 1 (November 1974): 80.

9. Earl S. Schaefer, "Parents as Educators: Evidence from Cross-Sectional, Longitudinal, and Intervention Research," *Young Children* (April 1972): 237.

10. Social Research Group, *Toward Interagency Coordination: An Overview of Federal Research and Development Activities Relating to Early Childhood*, Fourth Annual Report (Washington, D.C.: The George Washington University, 1974), p. 37.

11. Social Research Group, *Toward Interagency Coordination: An Overview of Federal Research and Development Activities Relating to Adolescence*, First Annual Report (Washington, D.C.: The George Washington University, 1973), p. 28.

12. Cited in Marvin Wyne, Kinnard P. White, and Richard H. Coop, *The Black Self* (Englewood Cliffs, N.J.: Prentice-Hall, 1974), p. 37.

13. Charles E. Bowerman and John W. Kinch, "Changes in Family and Peer Orientation of Children Between Fourth and Tenth Grades," in *Adolescent Development*, ed. Martin Gold and Elizabeth Douvan (Boston: Allyn and Bacon, 1969), p. 137.

14. Denise B. Kandel and Gerald S. Lesser, *Youth in Two Worlds* (London: Jossey-Bass, 1972), p. 126.

15. Gisela Konopka, *Young Girls: A Portrait of Adolescence* (Englewood Cliffs, N.J.: Prentice-Hall, in press).

16. John Condry and Michael L. Siman, "Characteristics of Peer- and Adult-Oriented Children," *Journal of Marriage and the Family* 36, no. 3 (August 1974): 552.

17. Bachman, p. 194.

18. Daniel Offer, *The Psychological World of the Teen-ager* (New York: Basic Books, 1969), p. 70.

19. John P. Hill, "Some Perspectives on Adolescence in American Society," (Paper prepared for the Office of Child Development, U.S. Department of Health, Education and Welfare, Washington, D.C., May 1973), p. 33.

20. The Group for the Advancement of Psychiatry, *Normal Adolescence: Its Dynamics and Impact* (New York: Charles Scribners' Sons, 1968), p. 66.

21. Charles E. Bowerman and Rebecca M. Dobash, "Structural Variations in Inter-Sibling Affect," *Journal of Marriage and the Family* 36, no. 1 (February 1974): 52.

22. Thomas S. Langner, telephone conversation, 18 November 1974, citing *Children Under Stress* (New York: Columbia University Press, in press).

23. Bachman, pp. 192-93.

24. Donald Cohen and Richard Frank, "Preadolescence: A Critical Phase of Biological and Psychological Development," in *Mental Health in Children*, vol. 1, ed. D.V. Siva (Westbury, New York: PJD Publications, Ltd., 1975), p. 138.

25. Joint Commission on the Mental Health of Children, *Crisis in Child Mental Health: Challenge for the 1970's* (New York: Harper and Row Publishers, 1970), p. 359.

26. Jerome Kagan, "A Conception of Early Adolescence," *Daedalus* 100, no. 4 (Fall 1971): 1010.

27. We are indebted to Sigmund Dragastin, formerly of NICHD and now at NIMH, for the description of Baumrind's work, which has been funded by the Grant Foundation and NICHD. Letter of 14 July 1974.

28. Diana Baumrind, "Early Socialization and Adolescent Competence," in *Adolescence in the Life Cycle*, ed. Sigmund E. Dragastin and Glen H. Elder, Jr. (Washington, D.C.: Hemisphere Publishing Corporation, 1975), p. 131.

29. Ibid., p. 133.

30. Bachman, p. 171.

31. Offer, p. 202.

32. Kandel and Lesser, p. 107.

33. Hill, pp. 23-24.

34. Alice Marcella Propper, "Relationship of Maternal Employment to Adolescent Roles, Activities and Parental Relationship," *Journal of Marriage and the Family* 35, no. 1 (1973): 421.

35. Glennard H. Elder, Jr., *Adolescent Socialization and Personality Development* (Chicago: Rand-McNally and Co., 1968), p. 46.

36. Stanley Coopersmith, *The Antecedents of Self-Esteem* (San Francisco: W.H. Freeman, 1967), p. 257.

37. Social Research Group, *Toward Interagency Coordination: Adolescence '73*, pp. 29-30.

38. Baumrind, pp. 128-29.

Chapter 5
Voluntary Youth-Serving Agencies

1. Reynold E. Carson and Robert F. Hanson, *Organizations for Children and Youth* (Englewood Cliffs, N.J.: Prentice-Hall, 1972), p. 4.

2. William W. Wattenberg, *The Adolescent Years*, 2nd ed. (New York: Harcourt, Brace and Jovanovich, 1973), p. 296.

3. Urie Bronfenbrenner, *Two Worlds of Childhood: U.S. and U.S.S.R.* (New York: Russell Sage Foundation, 1970. Cited Edition in Pocketbook, 1973), p. 170.

4. *Girl Scout Handbook for the Intermediate Program* (New York: Girl Scouts, 1942), pp. 4-11.

5. "The Improved Scouting Program" (New Brunswick, N.J.: Boy Scouts of America, 1972), p. 1.

6. *World Almanac and Book of Facts*, 1971 edition (New York: Newspaper Enterprise Association, 1973), pp. 259-62; 1974 edition, pp. 270-74.

7. Carson and Hanson, pp. 115-16.

8. *Youth Alternatives Newsletter* 1, no. 9 (September 1974): 3.

9. Carson and Hanson, pp. 151-54.

10. *Resources for Youth Newsletter* 2, no. 1:8.

11. Mildred McClosky with Peter Kleinbard, *Youth Into Adult* (New York: National Commission on Resources for Youth, 1974), pp. 2-5.

12. Gisela Konopka, *Young Girls: A Portrait of Adolescence* (Englewood Cliffs, N.J.: Prentice-Hall, in press), mss. p. 221.

13. "Community Participation Class," *Resources for Youth Newsletter* 3, no. 1:1-2.

14. Peter Kleinbard, National Commission on Resources for Youth, New York City, telephone conversation, 11 September 1974.

15. Emory J. Brown and Patrick G. Boyle, *4-H in Urban Areas* (Washington, D.C.: National 4-H Club Foundation, 1964), p. 31.

Chapter 6
The Young Adolescent in the Juvenile Justice System

1. *U.S. Code: Congressional and Administrative News*, Legislative History, 93rd Congress, Second Session, 1974, p. 5318.

2. Nicholas Hobbs, *The Futures of Children: Labels and Their Consequences* (San Francisco: Jossey-Bass, 1975), p. 2.

3. Robert W. Winslow, *Juvenile Delinquency in a Free Society* (Belmont, Cal.: Dickenson Publishing Co., 1968), p. 2.

4. *U.S. Code*, p. 5289.

5. *Annual Report of Federal Activities in Youth Development, Juvenile Delinquency and Related Fields* (Washington, D.C.: Social and Rehabilitation Services, 1971), pp. 1-2.

6. Diane Ravitch, "Crime Fighting as Part of Curricula," *New York Times* News of the Week in Review, 21 July 1974.

7. Winslow, p. v.

8. The President's Commission on Law Enforcement and the Administration of Justice, *The Challenge of Crime in a Free Society* (Washington, D.C.: U.S. Government Printing Office, 1967), pp. 56-57.

9. Jerald G. Bachman, *Youth in Transition*, Vol. 2, *The Impact of Family Background and Intelligence on Tenth-Grade Boys* (Ann Arbor, Mich.: Survey Research Center, Institute for Social Research, 1970), p. 165.

10. Marvin E. Wolfgang, Robert M. Figlio, and Thorsten Sellin, *Delinquency in a Birth Cohort* (Chicago: University of Chicago Press, 1972).

11. Ibid., p. 216.

12. Ibid., p. 104.

13. Ibid., p. 103.

14. Ibid., pp. 134-35.

15. *Annual Report of Federal Activities*, p. 2.

16. Sol Rubin, *Crime and Juvenile Delinquency* (New York: Oceana Publications, 1970), p. 35.

17. Anthony Platt, *The Child Savers: The Invention of Delinquency* (Chicago: University of Chicago Press, 1969).

18. Saleem A. Shah, "Perspectives and Directions in Juvenile Corrections," *The Psychiatric Quarterly* 47, no. 1:6.

19. Paul Lerman, "Child Convicts," *Trans-Action* (July-August 1971): 34-35.

20. Justine Wise Polier, "Myths and Realities in the Search for Juvenile Justice," *Harvard Educational Review* 44, no. 1 (February 1974): 115.

21. Ted Morgan, "They Think, 'I can kill because I'm 14,' " *New York Times Magazine*, 19 January 1975, p. 11.

22. Shah, p. 18.

23. Michael C. Dixon and William E. Wright, *Juvenile Delinquency Prevention Programs*, Institute on Youth and Social Development, The John F. Kennedy Center for Research on Education and Human Development, George Peabody College for Teachers (Nashville, October 1974), p. 11.

24. Ibid., p. 34.

25. Ibid., p. 4.

26. Ibid., pp. 63-77.

27. Edwin M. Lemert, *Instead of Court: Diversion in Juvenile Justice*, Crime and Delinquency Series, National Institute of Mental Health Center for Studies of Crime and Delinquency (Rockville, Md., 1971), pp. 73-74.

28. Shah, pp. 14-15.

29. Lemert, pp. 72, 89.

30. Ibid., p. 91.

31. James Q. Wilson, *Thinking About Crime* (New York: Basic Books, 1975), p. 177.

32. Ibid., p. 208.

33. Ibid., pp. 198-99.

34. Hobbs, p. 39.

35. *Annual Report of Federal Activities*, pp. 1-2.

36. Ohlin, Lloyd E. "Institutions for Predelinquent or Delinquent Children," in *Child Caring, Social Policy, and the Institutions*, ed. D.M. Pappenfort et al. (Chicago: Aldine Publishing Co., 1973).

37. Morgan, p. 22.

38. For studies supporting this view see R.A. Coward and L.E. Ohlin, *Delinquency and Opportunity: A Theory of Delinquent Gangs* (New York: Free Press, 1960); D.F. Duncan, "Stigma and Delinquency," *Cornell Journal of Social Relations* 4 (1969): 41-45; E.M. Schur, *Radical Non-Intervention* (Englewood Cliffs, N.J.: Prentice-Hall, 1973); H.S. Becker, *Outsiders: Studies in the Sociology of Crime* (New York: Free Press, 1963).

39. Wolfgang, Figlio, and Sellin, p. 252.

40. Polier, p. 118.

41. Rosemary Sarri and Paul Isenstadt, Remarks presented at the Hearings of the U.S. House of Representatives Select Committee on Crime, 18 April 1973 (Ann Arbor: University of Michigan Institute of Continuing Legal Education, 1973), p. 1.

42. Frank A. Orlando and Jerry P. Black, "The Juvenile Court," in *Issues in the Classification of Children*, ed. Nicholas Hobbs, 2 vols. (San Francisco: Jossey Bass, 1975), 1:354.

43. Mark Levin and Rosemary Sarri, *Juvenile Delinquency: Comparative Analysis of Legal Codes in the U.S.*, National Assessment of Juvenile Corrections (Ann Arbor: University of Michigan, 1974), p. 8.

44. Ibid., pp. 31-32.

45. Ibid., p. 34.

46. Ibid., p. 53.

47. Ibid., p. 56.

48. Ibid., p. 61.

49. Sarri and Isenstadt, pp. 4-8.

50. Lloyd E. Ohlin, Robert B. Coates, and Alden D. Miller, "Radical Correctional Reform: A Case Study of the Massachusetts Youth Correctional System," *Harvard Educational Review* 44, no. 1 (February 1974): 74-111.

51. Ibid., pp. 84, 93.

52. Ibid., p. 94.

53. Robert L. Smith, "Diversion from the Juvenile and Criminal Justice Process," in *Corrections*, ed. Allen F. Breed, California Youth Authority (Sacramento, Cal., 1973), pp. 3-4.

54. Lemert, p. 9.

55. Ibid., p. 92.

56. Ibid., p. 95.

57. President's Commission, p. 7.

58. California Youth Authority, *The Challenge of Youth Service Bureaus*, Report to State of California Youth Development and Delinquency Prevention Administration (Sacramento, Cal., 1973), pp. 18-20.

59. Sarri and Isenstadt, p. 11.

60. Selwyn Raab, "City Prison Reform Plan Called Failure," *New York Times*, 10 August 1975, p. 1.

61. Ibid., p. 4.

62. Ibid., p. 1.

63. Eleanor Harlow, J. Robert Weber, and Leslie T. Wilkins, *Community Based Correctional Program*, National Institute of Mental Health, DHEW No. (ADM)74-56 (Washington, D.C.: U.S. Government Printing Office, 1971), p. 5.

64. Ibid.

65. Ibid., p. 7.

66. Ibid., p. 12.

67. Ibid., p. 14.

68. Ibid., p. 16.

69. Winslow, p. 226.

70. Sarri and Isenstadt, p. 15.

71. Information concerning the development of the Achievement Place model, its evaluations, and specific guidelines appear in E.L. Phillips, E.A. Phillips, D.L. Fixen, and M.M. Wolf, *The Teaching Family Handbook* (Lawrence: University of Kansas Printing Service, 1972).

72. Stevens Clarke, *The Contribution of Juvenile Offenders Treatment and Service Programs to the Reduction of Juvenile Delinquency*, Mecklenburg Criminal Justice Pilot Project (Chapel Hill: University of North Carolina Press, 1973), p. 20.

73. Clarke, p. 27.

74. Martin Gold and J.R. Williams, "National Study of the Aftermath of Apprehension," *University of Michigan Journal of Law Reform* 3 (1969): 1-12.

75. Wolfgang, Figlio, and Sellin, pp. 174-92.

76. Clarke, pp. 27-28.

77. Urie Bronfenbrenner, *Two Worlds of Childhood: U.S. and U.S.S.R.* (New York: Russell Sage Foundation, 1970. Cited Edition in Pocket Book, 1973), p. 113.

78. Wolfgang, Figlio, and Sellin, p. 248.

79. Ibid., p. 254.

80. Sarri and Isenstadt, p. 19.

81. *U.S. Code*, p. 5291.

Bibliography

Abeson, Alan, and Fleury, J.B., eds. *State Certification Requirements for Education of the Handicapped.* Arlington, Va.: The Council for Exceptional Children, 1972.

Ayrault, Evelyn West. *Helping the Handicapped Teenager Mature.* New York: Associated Press, 1971.

Bachman, Jerald G. *Youth in Transition*, vol. 2, *The Impact of Family Background and Intelligence on Tenth-Grade Boys.* Ann Arbor, Mich.: Survey Research Center, Institute for Social Research, 1970.

Bachman, Jerald G. *Young Men in High School and Beyond: A Summary of Findings from the Youth in Transition Project.* Final Report. Washington, D.C.: Office of Education, U.S. Department of Health, Education, and Welfare, May 1972.

Bachman, Jerald G.; Green, Swayzer; and Wirtanen, Ilona D. *Youth in Transition*, vol. 3: *Dropping Out–Problem or Symptom?* Ann Arbor, Mich.: Survey Research Center, Institute for Social Research, 1971.

Banks, James A., and Grambs, Jean D. *Black Self-Concept: Implications for Education and Social Science.* New York: McGraw-Hill Book Co., 1972.

Baumrind, Diana. "Coleman II: Admixture of Utopian Fantasy and Sound Social Innovation." *School Review* 83, no. 1 (November 1974): 69-84.

Bazelon, David. "Implementing the Right to Treatment." University of Chicago *Law Review* 36 (1969).

Beck, Rochelle. "The White House Conference on Children: An Historical Perspective." *Harvard Educational Review* 43, no. 4 (November 1973): 662.

Begab, Michael J. "The Major Dilemma of Mental Retardation: Shall We Prevent It?" *American Journal of Mental Deficiencies* 78, no. 5 (1974).

Behn, W.H. et al. "School is Bad: Work is Worse." *School Review* 38 (November 1974).

Bennett, G. Vernon. *The Junior High School.* Baltimore: Warwick and York, 1919.

Birch, Herbert G., and Gussow, Joan Dye. *Disadvantaged Children: Health, Nutrition and School Failure.* New York: Harcourt, Brace and Jovanovich, 1970.

Bereiter, Carl. *Must We Educate?* Englewood Cliffs, N.J.: Prentice-Hall, 1973.

Blatt, Sol. "The Legal Rights of the Mentally Retarded." *Syracuse Law Review* 23 (1972).

Bloom, Benjamin. *Stability and Change in Human Characteristics.* New York: John Wiley and Sons, 1964.

Blos, Peter. *The Young Adolescent.* New York: The Free Press, 1970.

Borinsky, Mark E. *Provision of Instruction to Handicapped Pupils in Local Public Schools.* Washington, D.C.: U.S. Government Printing Office, 1974.

Bowerman, Charles E., and Dobash, Rebecca M. "Structural Variations in Inter-Sibling Affect." *Journal of Marriage and the Family* 36, no. 1 (February 1974): 52.

Bowerman, Charles E., and Kinch, John W. "Changes in Family and Peer Orientation of Children Between Fourth and Tenth Grades." In *Adolescent Development*, edited by Martin Gold and Elizabeth Douvan. Boston: Allyn and Bacon, 1969.

Boys Town Center for the Study of Youth Development. "The Boys Town Research and Training Complex." Mimeographed, n.d.

Boy Scouts of America. *The Improved Scouting Program.* New Brunswick, N.J.: Boy Scouts of America, 1972.

Briggs, Thomas H. *The Junior High School.* Boston: Houghton Mifflin Co., 1920.

Bronfenbrenner, Urie. *Two Worlds of Childhood: U.S. and U.S.S.R.* New York: Russell Sage Foundation, 1970. Cited Edition in Pocket Book, 1973.

Brown, Emory J., and Boyle, Patrick G. *4-H in Urban Areas.* Washington, D.C.: National 4-H Club Foundation, 1964.

Brown, Frank, ed. *Reform of Secondary Education.* Report of the National Commission on the Reform of Secondary Education. New York: McGraw-Hill Book Co., 1973.

Burnett, Jacquetta Hill. *Social Structures, Ideologies, and Culture Codes in Occupational Development of Puerto Rican Youths.* Vol. 1 of Final Report. Urbana: Bureau of Educational Research, University of Illinois, Spring 1974.

California Commission for Reform of Intermediate and Secondary Education. *RISE: Report of the California Commission for Reform of Intermediate and Secondary Education.* Sacramento: California State Department of Education, 1975.

California Youth Authority. *The Challenge of Youth Service Bureaus.* Report to the State of California Youth Development and Delinquency Prevention Administration. Sacramento, 1973.

Carson, Reynold E., and Hanson, Robert F. *Organizations for Children and Youth.* Englewood Cliffs, N.J.: Prentice-Hall, 1972.

Center for Youth Development and Research, *Youth Encounters A Changing World.* Minneapolis: University of Minnesota Center for Youth Development and Research, August 1972.

Chesney-Lind, Meda. "Juvenile Delinquency: the Sexualization of Female Crime." *Psychology Today* 8 (July 1974).

Children's Defense Fund, *Report of the Second Year Activities of the Children's*

Defense Fund of the Washington Research Project, Inc. Cambridge, Mass., 1974.

Clarke, Stevens. *The Contribution of Juvenile Offenders Treatment and Service Programs to the Reduction of Juvenile Delinquency.* Mecklenburg Criminal Justice Pilot Project. Chapel Hill: University of North Carolina Press, 1973.

Cohen, Donald, and Frank, Richard. "Preadolescence: A Critical Phase of Biological and Psychological Development." In D.V. Siva, ed., *Mental Health in Children*, vol. 1, Westbury, N.Y.: PJD Publications, Ltd., 1975.

Coleman, J.A. *Youth: Transition to Adulthood.* Report of the Panel on Youth of the President's Science Advisory Committee. Washington, D.C.: U.S. Government Printing Office, 1973.

Condry, John, and Siman, Michael L. "Characteristics of Peer- and Adult-Oriented Children." *Journal of Marriage and the Family* 36, no. 3 (August 1974): 552.

Cooper, Paulette, ed. *Growing Up Puerto Rican.* New York: New American Library, 1972.

Coopersmith, Stanley. *The Antecedents of Self-Esteem.* San Francisco: W.H. Freeman, 1967.

Daedalus 100 (Fall 1971). Special Issue: "Early Adolescence."

Daniel, William A., Jr., M.D. *The Adolescent Patient.* St. Louis: C.V. Mosby Co., 1970.

Deisher, Robert. "Youth Services in Europe." Mimeographed. University of Washington, Seattle, Wash., n.d.

de la Garza, O.; Kruszeruski, Z. Anthony; and Arciniega, Tomas A. *Chicanos and Native Americans.* Englewood Cliffs, N.J.: Prentice-Hall, 1973.

Dixon, Michael, and Wright, William E. *Juvenile Delinquency Prevention Programs.* Nashville: Institute on Youth and Social Development, The John F. Kennedy Center for Research on Education and Human Development, George Peabody College for Teachers, October 1974.

Douvan, Elizabeth, and Adelson, Joseph. *The Adolescent Experience.* New York: John Wiley and Sons, 1966.

Dragastin, S.E., and Elder, G., Jr. *Adolescence in the Life Cycle.* Washington, D.C.: Hemisphere Publishing Corporation, John Wiley and Sons, 1975.

Dupont, Henry, ed. *Educating Emotionally Disturbed Children: Readings.* New York: Holt, Rinehart and Winston, 1969.

Duran, Livie Isauro, and Bernard, H. Russell, eds. *Introduction to Chicano Studies.* New York: Macmillan Co., 1973.

Education Commission of the States. *Legislative Review* 4, no. 17 (12 August 1974).

Elder, Glennard H., Jr. *Adolescent Socialization and Personality Development.* Chicago: Rand-McNally and Co., 1968.

Elkind, David. "Egocentrism in Adolescence." *Child Development* 38 (December 1967): 1025-34.

Erikson, Erik. *Identity, Youth and Crisis.* New York: W.W. Norton, 1968.

Fader, Daniel. *The Naked Children.* New York: Macmillan Co., 1971.

Fantini, Mario D. *Public Schools of Choice.* New York: Simon and Schuster, 1973.

Farson, Richard E.; Hauser, Philip M.; Stroup, Herbert; and Wiener, Anthony J. *The Future of the Family.* New York: Family Service Association of America, 1969.

Feingold, Ben F. "Hyperkinesis and Learning Disabilities (H-LD) Linked to the Ingestion of Artificial Food Colors and Flavors." Presentation before the Committee on Education, California State Legislature, 31 July 1974. Mimeographed.

Fitzpatrick, Joseph. *Puerto Rican Americans.* Englewood Cliffs, N.J.: Prentice-Hall, 1971.

Foote, Nelson Northrup. "Family." *Encyclopaedia Britannica* 9. Chicago: Encyclopaedia Britannica, 1963.

The Ford Foundation. *A Foundation Goes to School: The Ford Foundation Comprehensive School Improvement Program, 1960-1970.* New York: Office of Reports, The Ford Foundation, November 1972.

Franks, D.J. "Ethnic and Social Status Characteristics of Children in EMR and LD Classes." *Exceptional Children* 37 (1971): 537-538.

Franks, Lucinda. "F.D.A., In Shift, Test Diet for Hyperactive." *New York Times*, 9 February 1975.

Friedenberg, Edgar Z. *The Vanishing Adolescent.* New York: Dell Publishing Co., 1959.

Frisch, Rose E. "Demographic Implications of the Biological Determinants of Female Fecundity." Paper presented at the Population Association of America Annual Meeting, New York, April 1974. Mimeographed.

Gallagher, James J. "Special Education: Trends and Issues." *Phi Delta Kappan* 55 (April 1974): 516-520.

Gallagher, J. Roswell, and Harris, Herbert I. *Emotional Problems of Adolescents.* New York: Oxford University Press, 1964.

Gallatin, Judith E. *Adolescence and Individuality: A Conceptual Approach to Adolescent Psychology.* New York: Harper and Row Publishers, 1975.

Gallatin, Judith, with Adelson, Joseph; O'Neil, Robert; and Miller, Lamar. "The Development of Political Thinking in Urban Adolescents." Mimeographed. Final Report, Project No. 0-0554, National Center for Educational Research and Development, U.S. Department of Health, Education, and Welfare, Washington, D.C., December 1972.

Gilligan, Carol. "Fostering Moral Development in Children." *EDC News* 4 (Spring 1974): 8.

Glazer, Nathan. "Ethnicity and the Schools." *Commentary* 58 (September 1974): 55-59.

Gold, Martin. *Delinquent Behavior in An American City.* Belmont, Cal.: Dickenson Publishing Co., 1970.

Gold, Martin, and Williams, J.R. "National Study of the Aftermath of Apprehension." *University of Michigan Journal of Law Reform* 3 (1969): 1-12.

Goldhammer, Keith et al. *Elementary Principals and Their Schools: Beacons of Brilliance and Potholes of Pestilence.* Center for the Advanced Study of Education, University of Oregon. Washington, D.C.: Capitol Publications, 1971.

Goldstein, Joseph; Freud, Anna; and Solnit, Albert J. *Beyond the Best Interests of the Child.* New York: Macmillan Co., 1973.

Green Alan C. "Planning for Declining Enrollments." *School Review* 82, no. 4 (August 1974): 595-607.

Greenbaum, William. "America in Search of a New Ideal: An Essay on the Rise of Pluralism." *Harvard Educational Review* 44 (August 1974): 411-440.

Greenberger, Ellen, and Sorensen, Aage B. "Toward a Concept of Psychosocial Maturity." *Journal of Youth and Adolescence* 3 (December 1974): 329-358.

Greif, Esther Blank, and Hogan, Robert. "The Theory and Measurement of Empathy." *Journal of Counseling Psychology* 20, no. 30 (1973): 281.

Grinder, Robert E., ed. *Studies in Adolescence: A Book of Readings in Adolescent Development.* 2nd ed. London: Macmillan and Co., 1969.

Group for the Advancement of Psychiatry. *Normal Adolescence: Its Dynamics and Impact.* New York: Charles Scribners' Sons, 1968.

Grumbach, Melvin; Grave, Gilman O.; and Mayer, Florence E., eds. *The Control of the Onset of Puberty.* New York: John Wiley and Sons, 1974.

Hallstrom, Betty J., and Banda, Joachim M. *The Provision of Health Care Services to Adolescents in the 1970's.* Minneapolis: Minnesota Systems Research, 1972.

Harlow, Eleanor: Weber, J. Robert; and Wilkins, Leslie T. *Community Based Correctional Program.* National Institute of Mental Health, DHEW No. (ADM)74-56. Washington, D.C.: U.S. Government Printing Office, 1971.

Harvard University Center for Law and Education. *Classification Materials.* September 1973.

Havighurst, J., and Dreyer, P.H., eds. *Youth: The 74th Yearbook of the National Society for the Study of Education.* Chicago: University of Chicago Press, 1975.

Heald, Felix, ed. *Adolescent Nutrition and Growth.* New York: Appleton-Century Crofts, 1969.

Herzog, Elizabeth. "Who Should Be Studied?" *American Journal of Orthopsychiatry* 41 (January 1971): 4-12.

Hill, John P. "Some Perspectives on Adolescence in American Society." Paper prepared for the Office of Child Development, U.S. Department of Health, Education, and Welfare, Washington, D.C., May 1973.

Hill, John P., and Palmquist, Wendy J. "Social Cognition and Social Relations in Adolescence: A Precursory View." Paper presented at the meeting of the Eastern Psychological Association, Philadelphia, April 1974.

Hobbs, Nicholas. *The Futures of Children: Labels and Their Consequences.* San Francisco: Jossey-Bass, 1975.

Hobbs, Nicholas, ed. *Issues in the Classification of Children.* 2 vols. San Francisco: Jossey-Bass, 1975.

Hogan, Robert. "Moral Conduct and Moral Character: A Psychological Perspective." *Psychological Bulletin* 79 (1973): 217-232.

Hutt, Max, and Gibby, Robert G. *The Mentally Retarded Child: Development, Education and Treatment.* Boston: Allyn and Bacon, 1965.

James, Charity. *Beyond Customs.* New York: Agathon Press, 1974.

James, Charity. *Young Lives at Stake.* New York: Agathon Press, 1972.

Johnson, G. Orville, and Blank, Harriet D., eds. *Exceptional Children Research Review.* Washington, D.C., The Council for Exceptional Children, 1968.

Johnson, Kenneth R. *Teaching the Culturally Disadvantaged: A Rational Approach.* Palo Alto: California Science Research Associates, 1970.

Joint Commission on Mental Health of Children. *Crisis in Child Mental Health: Challenge for the 1970's.* New York: Harper and Row Publishers, 1970.

Joint Commission on Mental Health of Children. *Mental Health: From Infancy Through Adolescence.* Reports of Task Forces I, II, and III and the Committee on Education and Religion. New York: Harper and Row Publishers, 1973.

Joint Commission on Mental Health of Children. *The Mental Health of Children: Services, Research, and Manpower.* Reports of Task Forces IV and V and the Committee on Clinical Issues. New York: Harper and Row Publishers, 1973.

Joint Commission on Mental Health of Children. *Social Change and the Mental Health of Children.* Report of Task Force II and Excerpts from the Report of the Committee on Children of Minority Groups. New York: Harper and Row Publishers, 1973.

Jones, Reginald L., ed. *Black Psychology.* New York: Harper and Row Publishers, 1972.

Kakalik, J.S.; Brewer, Garry D.; Dougharty, Laurence A.; Fleishauer, Patricia D.; and Genensky, Samuel M. *Services for Handicapped Youth: A Program Overview* R-1220. Santa Monica, Cal.: Rand Corporation, 1973.

Kandel, Denise B., and Lesser, Gerald S. *Youth in Two Worlds.* London: Jossey-Bass, 1972.

Kirk, Samuel A. *Educating Exceptional Children.* 2nd ed. New York: Houghton Mifflin Co., 1972.

Kirk, Samuel, and Elkins, John. *Characteristics of Children Enrolled in Child Service Demonstration Centers.* Final Report, Project No. H12-7145B, Grant No. OEC-0-714425, DHEW, U.S. Office of Education, Bureau of Education for the Handicapped, June 1974.

Kirp, David L. "Schools as Sorters: The Constitutional and Policy Implications of Student Classification." *University of Pennsylvania Law Review* 121 (1973): 731-737.

Kirp, David L.; Buss, William G.; and Kuriloff, Peter J. "Legal Reform of Special Education: Empirical Studies and Procedural Proposals." *California Law Review* 62 (1974): 58-96.

Kohlberg, Lawrence. "The Development of Children's Orientation Toward a Moral Order." *Vita Humana* 6 (1963): 11-33.

Kolata, Gina Bari. "!Kung Hunter-Gatherers: Feminism, Diet, and Birth Control." *Science* 185 (13 September 1974): 932-934.

Konopka, Gisela. "Requirements for Healthy Development of Adolescent Youth." *Adolescence* 8, no. 31 (Fall 1973): 291-316.

Konopka, Gisela. *Young Girls: A Portrait of Adolescence.* Englewood Cliffs, N.J.: Prentice-Hall, in press.

Lambert, B. Geraldine; Rothschild, Barbara; Altland, Richard; and Green, Lawrence. *Adolescence: Transition from Childhood to Maturity.* Monterey, Cal.: Brooks/Cole Publishing Co., 1972.

Larson, Meredith A., and Dittmann, Freya E. *Compensatory Education and Early Adolescence: Reviewing Our National Strategy.* Research Report EPRC 2158-7, Educational Policy Research Center, Stanford Research Institute (May 1975).

Larson, Meredith A., and Dittmann, Freya E. *Adolescence: Alternative Strategies For Compensatory Education.* Educational Policy Research Center, Stanford Research Institute. Prepared for the Office of the Assistant Secretary for Education, U.S. Department of Health, Education, and Welfare, Washington, D.C., July 1974.

Leet, Pauline M. "Socialization and the 'Middle' Child: A Twentieth Century Model of a Seventeenth Century Process." Paper presented at the 1974 Annual Meeting, American Educational Research Association, Chicago, April 1974.

Lemert, Edwin M. *Instead of Court: Diversion in Juvenile Justice.* Crime and Delinquency Issues. Rockville, Md.: National Institute of Mental Health, Center for Studies of Crime and Delinquency, 1971.

Lerman, Paul. "Child Convicts." *Trans-Action* (July-August 1971).

Lerner, Max. *America As A Civilization.* New York: Simon and Schuster, 1957.

Lerner, Michael, "Nutritional Therapy and Children with Learning Disabilities and Behavior Disorders Relating to Central Nervous System Disorders." A Report to the Carnegie Council on Children. Mimeographed, n.d.

Levin, Mark, and Sarri, Rosemary. *Juvenile Delinquency: Comparative Analysis of Legal Codes in the U.S.* National Assessment of Juvenile Corrections. Ann Arbor: University of Michigan, 1974.

Levine, Daniel. "Cultural Diffraction in the Social System of the Low Income School." *School and Society* 96 (March 20, 1968).

McClosky, Mildred, with Kleinbard, Peter. *Youth into Adult.* New York: The National Commission on Resources for Youth, 1974.

McGlasson, Maurice. *The Middle School: Whence? What? Whither?* Phi Delta Kappa Fastback No. 22. Bloomington, Ind.: Phi Delta Kappa Educational Foundation, 1973.

McNassor, Donald. "Social Structure for Identity in Adolescence: Western Europe and America." *Adolescence* 2 (Fall 1967): 311-334.

McPartland, James M., and Epstein, Joyce L. *Interim Report: School Organization and School Outcomes: A Study of the Effects of Open-Environment Schools.* Baltimore: Center for Social Organization of Schools, The Johns Hopkins University, December 1973.

Mangold, Margaret, ed. *La Causa Chicano.* New York: Family Service Association of America, 1971.

Mapp, Edward, ed. *Puerto Rican Perspectives.* Metuchen, N.J.: Scarecrow Press, 1974.

Martin, John Henry et al. *Report of the National Panel on High Schools and Adolescent Education.* Washington, D.C.: U.S. Office of Education, March 1974.

Masterson, J.R. "The Symptomatic Adolescent Five Years Later: He Didn't Grow Out of It." *American Journal of Psychiatry* 123 (1967).

Mercer, J.R. "Sociocultural Factors in Labeling Mental Retardates." *Peabody Journal of Education* 48 (1971): 188-293.

Metz, A. Stafford, and Cramer, H. Leslie, *Professional Staff for the Handicapped in Local Public Schools.* Washington, D.C.: U.S. Government Printing Office, 1970.

Miller, Derek. *Adolescence: Psychology, Psychopathology and Psychotherapy.* New York: Jason Aronson, 1974.

Miranda, Magdalena, ed. *Puerto Rican Task Force Report.* New York: Council on Social Work Education, 1973.

Morgan, Ted. "They Think, 'I can kill because I'm 14.' " *New York Times Magazine*, 19 January 1975.

Muuss, Rolf E., ed. *Adolescent Behavior and Society: A Book of Readings.* New York: Random House, 1971.

Muuss, Rolf E. "Jean Piaget's Cognitive Theory of Adolescent Development." *Adolescence* 2 (Fall 1967): 285-310.

National Academy of Sciences. *Extent and Meanings of Iron Deficiency in the United States.* Summary Proceedings of a Workshop of the Food and Nutrition Board, Washington, D.C., 8-9 March 1971.

National Academy of Sciences. *Maternal Nutrition and the Course of Pregnancy.* Summary Report of the Committee on Maternal Nutrition, Food and Nutrition Board. Reprinted Washington, D.C.: U.S. Government Printing Office, 1974.

National Association of Independent Schools Task Force. *Initial Position Papers and Accompanying Papers.* Mimeographed. Cambridge, Mass.: NAIS, 1975.

National Commission on Resources for Youth. *New Roles for Youth in the School and the Community.* New York: Citation Press, 1974.

National Institute of Child Health and Human Development. "Expanded Program in Adolescent Development." Mimeographed. Washington, D.C.: August 1973.

National Institute of Child Health and Human Development. "Nutrient Requirements in Adolescence." Recommendations of work group at Airlie House, Va., 3-6 June 1973.

National Institute of Education. *Conference on Studies in Reading.* Conference Guidance Materials. Washington, D.C.: 18-22 August 1974.

Obermann, C. Esco. *Coordinating Services for Handicapped Children.* Washington, D.C.: Council for Exceptional Children, 1964.

Offer, Daniel. *The Psychological World of the Teen-ager.* New York: Basic Books, 1969.

Ohlin, Lloyd E. "Institutions for Predelinquent or Delinquent Children." In *Child Caring, Social Policy, and the Institutions*, edited by D.M. Pappenfort et al. Chicago: Aldine Publishing Co., 1973.

Ohlin, Lloyd E.; Coates, Robert B.; and Miller, Alden D. "Radical Correctional Reform: A Case Study of the Massachusetts Youth Correctional System." *Harvard Educational Review* 44, no. 1 (February 1974): 74-111.

Piaget, Jean. "Intellectual Evolution from Adolescence to Adulthood." *Human Development* 15 (1972): 1-12.

Platt, Anthony. *The Child-Savers: The Invention of Delinquency.* Chicago: University of Chicago Press, 1969.

Polier, Justine Wise. "Myths and Realities in the Search for Juvenile Justice." *Harvard Educational Review* 44, no. 1 (February 1974): 112-124.

The President's Commission on Law Enforcement and the Administration of Justice. *The Challenge of Crime in a Free Society.* Washington, D.C.: U.S. Government Printing Office, 1967.

The President's Committee on Mental Retardation. *Islands of Excellence.* DHEW Publication No. (05) 73-7. Washington, D.C.: U.S. Government Printing Office, 1973.

Pringle, Ralph W. *The Junior High School: A Psychological Approach.* New York: McGraw-Hill Book Co., 1937.

Propper, Alice Marcella. "Relationship of Maternal Employment to Adolescent Roles, Activities and Parental Relationship." *Journal of Marriage and the Family* 35, no. 1 (1973): 421.

Quay, H.D. "Special Education: Assumptions Techniques, and Evaluation Criteria." *Exceptional Children* 40 (1973): 165-170.

Rabb, Selwyn. "City Prison Reform Plan Called Failure." *New York Times*, 10 August 1975.

Ravitch, Diane. "Crime Fighting as Part of Curricula." *New York Times* News of the Week in Review, 21 July 1974.

Resources for Youth Newsletter. The National Commission on Resources for Youth, 36 W. 44th Street, New York, N.Y. 10036.

Richmond, Julius B. "The Family and the Handicapped Child." *Clinical Proceedings Children's Hospital National Medical Center* 29 (July 1973).

Rogers, Dorothy. *Issues in Adolescent Psychology.* New York: Appleton-Century Crofts, 1972.

Rohwer, William D., Jr. "Prime Time for Education: Early Childhood or Adolescence?" *Harvard Educational Review* 41 (August 1971): 316-341.

Rohwer, William D., Jr. "Elaboration and Learning in Childhood and Adolescence." In *Advances in Child Development and Behavior*, edited by H.W. Reese. New York: Academic Press, 1973.

Rosenberg, Morris, and Simmons, Roberta G. *Black and White Self-Esteem: The Urban School Child.* Washington, D.C.: Sociological Association, 1971.

Ross, S.; DeYoung, H.; and Cohen, J. "Confrontation: Special Education Placement and the Law." *Exceptional Children* 38 (1971): 5-12.

Rubin, Sol. *Crime and Juvenile Delinquency.* New York: Oceana Publications, 1970.

Ruiz, Juliette, ed. *Chicano Task Force Report.* New York: Council on Social Work Education, 1973.

Rutherford, Andrew. *The Dissolution of the Training Schools in Massachusetts.* Columbus, Ohio: The Academy of Contemporary Problems, 1974.

Sarason, S.B. *The Culture of the School and The Problem of Change.* Boston: Allyn and Bacon, 1971.

Sarri, Rosemary, and Isenstadt, Paul. *Remarks.* Presented at the Hearings of the House of Representatives Select Committee on Crime, 18 April 1973. Ann Arbor: University of Michigan Institute of Continuing Legal Education, 1973.

Schaefer, Earl S. "Parents as Educators: Evidence from Cross-Sectional, Longitudinal, and Intervention Research." *Young Children* (April 1972): 237.

School Review 81 (May 1973). Special Issue: "The Future of Education for Black Americans."

Schur, E. *Radical Non-Intervention–Rethinking the Delinquency Problem.* Englewood Cliffs, N.J.: Prentice-Hall, 1973.

Shah, Saleem A. "Perspectives and Directions for Juvenile Corrections." *The Psychiatric Quarterly* 47, no. 1: 6.

Shah, Saleem A. "Juvenile Delinquency: A National Perspective." In *New Treatment Approaches to Juvenile Delinquency,* edited by J.L. Khanna, pp. 3-23. Springfield, Ill.: Charles C. Thomas, 1975.

Sheldon, Paul M. "Mexican-Americans and the Public Schools." In *Report of the Conference on Understanding and Teaching Mexican-American Children and Youth.* Sacramento: California State Department of Education, 1964.

Silberman, Charles. *Crisis in the Classroom.* New York: Random House, 1970.

Simmons, Roberta G.; Rosenberg, Florence; and Rosenberg, Morris. "Disturbance in the Self-Image at Adolescence." *American Sociological Review* 38 (October 1973): 553-568.

Simpson, Elizabeth Léonie. "Moral Development: A Case Study of Scientific Cultural Bias." *Human Development* 17 (1974): 81-106.

Smith, Robert L. "Diversion from the Juvenile and Criminal Justice Process." In *Corrections*, ed. Allen F. Breed, Sacramento: California Youth Authority, 1973.

Smithsonian Science Information Exchange. "Notices of Research Projects." Washington, D.C. Mimeographed.

Social Research Group. *Toward Interagency Coordination: An Overview of Federal Research and Development Activities Relating to Adolescence.* First Annual Report. Washington, D.C.: The George Washington University, 1973.

Social Research Group. *Toward Interagency Coordination: An Overview of FY '74 Federal Research and Development Activities Relating to Adolescence.* Second Annual Report. Washington, D.C.: The George Washington University, 1974.

Social Research Group. *Toward Interagency Coordination: An Overview of FY '74 Federal Research and Development Activities Relating to Early Child-*

hood. Fourth Annual Report. Washington, D.C.: The George Washington University, 1974.

Social Research Group. *Toward Interagency Coordination: FY '75 Federal Research and Development Activities Pertaining to Adolescence.* Third Annual Report. Washington, D.C.: The George Washington University, December 1975.

Stein, Howard F. "Ethnicity, Identity, and Ideology." *School Review* 83 (February 1975).

Stevens, Beth. "Symposium: Developmental Gains in the Reasoning, Moral Judgment, and Moral Conduct of Retarded and Non-retarded Persons." *American Journal of Mental Deficiency* 79, no. 2 (1974): 113-161.

Sue, Stanley, and Wagner, Nathaniel N., eds. *Asian-American Psychological Perspectives.* Ben Lomond, Cal.: Science and Behavior Books, 1973.

Sugarman, J. "Accountability through the Courts." *School Review* 82, no. 2 (February 1974).

Summers, Anita A., and Wolfe, Barbara L. "Which School Resources Help Learning? Efficiency and Equity in Philadelphia Public Schools." Federal Reserve Bank of Philadelphia *Business Review*, 1975.

Survey Research Center, Institute for Social Research, University of Michigan. *Adolescent Boys.* New Brunswick, N.J.: Boy Scouts of America, 1960.

Survey Research Center, Institute for Social Research, University of Michigan. *Adolescent Girls.* New York: Girl Scouts of America, n.d.

Taborn, John M. "Some Reflections on Meeting the Needs of Youth: Implications for Staff Awareness." *Center for Youth Development and Research Quarterly Focus* 1, no. 2.

Timpane, Michael; Abramowitz, Susan; Bobrow, Sue Berryman; and Pascal, Anthony. *Youth Policy in Transition.* A working note prepared for the Department of Health, Education, and Welfare by the Rand Corporation. WN-9309-HEW, December 1975.

Tompkins, J.R. "An Analysis: Needs, Progress and Issues in the Preparation of Personnel in the Education of Emotionally Disturbed Children." *Journal of Special Education* 3 (1969): 101-111.

Trudeau, Elaine, ed. *Digest of State and Federal Laws: Education of Handicapped Children.* Arlington, Va.: The Council for Exceptional Children, 1971.

Trump, J. Lloyd. "Dynamic Junior High-Middle-Intermediate Schools." *NASSP Bulletin* 58 (April 1974).

Tyack, David B. *The One Best System: A History of American Urban Education.* Cambridge, Mass.: Harvard University Press, 1974.

U.S. Code: Congressional and Administrative News. Legislative History, 93rd Congress, Second Session, Washington, D.C., 1974.

U.S. Congress, Senate, Select Committee on Nutrition and Human Needs. *To Save the Children: Nutritional Intervention Through Supplemental Feeding.* Washington, D.C.: U.S. Government Printing Office, 1974.

Van Geel, Tyll. "Does the Constitution Establish a Right to an Education?" *School Review* 82 (February 1974).

van Hilsheimer, George. *How to Live With Your Special Child.* Washington, D.C.: Acropolis, 1970.

Van Wyk, Judson; Underwood, Louis E.; Lister, Robert C.; and Marshall, Robert N. "The Somatomedins: A New Class of Growth-Regulating Hormones." *American Journal of Diseases of Children* 26 (November 1973): 705-710.

Waber, Deborah. "Developmental Trends and Biological Bases of Gender Differences in Mental Abilities." Ph.D. dissertation, Yale University, New Haven, Conn., n.d.

Walters, James, and Stinnett, Nick. "Parent-Child Relationships: A Decade Review of Research." In *A Decade of Family Research and Action*, edited by Carlfred D. Broderick. Minneapolis: National Council on Family Relations, 1971.

Warren, Marguerite Q. *Correctional Treatment in Community Settings: A Report on Current Research.* Crime and Delinquency Issues. Rockville, Md.: National Institute of Mental Health, 1972.

Wattenberg, William W. *The Adolescent Years.* 2nd ed. New York: Harcourt, Brace and Jovanovich, 1973.

Weiner, Irving B. *Psychological Disturbance in Adolescence.* New York: John Wiley and Sons, 1970.

Weinstein, Gerald, and Fantini, Mario D. *Toward Humanistic Education: A Curriculum of Affect.* New York: Frederick A. Praeger, 1970.

Weinstock, R., ed. *The Greening of the High School.* New York: I/D/E/A, Educational Facilities Laboratories, 1973.

Williams, Roger J. *Nutrition Against Disease: Environmental Prevention.* New York: Bantam Books, 1973.

Wilson, James Q. *Thinking About Crime.* New York: Basic Books, 1975.

Winslow, Robert W. *Juvenile Delinquency in a Free Society.* Belmont, Cal.: Dickenson Publishing Co., 1968.

Wirtz, Willard. "Summary Address," Universal Youth Service Conference. Franklin D. Roosevelt Library, Hyde Park, N.Y., April 10, 1976.

Wolfgang, Marvin E.; Figlio, Robert M.; and Sellin, Thorsten. *Delinquency in a Birth Cohort.* Chicago: University of Chicago Press, 1972.

Wunderlich, Ray C. *Allergies, Brains, and Children Coping.* St. Petersburg, Fla.: Johnny Reads, 1973.

Wyne, Marvin; White, Kinnard P.; and Coop, Richard H. *The Black Self.* Englewood Cliffs, N.J.: Prentice-Hall, 1974.

Daniel Yankelovich, Inc. *Is Scouting in Tune with the Times?* New Brunswick, N.J.: Boy Scouts of America, 1968.

Youth Alternatives Newsletter. The National Youth Alternatives Project, 1830 Connecticut Ave., N.W., Washington, D.C. 20009.

Youth Development and Delinquency Prevention Administration. *Annual Report of Federal Activities in Youth Development, Juvenile Delinquency and Related Fields.* Washington, D.C.: Social and Rehabilitation Services, 1971.

Zubin, Joseph, and Freedman, Alfred M., eds. *The Psychopathology of Adolescence.* New York: Grune and Stratton, 1970.

Index

Index

Abeson, Dr. Alan, 147
Abortion, and early adolescents, 138
Abstract thinking, 43. *See also* Formal operations
Acting-out adolescents, 136
Adelson, Joseph, 31, 37, 47-49
Adjudication process, 196
Adolescence. *See also* Early adolescence; Females; Males
  characteristics of, 3-8
  defined, 6
  life cycle, 6-7
  and nutrition, 16-21
  as a social process, 5-8, 13, 16, 42, 52
  stability in, xvi, 31, 33
  as transition period, 10, 30
Adolescence: Alternative Strategies for Compensatory Education, 101, 104
Adolescence in the Life Cycle, 4, 13, 26, 33
Adolescent Aggression: A Study of the Influences of Child-Training Practices and Family Interrelationships, 166
"The Adolescent as Philosopher," 46
Adolescents
  as children, xvi
  and conceptualization, 3-8, 40-42
  medicine for, 128-29, 133
  mental health of, 39, 134, 136
  with special needs, 19-20, 131
  stability of, 31, 33
Adult-oriented children, 163
Adults
  and negative attitudes, 118
  as role models, 113, 114
  and stereotyping of adolescents, 7, 28, 29
  and youth agencies, 178-79
Age (chronological), of adolescence, 3, 11
  and courts, 195
  and delinquency, 185-87
  and moral development, 45-47
  and myths of society, 16
  and political thought, 47-49
Agencies, for handicapped, 126. *See also* Youth agencies
Alcohol abuse, 139-40
Allergies
  and behavior problems, 19
  and dietary changes, 20
Allergy Section of Kaiser Foundation Hospitals, 20
Alternative schools, 97-100
"America in Search of a New Ideal: An Essay on the Rise of Pluralism," 109
American Indian culture, 112
American society
  vs. European, 91
  and the family, 159-60
  and myths about adolescents, xv-xvi, 28, 29, 33
  and problems for adolescents, 5
Anemia, 17
Anglo-Saxon society, 109, 111
Annual Report of the Youth Development and Delinquency Prevention Administration, 187
Anorexia nervosa, 136, 138
The Antecedents of Self-Esteem, 169
Artificial food additives, and behavior/learning problems, 20-21
Arts, and adolescent education, 100, 105-106
Asubel, David P., 162
Autonomy, of young adolescent, 30
Authoritarianism
  and early adolescence, 48-49
  as sex related, 166-67
Ayrault, Dr. Evelyn, 129, 131

Bachman, Jerald, 27, 28, 30, 165, 185
Bakan, David, 4-5
Barwick, J.M., 32

Baumrind, Diana, 166-67
"Beacons of Brilliance and Potholes of Pestilence," 95
Behavior modification, 201-202
Bennett, G. Vernon, 88, 89, 90, 92
Bereiter, Carl, 87, 120
Beyond Customs, 87, 99
Biological definition, of adolescence, 3
  research in, 12, 15-25
Black adolescents
  and abstract thinking, 43-44
  culture of, 112
  and identity problems, 108-109
  and political thinking, 49-50
Blatt, Sol, 151
Blood sugar levels, and maladapted child, 20
Bloom, Professor Benjamin, 36
Blos, Peter, 30, 31
B'nai B'rith Youth Organization, 175
Borinsky, Mark, 150
Bowerman, Charles, 162, 164
Boyle, Patrick, 179
Boys. *See also* Males
  and early maturation, 34, 35
  and suicide, 139
Boy Scouts (BSA), 173, 174, 179
Boys Town, 12
Brain dysfunction, and adolescence, 146
Briggs, Thomas, 89, 90
Bronfenbrenner, Urie, 81, 88, 124, 160-61, 171
Brown, Emory, 179
Burnett, Jacquetta Hill, 114

Cameron, Dr. Ross, 20
California's Commission for the Reform of Intermediate and Secondary Education (RISE), 116. *See also* RISE *Report*
California Youth Authority's Community Treatment Project (CTP), 200
Carolina Friends School, 83
Catholic Youth Organization (CYO), 175
Center for New Schools, 98
Center for Research for Mothers and Children (CRMC), 11
Center for Studies of Crime and Delinquency at the National Institute of Mental Health, 188
Center for Teaching and Learning at the University of North Dakota, 98
Center for Youth Development and Research, 12, 14
Cerebral lateralization, 44-45
Child care, defined, 87
Childhood, vs. adolescence, xvi, 4, 6, 10
Child labor legislation, 4
Children's Bureau of the Department of Health, Education and Welfare (DHEW), 183
Children's Defense Fund (CDF), 157
Children Under Stress, 165
Child Study Center, 14
Church-related organizations, 175
Clarke, Stevens H., 202
Clausen, John, 33-35
Clinics
  for adolescents, 141-43
  and research, 14
Cobb, Dr. Henry, 133, 149
Cognition, in adolescents, 12, 13, 15
  defined, 36-37
  and moral thought, 45-47
  and political thinking, 47-51
  in preadolescent, 29
  research in, 13, 36-56
  and schools, 123
Cohen, Donald, 13, 14, 25, 29, 30
"Coleman II," 100, 105. *See also* *Youth: Transition to Adulthood*
Community attitudes
  and school, 116-17, 123-24
  and youth groups, 177
Community-based treatment, 190, 200-202
Community schools, 117
Compensatory education, 101-105
Compensatory Education and Early Adolescence: Reviewing our

National Strategy, 101
Compulsory education, 4, 90, 92, 119-20
Condry, John, 163
Conformity, and early maturation, 34-35
Conley, R.W., 144
The Control of the Onset of Puberty, 22-25
Coopersmith, Stanley, 169
Courts, 143, 192-94, 195-96
  and change, 151, 156-57
  and schools, 119-20, 156-57
Crime, of juveniles, 184, 187, 191-92, 204, 208
Crippled Children's Service (CCS), 127, 129, 130
Culture
  American Indian, 112
  black, 112
  and ethnic schizophrenia, 114-15
  European, 91
  and moral development, 41, 45-47
  Spanish, 111-12

Davidson, Julian, 22, 23
Decade of Experiment: The Fund for the Advancement of Education, 1951-61, 86
Delayed intervention, 203-204
Delinquency, prevention programs for, 189-92, 194-205
Delinquency in a Birth Cohort, 185
Depressed adolescents, help for, 136
Detachment, defined, 30
Detention, and judicial system, 195-96
Developmental learning
  psychologists in, 9-10
  and retarded adolescents, 149
  theory of, 37-38
Diet, and adolescents, 18-19, 20-21
DiFranco, Sal, 96
Disadvantaged pupils, 103
  defined, 101
  vs. middle class, 101-102
  vs. normal, 103
"Disturbance in the Self-Image at Adolescence," 96
Disturbed adolescents, clinical neglect of, 143
Dittmann, Freya E., 101-105
Diversion programs, 198-200
Division of Personnel Preparation of the Bureau of Education for the Handicapped (BEH), 149
Douvan, Elizabeth, 31, 32
Dropout rate
  "leakage," 89, 90, 91, 92
  of minorities, 109-110
  as a myth, 28
  in 1896-1911, 89
Dropping out, 27-28
Drug abuse, 139-40

Early adolescence
  age group in, xv, 3, 10
  and authoritarianism, 48-49
  and Federal Reserve Bank report, 107
  and handicapped, 127
  in 1920s, 90-91
  and parenting styles, 167-68
  and political thought, 47-48, 50-51
  and psychosocial needs, 99-100
  research in, 10-12, 26-27, 161
  and RISE *Report*, 107-108
  and role models, 114
  variability of, xvi, 34
Early maturation
  effects of, 34-35
  and junior high school, 96
"Early Socialization and Adolescent Competence," 166
Economics, and delinquency, 185, 193
Edelman, Marion Wright, 119
Educable mental retardation (EMR), 144
Education
  and the arts, 100, 105-106
  compensatory, 101-105
  and compulsory attendance, 4, 90, 92, 119-20
  as a moral process, 87-88
  and skills of educators, 103-104

The Education of All Handicapped Children Act of 1975, 147
Educational Policy Research Center (EPRC), 101, 116
Educational system
  and cognitive abilities, 41
  and courts, 156-57
  as moral endeavor, 87-88
  special, 147, 149
Egocentrism, 39
  and RISE *Report*, 108
Elder, Glen, 6, 8, 31
Elkind, David, 37, 38-41, 43
Emotional development
  of young adolescents, 30-32
  of handicapped adolescents, 131-33
Emotionally handicapped, 133-34, 135-43
Employment and the Adolescent, 169
Endocrinology, 21-25
Epstein, Joyce L., 98
Erikson, Erik, 4, 6, 8, 31, 33
ESEA Title I program, 101, 103, 105
Ethnic minorities
  and cognitive development, 43-44
  and educational system, 109-111, 112
European society, 91
"Evils of adolescence," and junior high schools, 89, 90, 92
Extent and Meanings of Iron Deficiency in the U.S., 17
Eye contact, 112

Faigel, Dr. Harris, 128-29
Family
  and cognitive development, 42
  and delinquency, 185
  influence of, 159
  size, and effect, 165
  as social institution, 159, 164-65, 169
Fantini, Mario, 97
Farson, Richard, 159
Federal funding
  for adolescence research, 56-58, 60
  and delinquency, 59-60
  and education, 28, 100, 101, 180
  and family research, 161
  and handicapped youth, 129-30, 131
  and mental health, 136
  and pregnant teenagers, 137-38
Federal government
  and adolescence research, 11, 56-60
  and parent education, 180
Federal Reserve Bank of Philadelphia, 93, 106-107
Feingold, Dr. Benjamin, 20
Females. *See also* Girls
  and brain development, 40, 43, 44-45
  as delinquents, 184-85
  and early maturation, 35
  and "fear of success," 32
  and generation gap, 32-33, 34
  and growth, 21
  and life goals, 32
  and nutrition, 17, 19
  and parents, 163, 167
  and peer group, 162
  and privacy needs, 166
  as research subjects, 32
Fishman study, 199-200
Follow Through, 10
Food and Drug Administration, 20
Formal though (operations)
  and abstract thinking, 40-42
  and cognitive development, 37, 38, 39
  and egocentrism, 40
  and ethnic differences, 43-44
  and IQ, 43
  research in, 42
Foster home placement, 201
4-H Clubs, 176, 179
4-H in Urban Areas, 179
Frank, Richard, 13, 29, 165-66
Freud, Anna, 30, 31
Friedenberg, Edgar Z., 3, 5
Frisch, Rose, 21, 96
The Full Circle Residential Research and Treatment Center, 20
Funding. *See also* Federal funding

and early adolescence, 28
for mental health, 136
for special education, 100, 147

Gallagher, James, 54-55
Gallatin, Judith, 8, 33, 49-51
Gatewood, Thomas, 94
Gault decision, 195, 196
"Generation gap," 32-33
George Washington University, 56
Gifted adolescents, 54-55
Gilligan, Carol, 40, 46
Girls. *See also* Females
and anorexia nervosa, 136, 138
and drug abuse, 140
and justice system, 194
and pregnancy, 137-38
and sex, 137
and suicide, 139
and youth organizations, 178
Girl Scouts (GSA), 173, 174
Goldsmith, Joan, 118
Gorski, R.A., 23
Grade equivalent (g.e.) gains, 102-103
Grade organization, of schools, 94, 95
and self-image, 96-97
Grave, Gilman, 22
The Greening of the American High School, 105
Grinder, John, 63, 64
Grinder, Robert E., 25, 27
Group for the Advancement of Psychiatry, 136-37
Growth of Adolescence, 15
Growth and Development Branch of NICHD, 11
"Growth of Political Ideas in Adolescence: The Sense of Community," 48
Growth spurts, in adolescence, 21, 44-45, 123
Guided group interaction (GGI), 201

Halo effect, of drug programs, 140
Handicapped adolescents
education for, 147-49, 156-58
medical needs of, 128-31
and prevention, 129-30
problems of, 125-27, 132
research on, 57-58
Harris Survey, 122
Harvard University's Center for Population Studies, 96
Head Start, 10
Healy, Sandra, 29
HEW, and illiteracy, 121
Hill, John P., 5, 7, 8, 11-13, 26, 29-30, 31, 108
vs. Erikson, 33
and in-service training, 118
and parenting, 164, 167-68, 171
and research recommendations, 9, 10, 63, 74-77
and schooling, 116, 117
and self-concepts, 39, 40, 42-43
Hobbs, Nicholas, 125, 192
Hofmann, Dr. Adele, 128
Homosexual activities, in early adolescence, 137
Horner, Matina, 32
Hyperactive children, 19, 20
Hypoglycemia, 19, 20

Identification, and adolescence, 162, 163
Identity crisis, in adolescence, 4, 6, 29-35
and cognitive development, 39
and intergeneration conflict, 30, 32, 33
of minority adolescents, 108-109, 111, 114
and physically handicapped adolescents, 131-33
Identity: Youth and Crisis, 33
Illiteracy, 121
Incarceration, 197, 198
Income. *See also* Economics
and delinquency, 185, 193
and illiteracy, 121
Information Clearinghouse for Exceptional Children (CEC), 147
In-service training, 118-19
Instead of Court, 190

Institute of Human Development (Berkeley), 34
Institute of Open Education, 118
Institutions:
- and early maturation, 34-35
- and reform in Massachusetts, 197

Interactionist theories, 13
Interagency Panel on Early Childhood Research and Development, 11
Interagency Panel for Research and Development on Adolescence, 100, 105, 161, 170
- and federal research, 56-58, 59, 60-61, 77

Interdisciplinary approach, 13-14
Intergenerational conflict, 30-31, 32-33
IQ, 40, 43, 144
Isolation, and adolescence, 8
Israel, Dr. Richard, 133
Issues in the Classification of Children, 125, 157

James, Charity, 87, 99-100, 105, 118
Jewish Community Centers, 175
Johns Hopkins University, 54-55, 97
Joint Commission on Mental Health of Children, 5, 141
Junior high school movement
- and alternative schools, 98
- and community schools, 117
- and control, 99
- and handicapped adolescents, 148
- history of, 88-92
- problems with, 83-84, 89, 92
- research reports on, 106-107, 108
- and sociological demands, 91
- and students, 15, 87
- today, 92-93

The Junior High School (1919), 88
The Junior High School (1920), 89, 90
The Junior High School (1937), 91
Juvenile corrections system
- and child-saving movement (19th century), 188-89
- failure of, 204-205
- and status offenders, 188-89

Juvenile Delinquency Prevention Programs, 189
Juvenile delinquents
- defined, 183-85, 188
- and diet, 20-21
- number of, 183-84, 187-89

Juvenile Justice and Delinquency Prevention Act of 1974, 196, 204, 205
Juvenile justice system
- and diversion programs, 198-200
- failure of, 192-94

Kinch, John W., 162
Klotz, Sol, 19
Kohlberg, Lawrence, 37, 40, 46-47, 51-53
Konopka, Gisela, 6, 11, 32, 100, 137, 140, 163
- and multidisciplinary approach, 14-15
- and research recommendations, 76
- and youth-serving agencies, 178, 180-81

Koos, Leonard V., 95

Langner, Dr. Thomas, 164-65
Larson, Meredith, 101-105
Law Enforcement Assistance Administration (LEAA), 195, 199
Lawyers, and education, 151, 156-57
Learning disabilities, 145-47
Learning Disabilities Act of 1969, 146
Leet, Pauline, 98-99, 100
Legal counsel, for juveniles, 196
Legislation, and adolescents, 4, 156, 157
Lemert, Edwin, 190, 191, 198
Lerner, Max, 124
Lerner, Michael, 20
Levine, Daniel, 113
Life cycle
- and adolescence, 6-7, 8, 11
- and NICHD conference, 26
- and parents, 170, 171
- and research, 14, 75, 78

Lippmann, Walter, 85

Literacy Among Youths 12-17 Years, 121
Low-income adolescents, 43-44

Mainstreaming, and handicapped, 149, 151, 156-58
Males. *See also* Boys
  and brain development, 44-45
  as delinquents, 184-85, 187
  and dropout rate, 28
  and family size, 165
  vs. females, 32, 138
  illiteracy of, 121
  and longitudinal study, 27
  machismo of Spanish, 111-12
  and nutrition, 17
  and parents, 167, 168, 169
  and sexual maturation of, 23-24, 25
Malnutrition, 17
Martin, John Henry, 94, 95
Maslow, Abraham, 98
Massachusetts Department of Youth Services, 197
Mass media
  and cognitive development, 55
  and drug abuse, 140
  influence of, 28, 29
  and parenting, 171
  and schools, 85, 86
Masterson, J.H., 134
Maternal and Child Health Service (MCHS), 16, 184
  and handicapped adolescents, 129, 130
Maternal coldness, effects of, 165
McGlasson, Maurice, 93-95
McPartland, James, 98
Medicaid, and handicapped, 129-30
Mental health services, for adolescents, 134, 136, 141-43
Mentally handicapped
  education for, 147-49, 151, 156-57
  problems of, 143-47
  teachers of, 149-51
Michigan Bean Commission, 19
Middle School Journal, 94
Middle school movement, 93-97
Miller, Dr. Jerome, 197
Minnesota's Center for Youth Development and Research, 12, 108, 141
Minority students, and identity, 108-109, 111, 114. *See also* Identity crisis
Money, John, 24, 25, 208
Moral development, in adolescents, 45-47
  research in, 51-54
"Moral Development Research: A Case Study of Scientific Cultural Bias," 53
"Moral Judgment and Perceptions of Injustice," 52
Morgan, Ted, 193
Multiply handicapped, 127
Must We Educate?, 87
Myths, about adolescence, xvi, 27, 28, 29, 33

National Academy of Science's Food and Nutrition Board, 17
National Assessment of Juvenile Corrections (NAJC), 194-98, 201, 202
National Association of Independent Schools (NAIS), 116
National Association of Middle Schools, 94
National Commission on Resources for Youth, 177, 178-79
National Consortium for Options in Public Education (NCOPE), 98
National Federation of Settlements and Neighborhood Centers, 176-77
  and family integration, 179, 180
National Institute of Child Health and Human Development (NICHD)
  and *The Control of the Onset of Puberty*, 22-25
  and nutrition, 17, 18
  and research, 10-11, 26, 55-56
National Institute of Education, 20

National Society for the Study of Education (NSSE) Yearbook, 26
National Youth Alternatives Project, 177
NICHD. *See* National Institute of Child Health and Human Development
NIMH funding, 60-61
1970 White House Conference on Children and Youth, 144, 159
1974 International Conference of the Association of Children with Learning Disabilities, 145
Nixon, President Richard, 51
Nonresidential intensive treatment, 201
Normal Adolescence: Its Dynamics and Impact, 136-37
Nuclear family, 159, 160, 169
Nutrition, and adolescence, 16-21
Nutrition Against Disease: Environmental Prevention, 19

Obesity, 17
Offer, Daniel, 30-31, 163, 167
Office of Child Development (OCD), 180
Office of Education (OE), 27
Office, for youth affairs, 76
Open environment, 97-98
Otto, Herbert, 29

Palmquist, Wendy J., 39, 40, 42
Parent-child relationship
  and early adolescent (12-13), 163-64, 165-69
  and handicapped adolescent, 132
Parenting styles, 164, 165-69, 170-71
Patterns of Child Rearing, 166
Payne Whitney Clinic, 134
Pediatric allergists, 19, 20
Peer group
  and early adolescent, 162-63, 164, 166
  and radical nonintervention policy, 203
Peer-oriented children, 163, 164
Pennsylvania Association for Retarded Children v. Commonwealth of Pennsylvania (*PARC* case), 156
Perrone, Vito, 98
Personality, 25, 132
Peter Doe case, 119-20, 122
Physical changes, in adolescence, 131-33
Physically handicapped, 127-31
Physicians, and adolescents, 128
Piaget, 42, 45, 46
  and cognitive development, 37-38
Pinellas County Health Department, 20
Platt, Anthony, 188
Polier, Honorable Justice Wise, 188
Political thinking, in adolescence, 47-51
Positive Action for Youth (PAY), 201
Preadolescence, 29, 165-66
Pregnancy, of adolescents, 137-38
President's Commission on Law Enforcement and Administration of Justice, 184-85
President's Committee on Mental Retardation, 149
Pringle, Ralph, 91, 92
Probation, 200, 201
Professional Staff for the Handicapped in Local Public Schools, 150
Program development, 10, 58-59, 83-84, 126
Propper, Alice, 168
Provision of Instruction to Handicapped Pupils in Local Public Schools, 150
Principals, role of, 95
Promoting the Health of Mothers and Children, 16, 17
Psychiatric clinics, 134
"Psycho-endocrinology" counseling, 24-25
Psychological definition, of adolescence, 4-6
Psychosexual development, 25
Psychosocial development, 30, 99-100
Puberty, 15-16

defined, 3
delayed, 24-25
early, 34
and hormonal changes, 22-23
and retarded adolescents, 144
and weight gain, 21
Public Schools of Choice, 97
Putnam's Monthly, 109

Racism, in schools, 113-14
Radical nonintervention, 202-203
Rand report R-1220, 130-31, 134, 136
and retarded, 144
and special education, 147
Ravitch, Diane, 184, 208-209
Rebellion, in early adolescence, 30, 163-64
"Recent Research on Cognitive Development in Adolescence," 38
Recreation programs, and prevention, 190
Report of the National Panel on High Schools and Adolescent Education, 105-106
"Requirements for Healthy Development of Adolescent Youth," 11, 12, 100
Research, and early adolescence, 8-12, 13-15, 35-36
cognitive, 42, 55-56
delinquency, 59-60
dissemination of, 59, 61-62
family, 161-71
on handicapped, 133
and legal issues, 60
life cycle, 6-7, 8, 14, 76, 77
multidisciplinary approach to, 12-14
nutrition, 19
and program planning, 10, 58-59, 83-84, 126
puberty, 23-25
recommendations for, 74-77
socio-emotional, 12, 13, 15, 26-36
Researchers, and adolescents, 13-15, 18-19, 25-26, 36-37
Residential programs, 200-201
Right-to-Read, 105
RISE *Report*, 107-108, 116
Rites-de-passage, 5
Rivera, Richard, 109
Rogers, Carl, 98
Rohwer, William, 41
Role models, for minority adolescents, 113, 114
Rudd, Dr. Lucie, 137

Satellization theory, 162
Save the Children Federation, 177, 180
School personnel, 83, 103, 104
Schools
alternative, 97-100
community, 117
and community attitudes, 114-15
function of, 85-86, 87-88
and crime in, 184, 208
and minorities, 110-11, 112-15
organization of, 97-98
and pregnant adolescents, 137
problems with, 83-85, 122-24
racism in, 113
role models in, 114
size of, 95, 107
as socializing institution, 109
School Staffing Survey, 150
Secondary education, 150-51
and need for reform, 105-108
Self-image, of adolescents, 29-35
and cognitive development, 38-40
and community projects, 179, 181
and school grade organization, 96
Self-reliance, and open schools, 98
Services for Handicapped Youth: A Program Overview, 126, 127. *See also* Rand Report R-1220
Sexual maturation, 136-38, 144
Shah, Dr. Saleem, 188, 189, 191, 203
Sibling relationships, 164
Simmons, Roberta, 96
Simon, Michael, 163
Simpson, Elizabeth, 53
Skinner, B.F., 37-38
Smith, Vernon, 98

Social changes, and adolescence, 4, 5
Social institutions, 81-82
Social Research Group, 161-62, 170
Socialization, of adolescents, 13, 42, 52
  and maturation, 33-35
  and schools, 85, 109-11, 122-23
"Socialization and the 'Middle' Child: A Twentieth-Century Model for a Seventeenth-Century Process," 99
Society
  and delinquent youth, 205
  and early adolescence, 4, 5, 207
  and family, 160, 161
  and junior high school movement, 88-89
  and schools, 85-86, 115
Society for Adolescent Medicine, 128
Socio-historical perspective, 6-8
Somatomedin (growth hormone), 23
"Some Perspectives on Adolescence in American Society," 11
Spanish minorities, 111-12
Spatial skills, 44-45
Stability, xvi, 31, 33
Stanford Research Institute, 101
Status offenses
  vs. criminal acts, 195, 199
  defined, 187-88
  and girls, 194
  treatment for, 188-89
Stereotyping, of adolescents, 7, 28, 29
Students, 15, 89-90
Sturm und drang, 30-31, 42
Suicide, and early adolescence, 138-39
Supreme Court, 87
"The Symptomatic Adolescent Five Years Later: He Didn't Grow Out of It," 134

Tanner, James, 15, 16, 21, 22, 24
Task Force on Middle Schools, 83
Teachers
  education for, 117-19
  qualities of, 76
  and racism, 113-14
  and special education, 149-51
Ten-State Nutrition Survey of 1972, 17, 19
Therapist, and young adolescent, 142
Thinking About Crime, 191
Trainable mental retardation, 144
Training schools, 193
"Transescent" youth, xv, 95-96
Treatment
  for delinquents, 194-205
  for learning disabled, 146
Two Worlds of Childhood, 81, 88

Unemployment, effect of, 6
Unidisciplinary research, 13-14
Urban areas
  and delinquency, 185
  and youth-serving agencies, 173, 175, 179
U.S. Supreme Court, 151

Values
  of Anglo-Saxon society, 109, 110
  of children, 87, 88
  of ethnic minorities, 109, 110, 111-12
  of society, 85-86
  of youth agencies, 173
Vanishing Adolescent, The, 5
Van Wyk, Judson, 23, 24-25
Verbal skills, 44, 45
Veterans Administration programs, and handicapped, 130
Vocational training, 89, 91, 149

Waber, Deborah, 9-10, 44-45
Wells, Don, 83
Wilkins, Lawson, 24
Wilson, James Q., 191, 203
Women, and role change, 160
Working mothers, 168-69
Work experiences, for adolescents, 99, 100, 106, 177, 180

Yale University, 14
Yearbook on Youth, 105
Young adolescents. *See also* Black

adolescents; Early adolescence; Females; Males
and autonomy, 30
defined, 3
psychosocial needs of, 30, 99-100
rebellion in, 30
Young Girls: A Portrait of Adolescence, 32, 181
Young Lives at Stake, 87, 100
Youth agencies, 173-80
recommendations for, 181
Youth Service Bureau, 198-99
Youth: Transition to Adulthood, 100, 105. *See also* "Coleman II"
Youth in Transition study, 27, 165
Youth in Two Worlds, 163
YMCA, 173, 174-75, 179
YWCA, 173, 175, 179

About the Author

Joan Lipsitz is coordinator of development at the Learning Institute of North Carolina and half-time consultant to the Ford Foundation. She heads the Southeastern Committee on Young Adolescents, funded by the Mary Reynolds Babcock Foundation. Dr. Lipsitz is a member of the Middle School Task Force of the National Association of Independent Schools. She received the B.A. from Wellesley College, the M.A. in English from the University of Connecticut, and the Ph.D. in secondary curriculum and instruction at the University of North Carolina, School of Education, in Chapel Hill.